The Economy of Nature

❧ The ❧ Economy of Nature

Rethinking the Connections Between Ecology and Economics

William Ashworth

Houghton Mifflin Company

BOSTON NEW YORK 1995

For information about permission to reproduce selections from
this book, write to Permissions, Houghton Mifflin Company,
215 Park Avenue South, New York, New York 10003.

Library of Congress Cataloging-in-Publication Data
Ashworth, William, date.
    The economy of nature : rethinking the connections between
ecology and economics / William Ashworth.
        p.   cm.
    Includes bibliographical references.
    ISBN 0-395-65566-8 (cl)   ISBN 0-395-71817-1 (pbk)
    1. Economic development — Environmental aspects.
2. Economics.   3. Ecology.   I. Title.
HD75.6.A78   1994
333.7 — dc20

                                        94-28894
                                         CIP

Printed in the United States of America

BP 10 9 8 7 6 5 4 3 2 1

Book design by Melodie Wertelet

Printed on recycled paper

As art and industry advance, the materials of cloathing and lodging, the useful fossils and minerals of the earth, the precious metals and the precious stones should gradually come to be more and more in demand, should gradually exchange for a greater and a greater quantity of food, or in other words, should gradually become dearer and dearer. This accordingly has been the case with most of these things upon most occasions, and would have been the case with all of them upon all occasions, if particular accidents had not upon some occasions increased the supply of some of them in a still greater proportion than the demand.

— Adam Smith, *The Wealth of Nations*

Men have an indistinct notion that if they keep up this activity of joint stocks and spades long enough all will at length ride somewhere, in next to no time, and for nothing; but though a crowd rushes to the depot, and the conductor shouts "All aboard!" when the smoke is blown away and the vapor condensed, it will be perceived that a few are riding, but the rest are run over.

— Thoreau, *Walden*

The economy of nature, its checks and balances, its measurements of competing life — all this is its great marvel and has an ethic of its own.

— Henry Beston, *The Outermost House*

The first thing we do, let's kill all the lawyers.

— Shakespeare, *Henry VI, Part 2*

Acknowledgments

MANY OF THE IDEAS in this book were thrashed out over coffee and bagels in Milt Bloombaum's wonderful Key of C coffeehouse, just around the corner from the Oregon Shakespeare Festival in downtown Ashland. The principal participants with me in those conversations were Alan Reder of Rogue River, Oregon, coauthor of *Investing from the Heart: A Guide to Socially Responsible Investing* (Crown, 1992), and Liam Sherlock of Ashland, staff attorney for the Headwaters environmental organization. Milt frequently came out of the kitchen to join us. Others dropped in and contributed from time to time, including Rod Badger (biochemist), Bryan Frink (investment counselor), Yehoshah Ourshalimian (naturopath), J. P. Phillips (Shakespearean actor), Bill Purdom (geologist), Tom Ward (permaculture designer), and Rob Winthrop (anthropologist).

A number of people who never made it to our informal bagel symposia nevertheless contributed significantly to the book. My brother Robert Ashworth of Bellingham, Washington, will recognize several of the ideas I have shamelessly cribbed from him, particularly in the sections on growth and the fallacy of composition. Scott Walker of Big Thicket National Preserve in Onalaska, Texas, who has thought deeply about the matters I deal with in this book, proved particularly cogent and helpful, both in conversation and with follow-up letters and documents. Wayne Yarnall of Corvallis, Oregon; Barry Laing of Salem, Oregon; and David Benson of Pullman, Washington, formed a spontaneous lunchtime focus group at the 1992 Annual Session of North Pacific Yearly Meeting of the Society of Friends (Quakers) to help me properly launch my principal research trip. Ray Schaaf of Bishop, California, spent a much-appreciated evening explaining in detail why he no longer works for the Forest Service. My good friend Collin Boyd of Ashland held forth with me through numerous wide-ranging conversations (including several trips to Portland and Seattle and an excellent lunch at Geppeto's); my cousin Susan Kobza and her husband, John, of Reno, Nevada, not only put me up for three nights (one of them on extremely short notice) but hashed thoroughly through the ideas for the book as well; and Bonnie Messenger and Steve Mullinax of Portland, my assigned hosts following the 1992 Oregon Chapter–Sierra Club banquet, proved both patient and insightful when the breakfast conversation the next morning turned inevitably to my favorite topic.

Hosts who provided valuable R and R during the long summer of 1992 included my brother Jack Ashworth and his wife, Ruth Spangler, in Louisville, Kentucky; my uncle Walter Ashworth in Gainesville, Georgia; my sisters Lillian Ashworth and Judith Ashworth in Pullman, Washington; my cousins Lewis Sherman in St. Louis, Missouri, and Merton Sherman in Pierre, South Dakota, and their wives, Marie and Mary; Max and Pat Gartenberg in Livingston, New Jersey; Ron Wolff and his family in Micanopy, Florida; my brother-in-law Larry James and his wife, Dolores, in Issaquah, Washington; my niece Lauri Bliss and her husband, Dan, in Vass, North Carolina; and my aunt-in-law, Alice Berry, in Charlotte, North Carolina. Friends and family who responded magnificently to my request for relevant clippings included Jim and Margaret Frye in Fort Collins, Colorado; Alec and Eunice McKay in Prince George, British Columbia; Deb Rogers Miller in Rapid City, South Dakota; Lisa Morrison in Portland, Oregon; Scott Walker; Lewis and Merton Sherman; Max Gartenberg; and Jack Ashworth.

Conversations in passing with Dave Mazza in Portland,

Oregon; Ron Eber in Salem, Oregon; and Grady Clay in Louisville, Kentucky, contributed bits and pieces to the puzzle. My co-workers at the Ashland Public Library not only covered for me while I was gone for three months, but put up with the intensity of my mood swings while I was trying to get all this down on paper; Maria Bertram and Bob Wilson were particularly helpful and understanding. Numerous public-agency personnel contributed interview time and documents: among these, I would like to single out particularly Beth Anne Eichenser of the Environmental Protection Agency in what used to be Times Beach, Missouri; Bob Steele and Dave Gudgel of the Bureau of Reclamation's desalination plant in Yuma, Arizona; Betsy Lowe and Ellen George of the Adirondack Park Agency in Ray Brook, New York; and Betsy Ballard of Modoc National Forest in Cedarville, California.

Finally, I need to acknowledge the special contributions made by my daughter, Sara, and my wife, Melody. Sara was usually in the house while I was writing, and her patience in dealing with my outbursts of temper, anguish over deadlines, and compulsive need to talk through the organizational problems of the text as they arose were remarkable; there are probably more of her ideas in this book than either of us will ever recognize. For Melody I don't need to guess: I *know* a very large part of "my" thoughts are actually hers. Ten thousand miles of travel with her through America, looking and musing and tossing ideas back and forth, has led to such a close intermingling of our observations on this issue that I am no longer able to tell which of us was originally responsible for any of them. I am solely accountable for the way the ideas are put down on paper, together with any mistakes that may have crept in and any misunderstandings that may arise from them. I claim no such ownership of the ideas themselves.

Contents

Prologue:
The People of the Cliffs

ON AUGUST 10, 1776, while George Washington and his Continentals, dug in on Long Island, were still waiting impatiently for the first official British response to the Declaration of Independence, a ragtag band of ten men — five Spaniards and five Native Americans — crept down out of the La Plata Mountains of southwestern Colorado and set up camp beside a small, sluggish branch of the Mancos River. Rain was falling, and one of the Spaniards was sick. They had made less than five miles that day, but it was going to have to do.

The little body of men was under the command of a priest from a minor Spanish order, Father Silvestre Velez de Escalante, nominally assigned to the mission at Zuni Pueblo but currently on an expedition of discovery for the governor of New Mexico. They had left Santa Fe two weeks before, heading north and west with a specific goal: to find a new route from the Spanish colonies of New Mexico to their sister settlements near California's Monterey Bay, a route that would swing around the north end of the dreadful Canyon of the Colorado and thus avoid the vast expanse of desert that made travel so difficult to the south. They would prove unsuccessful. Stymied and bewildered by the basins and ranges of Nevada and the vast red maze of Utah, worn to the bone, they would stumble back to Santa Fe on January 3, 1777, leaving behind as their principal legacy three names on the landscape. The Escalante River. A spectacular Colorado River ford, deep in the labyrinth of the upper canyon country, known ever since as the Crossing of the Fathers. And, here on the Mancos, where the south wall of the valley is formed by one side of an immense, flat-topped, forest-covered butte, a pedestrian, almost offhand identifier. The Green Table. Mesa Verde.

Escalante did not climb up onto his Green Table: he did not even record the name in his otherwise meticulous journal. It was left for word of mouth to bring that down to us. Discouraged by the rain, tending his sick companion, the young priest had no way of knowing the importance future discoveries would attach to that prosaic-looking piece of ground. A few miles south of the tent where the Spanish leader sat brooding about the unbroken wilderness around him, hidden by the high sandstone cliffs of the mesa's edge, a group of cities stood, their windows hollow, the solid stonework of their walls crumbling into the ground. They were empty. They had been empty for more than three hundred years.

The lost cities of Mesa Verde have long ranked as one of the world's great mysteries. Tucked into soaring aeries beneath the lips of the mesa's canyons, fronted by often spectacular drops to the canyon floors, the carefully worked stone-and-mortar walls have the feel of structures built for the ages. On the mesa top lie the ruins of the people's fields, their stone fences fallen, their far-flung irrigation works choked by full-grown junipers. Here and there bits of pavement suggest a road network. The cities' builders — the people we know today as the Anasazi — clearly had a good working body of scientific and technical knowledge. They were astronomers; they were farmers; they were master masons. They designed and built sophisticated ventilation systems, multistory apartment houses, and some of the loveliest cookware ever to grace a kitchen. Who were these people? Where did they go? Why, after nearly eight hundred years of increasingly successful control over their environment, did they suddenly pack up and leave, a full three centuries before the standard villain in the scenario of indigenous American culture destruction — a white man with a horse — came anywhere near the place?

But there is an even more provocative question. For more than seven centuries — fully 90 percent of the time Mesa Verde was occupied — the Anasazi built their cities beside their fields, on the mesa top. Only in the last eighty of the people's nearly eight hundred years in this place were the cities moved to the cliff faces above the canyons. What was the cause? Why did the people of the plateau, so close to the end of the long life of their civilization, suddenly decide to become the people of the cliffs? We can abandon the obvious explanation: despite the clear defensive advantages of these cliff-face sites, which the architects of the cities appear to have been fully aware of, there were no enemy hordes on the horizon. Years of diligent searching by archaeologists have failed to turn up even a shred of evidence that the Anasazi were ever under outside attack.

Are the two mysteries related? Did the sudden, wholesale move to the cliffs have anything to do with the abandonment of the whole area a few short decades later? Can the new nation that was being born on the east coast of the continent at the same time as the first Europeans passed near the lost cities of Mesa Verde learn anything of significance from the Anasazi experience?

Here is a clue. Go to Mesa Verde. Stand by the ruin known today as Far View House, one of the last of the Anasazi's plateau-top cities. Look to the southwest. Thirty miles distant, beyond the New Mexico border, beyond the broad, dusty basin of the San Juan River, looms the great volcanic crag known to the Navajo as *tse bida hi* — the Rock with Wings — and to whites, only slightly more prosaically, as Shiprock. An Anasazi standing at this place would have been able to see every pinnacle. You will be lucky to make out more than a vague, indistinct outline.

THE INVISIBLE HAND

Let us return briefly to 1776.

On March 9 of that year, a little less than four months before the signing of the Declaration of Independence and almost exactly five months before the first Europeans passed by Mesa Verde, a small publisher on the London Strand brought out a long, dull, excruciatingly detailed treatise on political philosophy by a former professor of rhetoric at Glasgow University. Though few could have predicted it at the time, this minor publishing event, occurring without fanfare of any sort, would have at least as great an impact on the future of mankind as the media happening across the ocean in Philadelphia. The book was *An Inquiry into the Nature and Causes of the Wealth of Nations,* and the author was Adam Smith.

Smith is often referred to these days as the "father of economics," a title that would have surprised, amused, and probably alarmed the old Scotsman. He knew as well as anyone that his work was primarily derivative. Many of the ideas in *The Wealth of Nations* were borrowed from a French school of philosophy, contemporaneous with Smith, known as physiocracy; others can be traced back as far as Plato, Aristotle, and the Bible. The medieval Church had devoted a considerable amount of thought to economics, developing a body of theory known as *justum pretium* ("just price"). It was not exactly as if no one had ever thought before about how money worked.

The genius of Smith's work lay not so much in its originality as in the scope of its synthesis. *The Wealth of Nations* brings together an astonishing range of ideas from politics, philosophy, ethics, law, history, and many other disciplines, weaving them into a coherent, organized body of thought. It discusses property rights, the nature of value and wealth, the division of labor, the fundamentals of supply and demand, the theory of money supply, and a wide variety of related topics, in such a disciplined and carefully related fashion that the work remains a source of fresh insights today, well over two hundred years later. And buried deep in the book's more than one thousand pages, there is a single reference to a two-word image so powerful that it has thoroughly dominated the public perception of Smith's economic ideas — and, indeed, the science of economics itself — ever since. The image is that of an "invisible hand." The passage where it appears is worth quoting in detail:

> Every individual is continually exerting himself to find out the most advantageous employment for whatever capital he can command. It is his own advantage, indeed, and not that of the society, which he has in view. But the study of his own advantage naturally, or rather necessarily leads him to prefer that employment which is most advantageous to the society. . . . By preferring the support of domestic to that of foreign industry, he intends only his own security; and by directing that industry in such a manner as its produce may be of the greatest value, he intends only his own gain, and he is in this, as in many other cases, led by an invisible hand to promote an end which was no part of his intention. Nor is it always the worse for the society that it was no part of it. By pursuing his own interest he frequently promotes that of the society more effectually than when he really intends to promote it.

It is important to understand the context in which Smith wrote. The dominant economic paradigm of the day was mercantilism: the belief that there was a fixed amount of wealth in the world, and that the economic well-being of a nation depended entirely upon how high a proportion of this wealth it could concentrate within its own borders. Wealth was symbolized by hard currency — gold and silver — referred to in the texts of the day as *specie*. You could acquire specie by trade, or you could snatch it by force of arms: it really didn't matter. What mattered was the more you had, the less there was for others. The world economy was, in effect, a giant zero-sum game.

There was an important corollary to the theory of mercantilism. Since nations obtained their wealth exclusively from other nations, it followed that a nation's government, as the only proper conduit for business with other nations, was the only proper guardian of the nation's store of specie. This led to a great amassing of treasure in the hands of government. (We still refer to nations' centers of monetary policy as "treasuries.") It also led to a massive and highly intrusive body of rules and regulations governing the economic behavior of ordinary citizens. The people of one nation couldn't be allowed to trade directly with the people of another; such trades would function as leaks through which specie might dribble off. They also couldn't be allowed to trade freely among themselves because that was a mere churning of specie that didn't help it accumulate at the top. Thus taxes came into being for every transaction. "Mercantilist government," wrote the journalist Soma Golden on the two hundredth anniversary of the publication of Smith's book, "had bent the entire economy to the state's needs, weaving a tight web around individual economic activity — tighter, historians say, than anything the West has seen since then, except during wartime." It was mercantilist thinking that was responsible for the stifling trade rules that Britain had imposed on her American colonies, the infamous Stamp Act included, which led to the Boston Tea Party and the outbreak of the Revolutionary War. It was also, indirectly, mercantilist thinking that had driven Silvestre de Escalante into the wild unknown around Mesa Verde. The Spaniards were in the New World primarily to collect specie from it. The missions to the Indians were strictly an afterthought.

Smith challenged this paradigm in two important ways. He showed that wealth did not have to be accumulated, but could actually be created by the activities of individuals, through trade, through manufacturing, and through the investment of and return on capital. And since the activities of individuals created wealth, it followed that curbs on those activities would interfere directly with the process of wealth creation. The best thing governments could do to assure their nations' prosperity was to dismantle all those rules and regulations and get out of the way.

A cornerstone of Smith's thinking was what has since become known as the *labor theory of value.* According to this theory, value is not inherent in an object, but is a product solely of the labor that went into providing it. The value of an ear of corn depends on the amount of time spent preparing the ground, planting the seed, and tending and harvesting the growing crop. The value of a barrel depends on the labor necessary to make the staves, smelt and forge the nails and iron bands, and assemble and finish the product; though the cooper must pay others to obtain the materials he uses, such as wood and iron, the sums paid are dependent upon the labor the others went through to obtain the materials — to mine and smelt the ore, or to chop down the trees and mill them into barrel staves, and to carry them to the point of use. Specie, in this view, is essentially worthless. It is the effort that has gone into gathering it that counts.

The labor theory of value is so broadly and unquestioningly accepted today that it is sometimes difficult to remember that it was an extremely radical idea in its time. Smith and the physiocrats he had borrowed the idea from were flying directly in the face of centuries of accumulated thought. The Greek philosophers had taught that each object had a specific "innate worth," an abstract quality that determined its value to humans, and the entire structure of economic thought since then had been built on that concept. The Church's *justum pretium* was an attempt to make sure that prices reflected innate worth instead of being artificially inflated by human frailties such as greed and envy. The whole creaking weight of mercantilism rested on the assumption that specie *was* wealth, not merely a representation of it. The idea that value was an extraneous quality attached to objects by humans was thus not merely new: it was dangerously subversive. Just how subversive it was can be seen if you examine the works of Karl Marx.

Though it is usually held up as the antithesis of Smith's thinking, Marxist philosophy — like capitalist — takes as its starting point an unquestioning belief in the labor theory of value.

But this view of value was not merely new, subversive, and dangerous: it was also overstated. In his zeal to score points against mercantilism, Adam Smith had gone too far. The Greeks were right: some value is innate in all objects, and while labor can indeed add value to these objects, labor can also take value away. Far away from London, on the far side of another continent, the mute, deserted cities of Mesa Verde stood as eloquent testimony to precisely that uncomfortable fact.

THE OCEAN OF ORGANIC BEING

We now move forward almost precisely twenty-five years from the publication of *The Wealth of Nations,* to a new century and a new nation: March 14, 1801, in Woodstock, Vermont. On that date a Woodstock attorney and gentleman farmer named Charles Marsh became a father for the fifth time. The child was a boy. When they were sure he would live, his parents had him christened George Perkins.

George Perkins Marsh was a sickly child — scrawny, physically weak, and plagued by recurring problems with his eyesight. Of little use on his father's Ottauquechee River farm, able to attend school only in fits and starts, he spent his boyhood roaming the foothills of the Green Mountains, learning whatever it was the woods and rocks could teach him. He wished to become a naturalist. His stern father would have nothing of it. Charles Marsh was a Vermont district attorney who had served his state with distinction as a member of the U.S. House of Representatives. The boy's grandfather had been the state's lieutenant governor. The boy would follow the family trade.

The boy tried. Graduating from Dartmouth College in 1822 at the top of his class, he taught school for a time, then opened a law practice in Burlington, Vermont, dabbling in wool growing and shopkeeping and authoring a linguistics textbook. The law served, as it often does, as a springboard into politics: by 1840, Marsh was a U.S. congressman, and in 1848 he entered the diplomatic corps, serving as minister to Turkey for six years. In 1861, following a five-year hiatus back in Vermont, he was named ambassador to Italy for the incoming Lincoln administration. He was to remain in that position for twenty-one years, all the rest of his life.

Such are the surface facts of Marsh's biography. But surfaces can be opaque, and hide much. Close beneath that dignified surface, clawing and kicking, the boy who had wanted to be a naturalist was still striving desperately to get out.

The wooded mountains of Vermont never left him, not even in the ambassador's residence on the barren, sun-baked hills of Tuscany. He might struggle with his eyesight, but, as he himself put it, "sight is a faculty, seeing is an art." It was an art he practiced diligently. Sitting in Italy with little to do (his government was, those early years of the 1860s, rather heavily involved elsewhere), he mused deeply on the many things he had seen; and in 1864 he sent the fruit of those musings to his publisher, Charles Scribner, in New York. The manuscript bore the title *Man and Nature; or, Physical Geography as Modified by Human Action.* Like *The Wealth of Nations* eighty-eight years before, it would revolutionize the way humans thought about their relationship to the world.

There are other comparisons to the earlier work. Like Adam Smith's book, George Marsh's was immense in both size and scope, running roughly seven hundred pages and covering topics as diverse as the construction of the Suez Canal, the effects of forests on climate, and the life cycle of a coral reef. Like Smith's work, Marsh's was largely derivative, drawing on an immense variety of sources gathered from all over the planet (the bibliography in the front of the second edition ran to more than two hundred items, in at least twelve languages). Like Smith, Marsh had trouble parsing a simple sentence: the book's prose is thorny and dense, full of long, convoluted phrases that tumble back on themselves like Chinese blocks. There are so many footnotes, full of so many detailed observations, that at times they threaten to overwhelm the text. Most of the way through, the reader appears to be faced with two separate and only casually related books, set in different typefaces and running concurrently, one on the top and the other on the bottom half of the page.

And the book was brilliant. That is another thing Marsh's work shares with Smith's. Like *The Wealth of Nations, Man and Nature* is today considered seminal, and its author is referred to, reverently, as the father of his discipline. The discipline is ecology. The word is never used in the book — the word would not appear in print for another five years, and would not be in common use for more than a hundred — but the conceptual framework is all there.

All previous naturalists had written of organisms. Marsh wrote of relationships. He told how insect numbers were controlled by birds, which ate them — and how bird numbers were in turn controlled by insects, whose population size determined how much food the birds would have, and how many would eat, and how many would starve. He told how fish were dependent upon forests, because the forests held back the runoff from rains and kept the water clean and flowing steadily. He showed how too many animals grazing on a hillside would damage the health of the soil, reducing its ability to grow grass, so that fewer and fewer animals could find a living there, until ultimately no animals could graze there at all. He explained the role of soil microorganisms (he called them "animalculae") in keeping crops healthy. And he demonstrated how humanity, by ignoring these connections, had seriously undermined the resources of Europe and the ancient world, leaving in its wake "an assemblage of bald mountains, of barren, turfless hills, and of swampy and malarious plains . . . where the operation of causes set in action by man has brought the face of the earth to a desolation almost as complete as that of the moon."

The book almost didn't see the light of day. Charles Scribner worried that it would not sell. Marsh, he said, should return to linguistics. But the old man persisted, and eventually the publisher gave in — and found, to his amazement, that he had a bestseller. *Man and Nature,* as one critic put it a few years later, came "with the force of a revelation." It quickly ran through several printings. European editions were prepared; they too sold out. In 1874, bowing to the inevitable, Scribner's brought out a new edition in English. Based, curiously, on Marsh's own retranslation of the Italian edition of the original, the new version — in addition to correcting errors of fact and updating statistics — added several dozen pages of material, including the most succinct statement of the case for environmental activism that would come along until the work of Rachel Carson, nearly one hundred years later:

> [Mankind] is dealing with dangerous weapons whenever he interferes with arrangements pre-established by a power higher than his own. The equation of animal and vegetable life is too complicated a problem for human intelligence to solve, and we can never know how wide a circle of disturbance we produce in the harmonies of nature when we throw the smallest pebble into the ocean of organic being.

Was Marsh, like Adam Smith before him, overstating his case to make a point? Perhaps. Certainly the "harmonies of nature" were more resilient than he thought. The web of dependence among species which radiates and magnifies ecosystem damage also helps to provide ecosystem stability. Though Marsh fretted that the earth was "fast becoming an unfit home," the "depravation, barbarism, and perhaps even extinction" that he confidently predicted for the human race within the next few generations has yet to take place.

But before we become too sanguine about the situation, we

should reexamine Mesa Verde. The year is 1874. The second edition of *Man and Nature* has just been published; *The Wealth of Nations* is two years shy of celebrating its hundredth birthday. And deep in southwestern Colorado a photographer named William Henry Jackson, attached to the great western survey effort known as the Hayden Expedition, is sitting in a bar in Durango and listening to prospectors spin tales of old, empty stone houses somewhere up there on that big green table across the La Plata Mountains a few dozen miles toward the Arizona Territory.

Jackson was sufficiently intrigued to lug one of his huge, balky cameras up one of the Mesa Verde canyons. The pictures he brought back made their way east, where they met with polite comments but little real interest: the so-called Aztec Ruin down near Farmington, New Mexico, was far more impressive. But Jackson, it turned out, had seen only peripheral structures. It was not until Christmas Eve, 1888, when a couple of cowboys named Dick Wetherill and Charlie Manson came back from chasing stray cows over the mesa and started babbling about an immense palace plastered to the side of a cliff that scientific attention — and public curiosity — finally began focusing on the deserted cities of Mesa Verde. Who had built them? Why had they left? Where had they gone?

Answers to these questions eventually began to turn up. It is unlikely that either George Perkins Marsh or Adam Smith would have been surprised.

ABOVE THE GREEN CANYONS

At first the archaeologists assumed it had been an enemy invasion. After all, they reasoned, the cliff dwellings were clearly defensive in design. It was also clear, even before accurate dating was available, that the move to those well-defended sites had come after a long period of building on the mesa top but shortly before the whole area had been abandoned. There was even an available villain, the Navajo, a people of Athabascan stock who had moved into the area only a couple of centuries before the whites had. It was, in fact, a Navajo word the archaeologists were using to name the Mesa Verde people, a word that meant, when translated literally, "enemy ancestors." The Navajo and the Pueblo peoples of the Rio Grande area were in what could be described only as an armed truce when the Spaniards arrived on the scene in the late sixteenth century. Was it not obvious that this warlike tribe from the north had chased the Anasazi away?

The trouble was that it wasn't obvious at all. To begin with, the Navajo weren't living on the great mesa either. If they were the ones who had chased off the former owners, they hadn't done a very good job of commandeering the spoils. Also, there was no evidence of warfare in the cities themselves: no blackened walls, no butchered skeletons, no accumulations of projectile points. If there had been a war, it must have been curiously nonviolent. And where were the oral histories? The Navajo should have had some tales of taking the place. They didn't.

Finally, after a compulsive tree-ring counter named A. E. Douglass published his results in 1929, the whole "enemy" theory disintegrated. Tree-ring counting (technically known as dendrochronology) establishes precise dates by matching overlapping sequences of tree rings. All of the trees growing in any given region will put down identical sequences of growth ring widths as the climate fluctuates. If one tree dies while others nearby continue to live, the number of rings the living trees have added since the sequences in the dead and living trees last matched will tell you exactly how long ago the dead tree died — and if you can then match up earlier rings in the dead tree with late rings in a third, even older dead tree, you have a way to extend accurate dating back to a time before any trees now living were around. In this manner, using the wooden structural members the Anasazi and their Navajo and Pueblo successors had built into their dwellings, Douglass compiled a massive, detailed, year-by-year calendar reaching back through more than a thousand years of Southwest American prehistory. For the enemy-invasion theorists at Mesa Verde, the results were highly embarrassing. The cities on the cliffs had been abandoned before the beginning of the fourteenth century. The Navajo "enemy" hadn't arrived for at least another hundred years.

But the tree rings themselves provided a possible alternate explanation. In the last half of the thirteenth century, at precisely the time Mesa Verde was being abandoned, the growth rings of all trees in the American Southwest become so close together that they are barely countable. A major drought had clearly hit the region during that period. Had lack of water driven the Anasazi from their homes? For a time the evidence seemed overwhelming — until some spoilsport pointed out that the enigmatic move off the mesa top and onto the cliffs had happened well before the drought hit, that earlier and even more severe droughts (which the Mesa Verde people had cheerfully lived right through) could be found in the tree-ring record, and that over on the Rio Grande, where the drought had been at least as severe, cities were being *founded* even as the Mesa Verde culture was disappearing. It was, in fact, becoming increasingly evident that this was where the Mesa Verde people had gone.

Did an epidemic wipe out the population? Not from the evidence of the dead.

Did the soil develop too many gullies to be farmed? Unlikely: though arroyos are common enough in the old fields, most of them appear to have developed after abandonment, not before. The Anasazi knew about erosion control: check dams they built well before they abandoned the place are still doing a fine job of holding back the earth and preventing further gullying today.

For a while, factionalism seemed a promising theory. This variant of the outside-enemy hypothesis assumed an inside enemy instead, with internal bickering among the Anasazi leading to the breakup of their culture and the abandonment of their cities. But if there was factionalism, what were they fighting about? Social structure? Religion? Water holes? Family or clan ties? Did an unavenged murder set neighbor against neighbor, or was it a point of theology? And why did *everyone* leave — why didn't the winners stick around? This "answer" raises at least as many riddles as it solves, and today it too has largely been abandoned, at least as a single cause.

In fact, the single-cause theory itself has largely been abandoned. Archaeologists today are pretty well convinced that it was a complex of causes that led to Mesa Verde's abandonment. The drought probably figured; so did factionalism, and soil erosion, and possibly even epidemic disease. The Anasazi could have coped with any of these things by itself. All of them together would have been overwhelming.

And what would cause such a complex of misfortunes to strike at once? To understand, we will need to go back briefly to Adam Smith and George Perkins Marsh.

We will begin with Marsh. Recall the old lawyer-naturalist's basic premise: nature is composed of connections, and by severing too many of those connections humanity has been reducing the planet's productivity. The "barren, turfless hills" of the ancient world were not a natural phenomenon, according to Marsh, but the result of resource overuse. Technology can help overcome an area's resource limitations — the intricate and far-reaching irrigation network of the Anasazi is a perfect example — but if you burst through one limit you end up, because of the connections, pushing even harder against the rest of them. Eventually, inevitably, the resource base begins to crumble. The impoverished land, sapped of its strength, can no longer support the weight of the culture. The culture collapses. Marsh was fond of pointing to the stunted crops and barren fields of the Roman Campagna. There, he would say, was the Fall of Rome. The bread basket had failed. The barbarians only came along and mopped up the remains.

But if Marsh tells us what can happen to a culture when its resources fail, he is not very good at explaining what happens to the people. The two are not synonymous. Cultures rise and fall; people go on. Where do they go? Marsh cannot tell us. It is only when we turn to Smith that we begin to perceive the hint of what might be an answer.

Bring back to mind Smith's central axiom: labor creates value. There is an obvious corollary: the more labor, the more value. The more effort that goes into creating an object, the more that object is worth.

Notice that this relationship exists whether or not the extra labor is actually necessary to make the object useful. A Rolex and a Casio do the same job, and they do it in roughly the same way. The extra value of the Rolex lies in superior craftsmanship, not superior utility. One yearns for a Lexus; one makes do with a Toyota. But what if the Toyota itself becomes too expensive to purchase?

The answer is that one buys a bicycle, or walks. When an entire class of goods is priced out of reach, substitutes must be sought in other classes. But what if there are no substitutes?

Go back, now, to Mesa Verde. Consider the simple task of placing a meal on the table. The first step is to build a fire; but there are no longer any trees nearby for firewood. To obtain fuel you must walk many miles, using up valuable energy and time. There is no substitute for this commodity; you have to pay the price, or do without.

The second step is to put food on the fire. Where has the food come from? From fields on the mesa top. These fields are losing their fertility; each year, it takes more and more work to produce a crop from them. Again, however, there is no substitute. You either labor to coax a few more ears of corn out of the impoverished soil, or you go elsewhere.

Water is a special case. Your meal must include it. Where do you get it? From the rain that falls on the mesa top, or from the springs that seep out high up on the canyon walls.

(You may or may not understand that the springs themselves are dependent upon the rain.) In either case, you are dealing with a renewable resource. More rain comes; more water flows out of the ground. The problem here is not that there are no replacements; the problem is the limited rate at which replacement occurs. You cannot use water up, but you can use it faster than it is being replenished. Again, time and effort will be needed to overcome this problem. Again, the value — and the price — will climb.

In fact, the problems of the Anasazi most likely started with water. Mesa Verde is a dry land, and water on the plateau top is a scarce commodity. In the beginning there was probably enough for both domestic and agricultural uses; but as the population grew, the resource would have been stretched thinner and thinner. Eventually someone would have pointed out that there was a substitute for domestic purposes which could not be used for agriculture: the springs below the rim. It would be cheaper to develop this new source than to continue to divide up the old one. The move to the cliffs would have begun.

It was only a temporary fix. Crop yields continued to decline, keeping the price of food high. Firewood was becoming more and more expensive as the forests were exhausted. And water was still a problem. The best springs would be quickly staked out by the wealthy, who would erect barriers to keep out the riffraff. The rest of society would have to make do with lesser sites. It is no mystery why, even in the absence of a specific "enemy," a superb location like Balcony House has walls around it. Exactly the same situation can be found today in Beverly Hills or Miami Beach or St. Clair Shores.

Eventually, the cost of living would rise so high that people would begin to move away. Those for whom the cost of making the move was cheapest would go first: unattached young people, older people who had lost their families, the socially marginalized with few possessions and no homes worth hanging on to. As the cost of staying relative to the cost of moving continued to go up, more people would join the first. Drought would accelerate the process. Finally only a few diehards would be left; then nobody at all. Anasazi expert Linda S. Cordell of the University of New Mexico has given us a poignant description of those final days:

> They seem not to have been in any hurry to leave, because they took most of their portable household belongings with them. Perhaps their first new homes were built fairly close to their old cliff dwellings, so that they could visit their former houses and carry away items that were still useful. Eventually the people made their homes among other Anasazi living in the Rio Grande area, where their descendants still reside. Visits to the old homeland quietly ceased, and the cliff dwellings lay empty and brooding above the green canyons.

Note that the intention was not to abandon the cities. The intention was self-betterment. Staying was expensive; moving was cheap. The decisions were individual, but the result was collective. The invisible hand was at work. The society was better off over by the Rio Grande. Individuals seeking an improvement in their own economic status moved it there.

Marsh — and ecology — explains why life became so expensive at Mesa Verde. Smith — and economics — explains what happened when it did. Neither explanation can do the work of the other. Neither discipline can stand alone.

Come with me once again to Far View House. Climb the Park Service ladder to the top of one of the high walls at the rear of the complex. Look toward Shiprock. The haze that muddles your view is man-made; its principal source is the immense Four Corners power plant near the desert corner where Utah, Arizona, Colorado, and New Mexico meet. The loss of Far View's far view is one of the prices we pay for air conditioners and electric ranges and streetlights and much else that we take for granted in modern society. Is it too high a price? The question is meaningless without context. Too high compared to what? Too high for whom?

It is better to stick to more basic questions.

Why is the cost of living rising while the quality of living falls? Ask ecology.

How are we likely to respond to these two disturbing trends? Ask economics.

What is the *best* — as opposed to the *most likely* — response to the twin traumas of rising costs and declining quality of life? Ask both disciplines. Ask both.

One

The Deer in the Mall

Only One Household

THERE IS NO LONGER anyplace on the planet that the environmental crisis has not reached.

The litany of damage is numbing. Waste products spewed into the atmosphere have altered the Earth's climate and opened holes in the ozone layer. Deforestation is taking place on a continentwide scale. Rivers and lakes have become toxic cesspools; even water from remote wilderness streams is often too polluted to drink. Groundwater resources are used up, contaminated, or both, over much of the world. The air in our cities cannot be safely breathed. Garbage spills out of old, overcrowded landfills, and there is no place to put new ones. The gentle, life-giving rain has become sulfuric acid.

There is literally no place to flee. Not to the ends of the Earth; that is where the ozone holes are. Not to the equatorial jungles; they are falling to the axe so fast that, as an intact ecosystem, they are not likely to last out the century. Not to the floor of the sea; it is littered with household trash, and polluted dredge spoil, and canisters filled with radioactive waste and toxic chemicals, and a myriad of other things we have dumped there under the delusion that we were getting rid of them. And not even to the depths of the Earth; those too are polluted. For decades now, we have been injecting hazardous wastes into aquifers as much as 20,000 feet below the surface of the planet. According to current EPA and industry estimates, there are some six hundred active injection wells in the United States alone — and upwards of forty thousand abandoned ones. Approximately 60 percent of the toxic waste we produce in this nation is currently handled by this so-called deepwell disposal method, which threatens groundwater supplies, alters the structures of subsurface rock formations, and has been known (in at least one thoroughly documented case, near Denver, Colorado) to cause swarms of earthquakes.

Nor can we successfully escape to those little bits of nature we have drawn lines around and explicitly chosen to leave undisturbed. Our parks and wilderness areas are in at least as much trouble as the rest of the planet. Two recently released studies demonstrate just how deep this trouble may be. An internal audit of the National Park Service conducted by the inspector general of the Interior Department found most of the thirty-three parks studied suffering from "serious and irreversible degradation" due to Park Service budget priorities, which have for years been emphasizing visitor services (92 percent of moneys spent) over protection of park ecosystems (8 percent). And an even broader study by the National Academy of Sciences, released on January 13, 1993, found "virtually all" parks and wilderness areas in the United States suffering seriously from air pollution. "[S]cenic vistas in most U.S. parklands," stated the Academy, "are often diminished by haze that reduces contrast, washes out colors and renders distant landscape features indistinct or invisible." For parks and preserves established to protect scenery, this is more than a minor nuisance: it is an attack on the central reason for their existence.

These problems are by now widely recognized and endlessly talked about. What is not generally recognized or talked about is that they are economic problems as well as ecological ones.

The health of a society's economy depends to an overwhelming extent on its relationship to its environment. This is true whether the economy is built on free trade or command-and-control; whether the society's focus is material or spiritual; whether the resources it uses are obtained directly from the earth or through trade with other societies; or even whether or not the society is human. The birds of Alaska's Bligh Reef had a far healthier economy before the *Exxon Valdez* ran aground there than they had in the days and months immediately afterward. Island nations such as England and Japan remain prosperous only to the extent that they can trade ideas, such as manufacturing know-how, for the products of other peoples' environments. Monks in monastic retreats must either labor in their own fields and vineyards or depend upon the largesse of a religiously minded people around them. Communism fell in Eastern Europe in large part because the resource bases of those ancient countries had been so badly neglected and abused, in the name of "economic progress," in the four decades since the end of the Second World War.

All of a nation's physical resources come in some form or another from the earth. Food must be grown in the soil; lumber must be harvested from the forests; minerals must be ripped from the rocks or distilled from the salt-laden waters of the sea. There are no other sources for these materials. Even intellectual products derive ultimately from the environment, for the mind is housed in the body and the body must be fed and clothed. All of us — capitalist and communist, industrialist and environmentalist, pragmatist, reactionary, and wild-eyed radical — all of us make our living only with what the earth gives us. It is the only way we can possibly stay alive.

So it has been through the centuries. Today, however, we are being told over and over that the source of an economy's wealth — its surrounding environment — and the economy itself can not only be divorced from each other but are basically antagonistic. Environmental protection "costs jobs" and leads to an outflow of capital from the protected area. Economic development "rapes the environment," leading to the loss of species diversity, the destruction of natural beauty, and, ultimately, human sickness and death. Here is Thoreau, muttering about a farmer "who would carry the landscape, who would carry his God, to market, if he could get any thing for him"; over there is Dan Quayle, complaining about Democrats who "put people first, unless there happens to be a spotted owl or a great garter snake or some other endangered species, and then that needs to have priority. . . . We must give priority to economic growth and the creation of jobs." On this side is the activist and vegetarian George Wuerthner, lambasting his fellow environmentalists for their carnivorousness: "You can't support wolf reintroductions in Yellowstone while consuming a big thick steak or be opposed to predator control if you chew on hamburgers." On the other side of the dietary fence stands Richard Darman, budget director for the Bush administration, telling the press emphatically that "Americans did not fight and win the wars of the twentieth century to make the world safe for green vegetables." The rhetoric rolls on and on, escalating as it goes, eventually reaching beyond rhetoric and into violence: fistfights in bars, spikes in trees, firebombs in environmentalists' cars, sand in the gas tanks of developers' bulldozers.

But if economic well-being and environmental protection are so strongly opposed, why is it that we so often find them together? Shove the rhetoric aside for a moment and look at the land. You will rapidly observe a striking correlation: ecologically distressed areas are almost always economically distressed as well. This is most easily seen in urban sacrifice areas such as south Chicago, central Los Angeles, and east Newark, but it is equally true of rural America. From the coal country of Appalachia to the logging towns of the Pacific Northwest, industries that have ripped wealth out of the land have left behind raw pockets of aching, bleeding poverty. The coincidence of a degraded, polluted landscape and a depressed economy in such places as Forks, Washington; Lake Linden, Michigan; Hammond, Indiana; and Pineville, Kentucky, is no accident; it is an integral part of the way we Americans have been doing things.

In contrast to the stagnant state of these economic and ecologic backwaters is the condition of such places as Santa Fe, New Mexico; Hilton Head, South Carolina; Davis, California; and Burlington, Vermont. These widely diverse areas all hold two things in common. They are places where strict land-use controls and other environmental regulations are in place, enforced, and supported by the people. And they are among the wealthiest communities in America. Property values are high; local businesses are booming. Economic indicators are extremely healthy. Money is drawn to these areas precisely because they have taken care of their environments. Forests and streams as neighbors create good places to live. Steel mills and coal mines create bad ones. Straightforward market forces do the rest.

Environmentalists prepared to chortle over the failure of economic exploitation to provide economic success, though, had better hold their tongues. The unwelcome truth is that environmental protection has not really provided a sound environment, either. The Davises and the Burlingtons are prettier, cleaner, and healthier than the south Chicagos and the Lake Lindens; but under those shining, scrubbed facades the same dark problems hide. Our vast complex of laws and regulations, our widespread network of parks and preserves, and our libraries full of ecologically conscious literature have yet to do more than minor cosmetic damage to the juggernaut that is destroying the planet. We have dented a fender or two, but the bulldozers continue to plow ahead.

Despite the flurry of legislation following the publication of *Silent Spring,* pesticide use in the United States has continued to climb dramatically, up from 648 million pounds per year in Rachel Carson's day to about 2.5 billion in our own. Fertilizer use has approximately doubled in the same period, rising from 25 million to 54 million tons annually. Twenty years of clean-water and clean-air legislation have left us with only marginally cleaner water and air. (In many places, it is actually considerably dirtier.) And though wilderness and park acreage is up dramatically, there is little evidence that this trend has improved the overall state of the environment. The gross forms of degradation — clear-cuts, freeways, mines — have not gone away, but simply shifted elsewhere. The more subtle forms have continued unabated, undeterred by human-created boundaries. Species diversity is down within the preserves as well as outside them, and air and water pollution are up. Acid rain respects no borders: there are at least as many acidified lakes within the "protected" area of the Adirondack Forest Preserve as there are in the rest of upstate New York.

When I first began hiking the wilderness trails of the Pacific Northwest, back in the early 1960s, I could stick a cup directly into virtually any stream I came across, confident that the cold, clear, vibrantly fresh water would be safe to drink. Today one must carry a filter. In thousands of little ways like this, the wilderness becomes less wild. Our belief that we can "preserve" these lands may comfort us, but it is no less a delusion than that of the developers who believe they can draw boundless resources from them, for free, until the end of time.

It is always easy to lay blame, but the exercise is curiously unproductive. Workers blame environmentalists; environmentalists blame developers; developers blame regulatory agencies; and regulatory agencies blame voters, whose ranks include workers, environmentalists, and developers. The fingers point in a circle, and we are no wiser than when we began.

It is also easy to come up with alternatives. The use of fossil fuels, with all its attendant environmental costs, would clearly drop dramatically if we all switched to solar heat. Pollution could be slashed if wastes were recycled instead of discarded. More money would be available for improving the lot of the poor if the wealthy would forgo some profit. Unemployment would be reduced if corporate energy now wasted on meeting the increasingly arcane and complex demands of the regulatory process could be used instead to create jobs. The problem with these and similar solutions is not that they won't work; the problem is that no one is implementing them. Means of implementation have been suggested, but they remain untested. Everyone wants to live in Utopia, but no one wants to put out the energy necessary to get from here to there.

It is time to begin seriously rethinking the ways in which we approach these things.

The great English economist Alfred Marshall once compared supply and demand to a pair of scissors: one blade, he pointed out, was totally useless without the other. Exactly the same can be said of economics and ecology. The time has come when we must recognize that neither free enterprise in ignorance of ecological principles, nor legalistic protectionism in ignorance of the laws of economics, is going to do more than temporarily improve our position on the planet. The time has come to look for the point where the scissors meet — the point where we recognize the truths of both ecology and economics, the point where each action we take is tested and judged by its conformance to both of these sciences.

The Greek root *oikos* means "household"; *nomos* means "management." The word *economics,* derived from these roots, thus means literally "household management," and originally that is exactly what economics involved. Economists planned purchases, kept track of income and outgo, and generally made sure that household affairs ran smoothly. They still do that, but today *household* has taken on a considerably larger meaning. Ever since Adam Smith demonstrated that the behavior of individual households could not be considered apart from one another, but had to be seen in the much broader context of markets, the *oikos* of economics has been understood to mean not just a household enclosed by four walls, but the household that belongs to all of us. The planetary household: indeed, the planet itself.

The Greek root *logos* means "study." *Ecology* thus means literally "household study"; but, unlike *economics,* the word *ecology* was never meant to apply to a literal, four-walled household. The term was coined in the nineteenth century by natural scientists who were consciously basing their choice of roots on the newly expanded meaning of the older term. The "eco" in *ecology* has always referred to the planetary household.

Ecology and economics are often pictured as implacable foes. But there is only one household. Ultimately, if economics and ecology are both true, they cannot possibly conflict with one another.

Of Laws and Regulations

A FEW MONTHS AGO in Florida, a real estate developer called a small group of his employees together for an unusual hunting trip. The venue was a large piece of private land on which he held development rights; the quarry was a bird on the endangered species list. The developer knew that if this bird were found on his land, he would have to curtail his building plans severely, perhaps even abandon them, under the terms of the Endangered Species Act. He was determined that no such finding would take place. "Gentlemen," he told the group, holding aloft a specimen of the endangered bird, "this is the enemy."

The Florida developer's action was particularly blatant, but it was not otherwise especially unusual. Polls may show that Americans support environmental legislation, but the record of compliance speaks otherwise. Indeed, there is probably no other class of laws that is so routinely evaded, violated, and ignored as those that have to do with environmental protection. On paper, our environmental protection mechanism is regulated as tightly as a fine watch. In practice, it is more like a wind-up clown with a drum — making a lot of noise, running around in circles, and running down almost immediately.

Take Superfund, for example. Passed in 1980 as the centerpiece of Congress's response to the hazardous waste crises that had been uncovered in the late 1970s at Love Canal near Niagara Falls, New York; Valley of the Drums, south of Louisville, Kentucky; White Lake, just outside of Muskegon, Michigan; and others, the Superfund Act — officially, the Comprehensive Environmental Response, Compensation and Liability Act of 1980 (CERCLA) — established a massive pool of funds, to be collected from taxes and other levies on companies that manufacture hazardous materials. The EPA was supposed to use the funds to identify and clean up the nation's huge backlog of toxic waste disposal sites. The original legislation included no deadlines; the size of the funding pool was set at a then astounding $1.6 billion. Six years later, frustrated by the lack of observable results, Congress passed what has come to be known as SARA (Superfund Amendments and Reauthorization Act). SARA jacked the size of the funding pool up to $10.1 billion and demanded that the EPA begin work on at least 375 sites by 1991. Another $5.1 billion was added to the fund's authorization in 1990, bringing the total pool to $15.2 billion — nearly ten times its "astounding" size just a decade before.

But CERCLA and SARA have done very little good. Of the roughly 400 sites on the original 1980 Superfund list, exactly 38 had been cleaned up as of May 1992. Another 312 were at some stage of the process. Meanwhile, the list had ballooned upward to 1,207 sites, with another 900 expected by the end of the decade. Cost estimates had shot up as well, with the entire bill expected to come in at around $300 billion — nearly twenty times the amount in the already bloated fund, and *two hundred times* the original estimate. And even at the sites where work had taken place, the results were questionable. In a yearlong study conducted between March 1991 and March 1992, the General Accounting Office found that the EPA's standards for declaring decontamination "successful" varied by as much as 360,000 percent from site to site. Soil cleanup goals for polyaromatic hydrocarbons (PAH), for example, ranged from 0.19 parts per million at the low end to 700 ppm at the upper limit. Similarly broad ranges were found for several other materials, including arsenic, chromium, and pentachlorophenol. And even the high figures were misleading, because they applied only to the minority of sites where some form of decontamination had been attempted. Of the 317 sites examined by the GAO, treatment of the contaminated materials had actually taken place at only 106. At the other 211, "cleanup" was really only containment.

Or look at the Great Lakes Water Quality Agreement of 1978 (GLWQA). Hailed widely at the time for its "dramatic new initiatives" in international environmental law, this "precedent-setting" treaty, signed at Ottawa on November 22, 1978, committed the United States and Canada to manage the shared resource of the Great Lakes in such a way as to achieve "zero discharge" of persistent toxic substances into their waters. To achieve this and other goals, the GLWQA required its signatories to take what has since been termed the "ecosystem approach" to pollution control, looking not only at the lakes themselves but also at the rivers draining into them; the farms, forests, and urban areas bordering the rivers; and the air arching over the whole thing. The language of the agreement was very explicit. Certainly now, environmentalists thought, we will get someplace.

But, of course, they didn't. "We were shocked to see so many blatant violations of those promises," wrote one pair of activists, John Jackson and Tim Eder, after touring the lakes on behalf of a labor-environmental coalition called Great Lakes United in the summer and fall of 1986:

> Plumes of black contaminants still reach out into the Lakes. Large cities still dump sewage that has only received primary treatment. Industrial smoke stacks still belch contaminants into the air. Old dump sites continue to leak dioxins, PCBs and numerous other insidiously destructive chemicals into rivers and lakes. Agricultural runoff continues to release massive quantities of pesticides and phosphorus-laden fertilizers into the Basin's waters. Dredging operations still pour toxic sediments into open waters. Every day hundreds of trucks still dump contaminated fill into the Lakes.

The context of these remarks is itself interesting: frustrated by the near-total lack of public hearings on treaty enforcement mechanisms, Great Lakes United had held its own set of hearings on progress under the Water Quality Agreement. At considerable expense and effort, the group took testimony from 382 people — public officials, fishermen, water activists, labor leaders, and just plain citizens — at nineteen separate sites around the Great Lakes basin over a four-month period. The results, professionally prepared, edited, and bound, were officially presented to the governments of both nations and to the International Joint Commission, the body charged with enforcing the agreement, in February 1987. It is almost too kind to say that the entire effort was ignored. By October 1991, frustration levels had reached such a height that Great Lakes United was calling for the abolition of the International Joint Commission's Water Quality Board and was actively petitioning the United Nations to crack down on its member nations for refusing to take any significant steps to abide by their own treaties. "In light of the failure of the governments to comply with the Great Lakes Water Quality Agreement," the organization wrote to Secretary-General Javier Pérez de Cuéllar, "we hereby formally request that the United Nations investigate the breaches of the Agreement. The critical state of the Great Lakes leaves us no choice but to request your intervention in this matter." The story was familiar: thirteen years after the agreement had been signed, not even basic inventories of toxic substances, point source impact zones, and wetlands had been completed. In most cases, they had barely been started.

Late in 1991, in preparation for the twentieth anniversary of the federal Clean Water Act, a group of reporters at the *Washington Post* began looking into what the nation's premier water pollution law had accomplished over its first two decades of life. It was no secret that the act's lofty goals — "fishable, swimmable waters" throughout the nation by 1983, "no net discharge" of pollutants into navigable waters by 1985 — had not been met. How far had enforcement fallen short, and what remained to be done?

It is probable that even the most cynical of the *Post*'s reporters were shocked by what they turned up. Nineteen years after passage of the act, and six years after it was supposed to be in full effect, the Environmental Protection Agency, charged with enforcing the legislation, had not even written the rules covering four-fifths of the industries that it was supposed to regulate. Industries with no rules in place included hazardous waste treatment facilities, commercial solvent recyclers, industrial laundries, hospitals, and chemical-drum recyclers. Machinery manufacturers remained unregulated; so did used-oil recyclers and much of the transportation industry. All in all, of some 75,000 industrial facilities around the nation that the Clean Water Act was supposed to police, 60,000 did not even have standards in place for judging their performance. Nor did there seem to be much hope that the situation would improve soon. Wrote the *Post* reporters, sounding somewhat disgruntled:

> Four years ago, frustrated by the EPA's inertia and the growing toxic threat, Congress ordered the agency to identify unregulated industrial sources of toxics, to start regulating them by February 1991, and to update the standards set as far back as the 1970s.
>
> A year after the deadline, the EPA has not issued a single new guideline.

It would be bad enough if these were isolated examples. Unfortunately, they are not. Virtually every one of the nation's showcase pieces of environmental legislation is afflicted, to a greater or lesser degree, with the same lackadaisical level of enforcement as Superfund and the Great Lakes Water Quality Agreement and the Clean Water Act. The difficulty of enforcing most of these laws, and the less-than-wholehearted attention given to them by the enforcement agencies, keeps violators fairly secure; and since the penalties for being caught rarely match the gains possible from continued violation, even strict enforcement is not usually enough to guarantee full compliance. What the *Post* termed the EPA's "default" on clean water standards is the norm, not the exception.

The damages resulting from these defaults vary widely. Often they are relatively minor: trash dumped along forest roads, untreated wastes discharged from pleasure boats into rivers or lakes, nearly unmeasurably small amounts of hazardous substances in the outfalls of industrial plants not quite in compliance. At other times they may be substantial: wetlands drained and filled without permits, endangered species lost due to deliberate habitat destruction, rivers polluted badly enough to kill their fish or to render them unfit for human consumption.

Sometimes the violations are only technical. In a 1992 case in South Dakota, for example, thirty-eight truckloads of infectious medical wastes were buried on a Mellette County ranch without a landfill permit, and the hospitals and clinics that were the sources of the wastes received falsified papers stating that the materials had been incinerated. Though obviously illegal, the operation had caused little environmental harm: the operators had followed good landfill practices — construction and backfilling of the site, they later testified, had cost them more than $20,000 — and a thorough examination by local health officials turned up no environmental hazards. At other times, the damage is almost literally incalculable. In Virginia, a company called Avtex Fibers was cited repeatedly by state and federal authorities over a period of nine years for a long list of offenses which included waste discharges into the Shenandoah River (at least 1,600 times), groundwater contamination, and air quality violations that reached as much as 770 times the allowable discharge rate for carbon disulfide. When the company was finally closed down, in November 1989, the plant site was found to be so heavily contaminated that it was immediately placed on the Superfund cleanup list, where officials estimated that it would probably incur cleanup costs "among the highest to date." The company, which had declared bankruptcy, could not be held financially liable.

Do regulations ever work? Occasionally. Certainly the air in America's urban areas is cleaner today than it was in the late 1970s, and there is no question that the 1972 Clean Air Act played a major, if belated, role. There has been a 97 percent reduction in atmospheric loadings of lead over the same period, due in no small part to the fact that cars burning leaded gas can no longer be legally manufactured for sale. Water, too, is cleaner than it once was. On June 22, 1969, the Cuyahoga River in downtown Cleveland, Ohio, caught on fire, and the fireboat *Anthony J. Celebrezze* had to be called out from its berth on the city's Lake Erie waterfront to go upstream and put out the river. The Cuyahoga is still not drinkable or even swimmable today, but at least it is no longer flammable. Clevelanders, who once stayed away from their river in droves, are beginning to trickle back, drawn by restaurants, boat tours, and other businesses that have taken advantage of the revitalized river. It would be foolish to deny that these gains exist, or to imply that the regulatory requirements of the Clean Water Act, the Toxic Substances Control Act, and similar pieces of legislation have not been major contributors to this improvement.

But it would be equally foolish to state that these successes, however laudable, mean that environmental regulation is doing its job. To do so would be to ignore the Great Smoky Mountains, where man-made smog now exceeds the mountains' famous natural haze by a ratio of better than two to one. It would ignore northern New Hampshire, where ozone levels at the top of 6,288-foot Mount Washington — the highest peak in the northeast — now regularly exceed the levels set by federal standards for downtown Los Angeles. And it would also ignore Los Angeles. The city that invented photochemical smog is still massively plagued by it, so much so that in 1989 California's South Coast Air Quality Management District, which oversees air pollution goal enforcement in the Los Angeles basin, adopted a truly draconian set of rules, known collectively as The Plan, which regulate (among other things) the commercial formulas for hair spray, nail polish, and barbecue lighter fluid; the exhaust gases of lawn mowers and chain saws; the disposal of cow manure on those few farms that still remain in the basin; and the operation of ships as far as 60 miles out to sea. "It's an Orwellian nightmare," grumbles Los Angeles County Supervisor Mike Antonovich. It may also be futile. Los Angeles authorities are likely to run into the same massive noncompliance faced by the Italian government in January 1993, when it attempted — in the face of smog problems at least as severe as those encountered in the City of Angels — to shut down private automobile traffic completely for parts of each day in a number of major cities, including Rome, Milan, Naples, Trieste, and Florence. The first three hours of the ban saw more than seven thousand tickets written by police in Rome alone, despite the imposition of a compulsory seventy-dollar fine for each offense. "I'd rather pay the fine than leave the car" was one driver's angry response to a reporter's question. Angelenos may not feel the same way about their hair spray, but the precedents are not promising.

It can be argued, of course, that most of this is irrelevant to whether or not environmental protection measures, as currently conceived, are working. Naturally, one is tempted to say, laws that are being evaded are not doing their job. That is not a problem of the law but of enforcement. If the authorities would crack down, we could get someplace.

Naturally. I have no quarrel with enforcement, certainly; I have applauded as earnestly as any other environmentalist when the courts, under prodding from citizen groups, have forced federal agencies to follow the law — to protect the spotted owl and the marbled murrelet and the red-cockaded woodpecker, to file environmental impact statements, to get out of bed with the polluters and start cracking down on them. Given the damage, the laws that we have in place, and the political climate, enforcement is clearly good, necessary, and in too many cases long overdue.

I think it is necessary, however, to raise a couple of cautionary flags.

The first is that environmental damage is often irreversible. Once extinct, a species cannot be brought back; once cut down, an old-growth forest will not regenerate, at least not in the next several human lifetimes. Punishing the perpetrators of these desecrations after they have occurred may be good morals, but it is bad management. What we need is some means of preventing environmental damage from occurring. Laws that are opposed on principle, as many environmental laws are, will not do this. The landowners in southern California who have cut down all the coastal sage scrub on their lands to prevent the California gnatcatcher from nesting there will not be deterred by fines, or probably even jail sentences. They consider private property rights a sacred principle, and sacred principles are worth suffering for. Environmentalists, of all people, should understand that.

Second — and more important — the evidence suggests strongly that environmental laws, *even when fully enforced,* are not doing their job. Probably they cannot. Laws prescribe behavior, and prescribed behavior is necessarily inflexible and unchanging. But the essence of natural systems is change. Caught by this dichotomy, thoroughly imbued from conception with a worldview diametrically opposed to the systems it is designed to defend, our heritage of environmental law is creating failure through the offices of its own high designs.

To regulate is to prescribe certain forms of behavior and proscribe others. These prescriptions and proscriptions are necessarily based on current knowledge. When knowledge changes, the regulations are left behind. The behavior that the regulations control is forced to stay behind as well.

When regulations mandate the use of low-sulfur coal, utilities that develop technology to burn high-sulfur coal cleanly cannot use it because they cannot legally obtain the coal.

When regulations mandate the installation of septic tanks in rural areas, homeowners who wish to reduce their water consumption by recycling their wastes into fertilizer through the use of composting toilets will find themselves breaking the law.

When regulations mandate catalytic converters as a means of controlling pollutants in automotive exhaust, companies will be deprived of incentives to develop more effective pollution-control devices, and if by chance a company should develop such a device it could not legally be installed.

To depend on regulations of this nature is to fall into what can only be described as a lose-lose situation. The economy suffers because time, energy, and capital that should go into improving production methods are instead siphoned off into attempting to assure compliance with an ever more bewildering set of hoops to jump through. And the environment suffers because innovative approaches that might protect it fail to match the increasingly intricate cookie cutters wielded by the bureaucracy, and so cannot be implemented.

The real problem with the regulatory approach, it turns out, is not that the regulations are too long, or too full of burdensome paperwork, or too self-contradictory, or too intrusive into people's lives for any realistic chance for compliance. The real problem is simply that regulations regulate.

But this is really just a small part of a larger problem. Regulations, after all, do not arise in a vacuum. Regulations flow from a specific set of assumptions about the world. Among these, two stick out as particularly troublesome. One is *stasis:* the assumption that things can be trusted not to change unless we change them. The other is *separability:* the belief that it is possible to isolate the effects of an action to just those parts of the world we wish to act upon. The regulatory approach depends on stasis to ensure that rules, once in place, will remain valid for long periods of time. It depends on separability to assure proper targeting: regulations aimed at cleaning up water, for example, should not interfere with those aimed at cleaning up the air.

Unfortunately, neither of these comfortable assumptions is true. Both nature and human society are comprehensively dynamic and interconnected. Any attempt at environmental protection which does not deal with this basic fact is ultimately doomed to failure. To see the scope of that failure, one need only look at the current state of what is usually considered the crowning achievement of the American environmental movement: our great, continentwide system of parks, wilderness areas, and nature preserves.

Of Parks and Preserves

THE NATIONAL PARK was invented by Cornelius Hedges on September 19, 1870, beside a campfire at the junction of the Gibbon and Firehole rivers in northwestern Wyoming, where a survey party led by Henry Dana Washburn was bedding down after twenty-five days of exploration through the canyons and geysers of the country known today as The Yellowstone.

Or so goes the legend. Reality, as usual, is quite a bit messier.

Nations and their rulers have been setting aside nature preserves at least since the beginning of recorded history. Throughout most of that time, these areas have been primarily or exclusively for the use of the ruling classes — Robin Hood, you will remember, first got in trouble for shooting deer in the king's preserve in Sherwood Forest — but there has always been an undercurrent of populism that demanded parks for the people, too. The Greek city-states may have pioneered the modern park concept with the *agorae,* which were clearly set aside and maintained for the citizens at large, though they were more akin to village squares than to nature preserves. In more recent times, Victorian England set aside a number of large open spaces for the use of the common people, beginning with Victoria Park on the outskirts of London in 1842; France followed suit ten years later by deroyalizing the Bois de Boulogne. The Industrial Revolution was in full swing, and clean air and greenery had moved from being something one could take for granted to something one had to demand. Fifty years earlier, Ned Ludd and his followers had protested industrialization by smashing up factory machinery. But the Luddites were dead now, and the machinery had won. The best one could hope for was a little taste of rural life on one's day off.

On this continent, sentiment for preserving natural "wonders" dates back at least to Alexis de Tocqueville's 1831 plea to his friends that they should go to see Niagara Falls before America "spoiled" it with factories and waterwheels. But the real chance to preserve preindustrial landscapes lay in the undeveloped West. Just a year after Tocqueville's entreaty, the painter George Catlin was urging his countrymen to set aside most of the Great Plains and the Rocky Mountains as "a *nation's Park,* containing man and beast, in all the wild and freshness of their nature's beauty." That same year, 1832, saw the first national park actually created, at Hot Springs, Arkansas, though it was termed a "reservation" rather than a park. On June 30, 1864 — still more than six years before Cornelius Hedges's famous exhortation to his companions on the Washburn Expedition — the Yosemite Valley was deeded over to the state of California by Congress for the express purpose of protecting its scenery "inalienable for all time." (It would be returned to federal hands, at Congress's request, in 1905. California wasn't treating it inalienably enough.)

The Yellowstone Act of 1872 did, however, mark a pair of significant milestones. It was the first piece of legislation in which the term *national park* was actually used. And it was the first time a large, wild piece of land was set aside specifically to be preserved in its natural state. The original Yosemite bill had encompassed only the forty square miles of land immediately surrounding the valley itself and, as a separate four-mile-square unit, the Mariposa Grove of Giant Sequoias. Yellowstone was more than eighty times as large — nearly 3,500 square miles. Hedges and his companions were clearly serious about the job.

There is nothing in the Yellowstone legislation suggesting that its backers thought of it as only a beginning; but that, of course, is precisely what it turned out to be. Today, the national park system protects some 75 million acres of land spread over more than 330 separate areas in all fifty states, plus Guam, the Virgin Islands, and Puerto Rico. These areas carry a variety of labels: not only national parks but national monuments, national lakeshores, national seashores, national recreation areas, national rivers, and national preserves. Whatever they are called, all share a common mandate: to preserve and protect the scenic, scientific, and recreational values of natural landscapes "for the benefit and enjoyment of the people." Those words, which appear in the original Yellowstone Act, still guide Park Service policy. The national parks are really just the Bois de Boulogne, transplanted to the fertile soil of America and allowed to grow.

Wilderness areas show a similar historic dynamic. Officially, the first protected wilderness in the United States was the Gila, set aside in New Mexico by the Forest Service — at the urgings of a young assistant regional supervisor named Aldo Leopold — in 1924. Actually, the state of New York had beaten the Forest Service to the punch by nearly thirty years. Not just state law, but the state constitution, had, in an amendment that took effect on January 1, 1895, set the Adirondack Forest Preserve aside to "be forever kept as wild forest lands." Nor was New York alone. Californians had begun quietly setting aside small groves of redwoods marked for total preservation — that is, wilderness — as early as 1867, though these were rarely more than a square mile in size. At the other end of the scale, President Theodore Roosevelt's March 2, 1909, proclamation that created the Mount Olympus National Monument in the state of Washington was worded strictly enough to set the entire 600,000-acre area off-limits to virtually all forms of development, making it a wilderness rather than a park in everything but name, even if the actual author of the proclamation, Washington congressman W. E. Humphreys, would protest later that he didn't really mean it.

So the Gila, like Yellowstone, was not really a first. But the Gila — also like Yellowstone — did establish a significant pair of precedents. It was the first area specifically to be called a "wilderness." And it created a generic wildlands-preservation pattern that could be followed elsewhere. It was. Today there are roughly 89 million acres of declared wilderness in the United States, mostly in the West (though outstanding examples also exist in New England and the central Appalachians). Since 1964, these areas have been congressionally protected as national wilderness areas, rather than being proclaimed by Forest Service edict, granting them considerably improved security against shrinkage and piecemeal erosion of their wild character.

There are other preserves besides national parks and national wilderness areas. There are national wildlife refuges (more than 400 of them), national wild and scenic rivers (115, with a combined length of some 9,300 miles), and various networks of administratively protected federal lands, such as the Forest Service's special interest areas and the Bureau of Land Management's areas of critical environmental concern. There are also state preservation systems — state parks, state forests, state wildlife preserves — many of which match the national preserves in caliber. (Adirondack Park is still the best of these, but Michigan's Porcupine Mountains Wilderness Park and California's Anza-Borrego Desert Park are not far behind.) There are even a few city- and county-owned "urban wildernesses," such as Chicago's Cook County Forest Preserve and Portland, Oregon's immense Forest Park. Private landowners have also gotten into the act. Private wildernesses of significant size exist in every part of the country; these range from one-shot preserves like the Huron Mountain Club's holdings on Michigan's Upper Peninsula to the vast, far-flung system of nature reserves (more than 900 of them, in all fifty states) run by the Nature Conservancy.

All of which sounds as though nature preservation by boundary and fiat is working splendidly. Unfortunately, even a cursory examination of the preserves themselves shows that this is not true.

On the 8,000-foot-high southwest shoulder of Bearcamp Mountain in California's remote, spectacular Warner Mountains lies a series of four clear-cuts, half in and half out of the South Warner Wilderness. The wilderness area was there before the clear-cuts. Modoc National Forest, the federal agency responsible for this outrage, has blamed the intrusion on poor internal communication: its timber planners thought the wilderness boundary was farther north than it had actually been drawn. Trees on approximately 262 acres within the "protected" area were felled before a visiting Sacramento-area environmentalist pointed out to forest officials, with some alarm, exactly what was going on.

A similar situation exists in the Oregon Cascades. There, sometime in the 1980s, timber planners for Willamette National Forest attempted to wrap a clear-cut around a square corner of the Three Sisters Wilderness. They missed. The result was an L-shaped bare patch with two ruler-straight edges, lying almost entirely on what is officially "wilderness" land.

Early in 1993, a Park Service ranger in West Virginia discovered signs of fresh logging in a remote corner of the 62,000-acre New River Gorge National River. Investigation revealed that a local timber operator, one Richard Bailey, had constructed more than a mile and a quarter of road within the park boundaries and had used this road to log approximately 75 acres of National Park Service land. Bailey told park officials that he thought he was logging timber he had leased from a private landowner, and that he was "unaware of any NPS property in the area." At the time, the land in question had been part of the national park system for nearly fifteen years.

Logging in protected areas is clearly illegal. But perfectly legal environmental damage goes on within our so-called preserves as well. Loopholes in the enabling legislation have allowed, among other things, chromium mines in Oregon's Kalmiopsis Wilderness, gold and silver mines in Montana's Cabinet Mountains Wilderness, and geothermal steam wells in California's Salton Sea National Wildlife Refuge. Grazing is an allowed use on virtually all national forest lands, including designated wilderness, and many of the high-country wilderness areas in the Sierras and the Rocky Mountains are consistently overgrazed by cattle and sheep, to the point where some presumably "protected" ecosystems bear almost no resemblance to the natural ecosystems supported by the areas before the arrival of domestic livestock. Despite the title "wildlife refuge," hunting, livestock grazing, and even a limited amount of crop raising all take place regularly — and legally — on refuge lands.

Allowed but incompatible uses are not the only, or even necessarily the worst, legally sanctioned problems these areas face. Parks, wilderness areas, and other preserves are also in danger of being destroyed by their own success, mobbed and mauled by scenery-lovers like matinee idols in a crush of teenage fans. Trails in most of the nation's backcountry areas have been broadened and deeply rutted by the passage of thousands of booted feet, to the point where some wilderness-preservation advocates have begun requesting plaintively that hikers replace their traditional "waffle-stomper" boots with treadless footgear. Meadows are crisscrossed by way trails and marred by trampled and threadbare patches at particularly choice, and therefore heavily used, campsites. Soil, laid bare, is eroding into popular streams and springs. High-country lakes are ringed by closely spaced stone fire circles that make the "pristine" wilderness resemble a megalithic cemetery.

Most of the picturesque weathered snags that were once scattered widely through the high sierra have gone into campfires, and the woodpeckers and other wildlife that depended on them have become rare. Litter and other signs of human carelessness have proliferated, some of it caused by the areas' supposed "protectors." I once led a Sierra Club outing to a small subalpine lake in northern California's Siskiyou Mountains, in the heart of a roadless area we were trying to get protected as wilderness. At the lake were the remains of a very recent and extremely sloppy camp. Horse excrement fouled the lake water; the remains of a campfire still smoldered, waiting for a wind to fan it into flame and into the nearby trees. Cardboard and other litter blew about the area. When picked up, the cardboard proved to be part of a large delivery box. Prominent on one section was the name of the addressee — the local headquarters of the national forest on whose ground the camp was located.

Park Service areas probably suffer the most. Their legislated mission statement has a great deal to do with this. When your mandate is "the benefit and enjoyment of the people," nature necessarily takes a back seat. Thus we get extensive road systems, and paved trails, and parking lots, and hotels. We get pizza parlors and video-rental shops amid the wall-to-wall cars on the floor of Yosemite Valley. In the fall of 1992, the Park Service's Southwest Region adopted a set of thirty-two "goals and objectives" to guide it through 1993. An employee at one of the region's parks sent me a copy of the document laying out these goals and objectives, along with a tally he had made dividing them into "environmentally oriented" and "human oriented" categories. The human goals outnumbered the environmental goals by a ratio of eight to one.

All of these problems, of course, represent matters that can be dealt with in one way or another. Perpetrators of illegal activities can be prosecuted; loopholes can be closed, and users (and protectors) can be educated. Overuse can be curtailed through permit systems. Pavement can be torn out. Mission statements can be changed. What cannot be changed is the preserves' relationship to the larger environment they are in. And that, it turns out, is a bigger problem than all the rest of them put together.

We "preserve" areas by drawing boundaries around them. But boundaries are political creatures, and nature knows no politics. An arbitrary line on the ground means nothing to the wildlife that roam back and forth across it, the plant communities that advance or retreat in spite of it, or the air that moves above it.

Designating an area a preserve may prevent humans from directly damaging it. But it does nothing to prevent indirect damage. Boundaries may stop loggers (most of the time), but they are no barrier at all to air pollution. They may prevent hunting, but they do not guarantee that animals will have sufficient room to find food and homes and to raise offspring. They may be impenetrable by roads, but they are totally transparent to invading plants species, to waterborne chemicals or pathogens, to insects, and to fire.

At Devils Tower National Monument, in the northeastern corner of Wyoming a few miles west of the town of Sundance, the cottonwoods are dying. Park naturalists have traced the problem to heavy pesticide and herbicide spraying in the agricultural lands along the Belle Fourche River above the park. The river carries the chemicals across the boundary; the "preserved" trees absorb it through their roots and are slowly poisoned. The Park Service is planting new cottonwoods and negotiating with upstream landowners to try to find methods of preventing agricultural chemicals from reaching the river.

On Clingman's Dome in Great Smoky Mountains National Park, and at high points along the Blue Ridge Parkway from the Smokies north into Virginia, visitors are struck by the sight of hillsides full of bare, silvered tree trunks. They are nearly all that remain of these parks' fabled stands of Fraser fir. A close relative of the fragrant balsam fir that sweetens the north woods of Canada and New England, the Fraser fir is a cold-loving species that has managed to hang on in the American South due to the high elevations and rocky, acidic soils of the southern Appalachians. More than 70 percent of the tree's range is on "protected" lands. But protection hasn't stopped, or even slowed, the spread of an insect pest, the woolly adelgid, which was accidentally introduced into New England from Europe and has slowly spread south. The woolly adelgid eats fir needles. The Park Service estimates that 95 percent of the world's known Fraser firs have been largely or completely defoliated by the adelgid in the past thirty years. Nearly all of these have died. Air pollution is probably partly responsible: as noted earlier (in the Prologue), more than 70 percent of the Smokies' smoke is now smog. Breathing smog weakens the immune systems of trees, as it does those of humans. The firs are not the only casualties of this pollution-induced immune-deficiency disease; pines are also dying in the Smokies, and tulip trees, maples, sycamores, and a host of other trees, shrubs, and flowers — ninety-six plant species in all — have shown significant damage from the smog's ozone content. Great Smoky Mountains National Park has been designated an international biosphere reserve by the United Nations, but in a few decades there may not be enough of the park's biosphere left to make that designation meaningful.

Michigan's Isle Royale National Park is also an international biosphere reserve. Surrounded by the vast, 30,000-square-mile sweep of the largest body of fresh water on the planet — Lake Superior — this 40-mile-long island of polished rock, glacial lakes, and dark spruce forest is about as well protected as a preserve can be. (The *narrowest* boundary is 15 miles of open water.) There was some copper mining there once, but the last mine closed down more than one hundred years ago; the National Park Service acquired the entire island in 1940 and has maintained it strictly as wilderness ever since.

But pollution has made serious inroads here, too. The island's lakes are contaminated with a variety of man-made toxic organic chemicals, most of which were not in widespread commercial use until well after Isle Royale was "protected." A 1978 study by Environmental Protection Agency limnologist Wayland R. Swain found PCBs and DDT present in fish from Siskiwit Lake — Isle Royale's largest — at levels up to twice those found in fish from Lake Superior itself. The source is the atmosphere. Pollutants blown into the air from as far away as Chicago and North Dakota have found their way into the lakes' waters via rainfall, snowfall, and what air pollution regulators refer to somewhat anthropomorphically as "fugitive dust." Despite long-standing bans on the use of most of these chemicals in the United States and Canada, levels of them in the island's waters continue slowly to increase. As in the Smokies, the "international biosphere reserve" label here may eventually become nearly meaningless.

In Texas, a vast, tangled complex of forests, bayous, and small, slow-moving rivers known to settlers simply as the Big Thicket once clothed a swath of low hills extending west and north from the mouth of the Sabine River for more than one hundred miles — 3 million acres in all. By the time Congress got around to establishing the Big Thicket National Preserve in October 1974, farming and logging operations had made enough inroads that no large core area remained to be preserved, so lawmakers had to be content with creating a network of twelve small units partially linked by corridors along waterways and roads — a combined total of fewer than 85,000 acres. It is nowhere near enough. "Technically I think this area should be called Big Thicket Temporary Refuge and Preserve," ranger Scott Walker wrote to me at Christmas, 1992. "The majority of the units are not large enough to house a viable population of large animals. . . . The large carnivores, if they can survive the hunters and are able to reproduce to a sufficient population, are doomed to extirpation due to the lack of genetic diversity as a result of insufficient habitat." The linking corridors are next to useless, because the migrating animals they are meant to help cannot easily locate them; as Walker writes, "I have yet to come across a racoon who can read the boundary signs."

And so it goes. All the national parks of the American Southwest, not just Mesa Verde, suffer visibility problems caused by smog from the Four Corners power plant: a nearly constant pall of particulates — a "haze hood," in the language of urban air pollution specialists — hangs in the once crystalline desert air over Monument Valley, and views from the rim of the Grand Canyon are often rendered hazy and indistinct. At Oregon Caves National Monument in southwest Oregon, drinking water for park visitors comes from a spring in the middle of a grazing unit on Forest Service land, and the park has had recurring trouble keeping it fenced and clean; clear-cuts reaching right up to the boundaries of the 480-acre park create visual blight and have served as springboards for invasion by at least twenty species of non-native plants (volunteers uprooting non-native vegetation by hand destroyed more than 68,000 seedlings in one recent three-year period). At the Herbert Hoover National Historic Park in Iowa, volunteers and park personnel have patiently and laboriously reconstructed several acres of native prairie. When my wife and I visited the site in the summer of 1990, the most prominent blooms in the "native" grassland were on fireweed — a species imported from Europe.

Possibly the hardest-hit preserve of all has been Everglades National Park. The Lower Forty-eight's second-largest park (after Yellowstone), Everglades sprawls over more than 1.4 million acres of the southern tip of Florida. Virtually all of that acreage is wetland — a vast, almost perfectly flat expanse of limestone plateau tilted imperceptibly to the south and gradually sliding under the sea. Fresh water runs down from the north in a broad sheet, draining out of Lake Okeechobee; where it meets the salt waters of the Gulf of Mexico, mangroves flourish. Hummocks covered with thick mahogany-dominated forests rise at widely spaced intervals out of the sawgrass, twined about with subtropical flowering vines like a neo-Hollywood vision of Africa. Living things abound: 1,600 species of plants, more than 300 species of birds, uncountable numbers of insects.

The life of the Everglades — the whole complex, interconnected system — depends for its existence on the continuous flow of fresh water from the north. That flow began to be interrupted in 1882 with the first tentative drainage of South Florida wetlands for agriculture, near Fort Myers. In 1928 a two-lane highway, the Tamiami Trail, was completed across the center of the wetlands region, cutting off the fresh-water flow entirely; when it became apparent that this was killing the Everglades, the U.S. Army Corps of Engineers was called in to create floodgates, four of them, at widely spaced intervals along the trail. Through these control structures now flows virtually all the water the Everglades receives, except for rain.

Everglades National Park was created in 1947, covering much of this already dying ecosystem. It has struggled for water all its life. At first, the struggle was largely political: the Corps's floodgates could move enough water to nourish the ecosystem adequately, but they were often prevented from doing so by farmers and developers whose water rights were in conflict with those of the park. Then, in the late 1960s, a new player entered the scene: a canal called C-111, constructed by the Corps itself along the park's eastern boundary. The agency's floodgates had granted the park water, and now its canal would take it away again. Drainage and development began in the region known as the East Everglades, between the park and the city of Miami. Water from the easternmost of the Tamiami Trail floodgates, which had been flowing into the park through the East Everglades, was drained off to the sea. During the dry summers the park burned, large stretches of sawgrass going up in smoke. By the end of the 1980s only about 10 percent of the "protected" area's original wealth of wildlife remained.

The park's defenders fought back, pressuring Congress for reforms. In a radical departure from standard National Park Service policy, park rangers openly lobbied the tourists they served, asking them to contact their congressmen. Visitor-center displays emphasized threats to the park; nature walks became lessons in human effects on ecological systems. After two decades, this approach led to victory. In December 1990 more than 100,000 acres of the East Everglades were added to Everglades National Park. The Corps was ordered to close and fill Ditch C-111. Exuberant Everglades officials headlined the event in the park's *Visitors' Guide:* OPENING THE TAP IN THE EAST EVERGLADES: EAST EVERGLADES RESTORATION BEGINS. Fortunately for their reputations for reliability, the writers began the article with the words "If all goes as planned . . ."

All didn't. In August 1992 Hurricane Andrew struck.

Andrew nearly leveled South Florida. Sixty thousand homes were damaged or destroyed, leaving an estimated 250,000 people homeless. Businesses, highways, and farms also fell before the 140 mph winds. Financial estimates of damage ranged as high as $20 billion. In the park, both major visitor centers and most of the connecting roads were destroyed — an estimated loss of $27 million. Thousands of trees were uprooted or broken off; at least 10,000 acres of mangroves were destroyed.

It wasn't these things that had park officials worried the most, however. It was the exotic species.

At least two hundred licensed exotic-animal facilities, mostly tourist attractions, had been operating in southern Dade County before the storm. Virtually all were destroyed, allowing the surviving animals to escape. Two thousand monkeys and five hundred baboons at the Mannheimer Primatological Center, adjacent to the park, were freed from their cages by the storm and "ran off into the night." They were joined by Asian deer, South American reptiles, numerous exotic birds, and at least one lion. "It's an ecological disaster," Florida wildlife inspector Tom Quinn told a reporter for the Baltimore *Sun*. "Even before the hurricane you had things in the Miami area running around and propagating, setting up miniature ecosystems. Now they're all over the place."

Even worse were the plants. For years, park officials had been fighting a desperate battle against an invasion of Brazilian pepper trees, Australian pines and melaleucas, and other imported species. Now the war was over and the enemy had won. Seeds of the hardy imports were blown all through the park, where they took root in the openings created by the destruction of the native species. Most of them had the potential to outcompete the Everglades' own plants. "They grow like wildfire and drive out the native vegetation," park spokesman Jim Coleman worried to the *New York Times*. Six months later the problems showed no signs of abating. "We're scared to death about the exotic question," the Park Service's Marty Fleming told *Nature Conservancy* magazine. The park was negotiating with the Corps of Engineers and surrounding landowners to keep water flow artificially high for the summer of 1993 in order to drown the exotic species' seeds and seedlings, but they did not have high hopes for success. The Everglades' remarkable, ancient ecosystem had almost certainly been radically, and perhaps permanently, transformed.

Like Oregon Caves. Like the Smokies. Like the thirty-three parks an internal Interior Department audit released in November 1992 found to be suffering from "serious and irreversible degradation." Like "virtually all the nation's federal parks and wilderness land" reported by the National Academy of Sciences to be suffering from air pollution damage.

"Previously, it was thought, islands of land could be preserved forever by simply drawing national park boundaries," wrote the Park Service in its 1990 brochure *Everglades: Your Park in Danger.* "Today it is clear that this is untrue. National parks are not islands. They are greatly impacted by what happens outside their boundaries." It is time to heed not just the letter but the spirit of those words. We need to stop depending upon preserves that don't preserve and boundaries that fail to bound and regulations that seldom regulate. After one hundred years of increasingly desperate failure, it is time for the environmental movement to take another tack.

Private Rights, Public Wrongs

LOOKING AT THE NUMEROUS WAYS in which our environmental protection laws are breaking down, and at the apparent inability of governments and regulations to deal with these breakdowns, it is easy to conclude that government itself is to blame. If government manipulation is demonstrably not working, it is tempting to say, freeing up a totally unregulated, laissez-faire market and converting public lands to private ownership must be better.

Such a conclusion would be wrong.

In meeting goals for the protection of clean air, clean water, stirring scenery, and viable ecosystems, private land ownership rights and unregulated market mechanisms have no better record than the government does. In fact, their record is, on the whole, very much worse. The history of this continent since 1492 points inexorably and inescapably to that conclusion.

It is important to be extremely clear about this point. If we wish to make progress, it will do us no good to replace one failed system with another that has failed just as badly. Government regulation, after all, did not fall out of the sky; it was erected, piece by piece, as an attempt to deal with the damage caused by unrestrained property rights and the unregulated free-market system. That the attempt has been less than satisfactory does not mean that it is better to move backward. We do not need to deconstruct regulation, but to reconstruct it. We need a new regulatory paradigm.

A totally free-market approach to environmental protection is attractive in theory, but it is thoroughly flawed in practice. Free-market enthusiasts such as Ronald Coase and the New Chicago School of economists argue passionately that placing all property in private hands and then using the old, well-established common-law principles of nuisance and trespass can deal with environmental harm more effectively and efficiently than governments can. They make an excellent case. But reality makes a better one.

The record of massive environmental damage caused by private enterprise is so well documented and widely known that it seems hardly necessary to repeat very much of it here. A few examples should suffice. We can begin with the obvious: it was no government, but a private corporation, that held title to the *Exxon Valdez* when it hung up on Alaska's Bligh Reef on a March midnight in 1989 and spilled nearly 11 million gallons of crude oil into the cold, bird-teeming waters of Prince William Sound. It was private corporations that produced, promoted, and sold DDT at levels that nearly exterminated bald eagles, peregrine falcons, and other raptors back in the 1960s — and still sell it today, despite its well-known and thoroughly dismal environmental record, in Third World countries where governments have not yet intervened. Private speculators, not public agencies, were behind the nearly complete denuding of Michigan and Wisconsin by cut-and-run logging in the late nineteenth century, an era now christened, with well-deserved capital letters, the Big Cut. Private companies created the blackened, blasted hillsides and poisoned farms and creeks of the Appalachian coal country. Private money sprawls subdivisions over open spaces on the outskirts of our cities, and gushes wastes into our water and our air from tens of thousands of industrial plants, and pours fertilizers and pesticides and Lord knows what else into our groundwater. Private enterprise does not have a good environmental track record at all.

A few bad apples — even gigantic apples like these — do not, of course, mean that the whole barrel is necessarily rotten. It is at least theoretically possible that an enlightened free-enterprise system could correct its own excesses and turn environmental piracy into environmental protection all on its own, without government intervention — indeed, better than with government intervention. There are even a few models that lead in that direction. Privately owned scenic attractions such as New York's Ausable Chasm, Pennsylvania's Bushkill Falls, and California's Shasta Caverns are usually at least as careful of environmental values as their public counterparts, and are often more so. These, and the preserves and wildlife refuges run by private organizations like the Nature Conservancy and the Audubon Society, tend to be managed more soundly on ecological principles than those run by the government, a fact that is perhaps less than astounding when you remember that governments must please a large and often conflicting set of constituencies, while private landowners, as long as they remain within legal bounds, must please only themselves. If the Nature Conservancy wishes to keep all humans out of one of its private wildernesses in order to protect the three-toed salamander, it can do so relatively easily. If the Forest Service wants to do the same thing, it will find itself the center of protests and appeals and letter-writing campaigns and even lawsuits, accusing it of failure to protect the rights of hunters or hikers or rockhounds or picnickers or any of numerous other groups who feel strongly, and with justification, that the term *public lands* means that these lands belong to the citizens of the United States, not the three-toed salamander, and that their owners should have free access to enjoy them.

But the better wilderness-management practices that often accompany private ownership of nature reserves do not suffice for everything. In particular, private ownership cannot protect these lands against the same nagging problem faced by the public preserves — the problem of boundaries. Private preserves are bounded by political lines, just as public ones are, and they experience the same difficulties with nonhuman forces that do not recognize NO TRESPASSING signs.

No, that is not true: they experience, not the same difficulties, but more. Private reserves are, on the average, much smaller than their public counterparts. And with natural systems, resiliency is largely a function of size.

It is, in fact, the size problem that is free enterprise's most obstinate and significant failing. The patchwork of small holdings typical of a private-property system leads to a fragmentation of management that is almost impossible to reconcile with ecological principles. Neighbors with differing goals work at cross-purposes to one another. The Nature Conservancy may own nine-tenths of the critical habitat of an endangered species it wishes to protect, but the species will be doomed anyway if the owner of the remaining 10 percent decides to put condominiums on it. A landowner can protect the environs of a spring on his own land, together with its associated stream and riparian vegetation, but he cannot keep it from drying up if the water table is drawn down by heavy irrigation on the next farm. A rancher can keep her cattle away from the banks of a river, but if her neighbors do not follow suit the river will be dirty anyway.

I have a daughter and son-in-law who are attempting to rehabilitate an old farm on a branch of Sucker Creek in southern Oregon's broad, fertile Illinois Valley. They use no agricultural chemicals and would like to have their produce certified as organic. Their chemical-using neighbors, however, make this impossible. The excess water from upstream irrigation systems flows back into the creek, carrying fertilizers and pesticides from the fields it has crossed. Irrigating their fields with that water — the only practical course — puts the fertilizers and pesticides on my daughter and son-in-law's crops, too.

It can be argued, of course, that the difficulty here is really not ownership but coordination and motivation. The solution would seem to be simple: if all the farmers along Sucker Creek practiced organic farming, organic certification for any of them could follow as a matter of course. The problem thus shifts from enforcement to education. What Aldo Leopold called the "land ethic" simply needs to be inculcated in everyone. In such an enlightened world, the argument goes, environmental protection would become automatic and the whole regulatory complex would shrivel into irrelevancy.

Indeed it would. Those who believe, however, that education of private landholders would be a trustworthy and efficient solution to environmental problems should review the story of Dorothy Irwin and her Enchanted Forest.

In the summer of 1937, Irwin, an artist and sculptor, and her husband, Henry, a San Francisco attorney, built a log cabin in the woods a few miles west of Healdsburg, California, on land they had purchased for that purpose a few years before. The land lay near the Russian River where it cuts through the California Coast Range, and the woods were redwoods — immense, towering trees shading a damp, moss-hung understory of maple and dogwood and head-high ferns. Light among redwoods does not shine: it seeps in, one ray at a time, probing between the great trunks, examining the treasures of the forest one at a time, like a furtive dwarf in a dragon's hoard. That is undoubtedly why the Irwins called the place enchanted. They spent every available weekend there, and, after Henry retired in 1957, they made it their permanent home.

Henry Irwin died in 1977, bringing Dorothy face to face with a quandary. What would happen to the land when she, too, died? She wanted it preserved and enjoyed as she and her husband had preserved and enjoyed it. Who could be trusted with that task?

Within a year she had made up her mind. She drew up a will leaving the Enchanted Forest to her alma mater, the California College of Arts and Crafts in Oakland. The land, said the will, was to be treated as a "living monument" to the memory of her husband, "who worked tirelessly for many years embellishing this beautiful creation of nature." That part of the will was never carried out; two years after signing it, Dorothy Irwin deeded the land directly to the college, making the provisions of the will moot. The deed carried no restrictions. Irwin probably thought she wouldn't need any.

She was wrong. In the summer of 1992, two years after Dorothy Irwin's death, the California College of Arts and Crafts sold 80 percent of the Irwins' Enchanted Forest to a Healdsburg development corporation, Schooner Creek Ranches, for $760,000. Logging began immediately. Healdsburg residents were incensed but powerless: the logging, and the contract, were entirely legal. "She trusted these people and look what they have done," fumed former Irwin neighbor Al Slendebroek to the *San Francisco Chronicle*. "If they had told Dorothy this is what they were going to do, she would have chased them off her land with a shotgun."

Such is the power of private ownership and the land ethic to protect land. It may work after a fashion while land-ethic people are in control. As soon as they are not, though, all protections disintegrate. A thousand successive owners may manage a piece of property soundly, but if the thousand-and-first rapes it, the work of the thousand is for naught. It takes three thousand years to grow a mature redwood. It only takes about three hours to cut one down.

Five hundred years of free enterprise and private-property rights on this continent have left us with a land transformed, its face largely unrecognizable, its natural systems running a narrow gamut from "modified" to "destroyed." The basic nature of free enterprise and private property suggests that this is their unavoidable legacy. For this reason we have built a fence of regulations around them. It has not been a very good fence; it carries its own fundamental flaws, flaws that not only render it ineffective but cause damage in their own right. But it will not help us merely to tear it down. We do not simply need an absence of fence: we need a presence of better means of control.

The Mirror Failure

READING OVER most contemporary environmental literature — including (let us be honest here) almost all of my own — it is easy to conjure up a mental image of ecocide-by-finance: the economy as Sherman tank, crushing its way across an ineffectual fence of regulations and careening through the Elysian Fields of the environment. But this picture is false. There is in fact a strong association between economic activity and ecosystem destruction; but association does not prove causation. Economic forces are not destroying the environment; our economic structure is too sick for that. Despite years of propping it up and treating it with a variety of medications ranging from Keynesian price supports to Laffer curves, America's economy is almost as moribund as its environment.

Signs of economic failure are somewhat more difficult to read than are signs of environmental failure, primarily because the two so often become confused with each other. It is common to blame economic problems on regulation, especially on environmental regulation. At a Denver conference called by the conservative Mountain States Legal Foundation in February 1993, this view was expressed as forthrightly as possible. We cannot let the environmental radicals succeed, thundered one conference speaker, Stone Forest Industries, Inc., president Gerald M. Freeman; if we do, "billions of dollars in our national economy would be lost and we would experience inflationary spirals unprecedented in the nation's history." Freeman would undoubtedly have agreed with the Klamath Falls, Oregon, man who wrote to Congressman Bob Smith

(R-Oregon) at about the time the Mountain States Legal Foundation's conference was getting under way. Congress, demanded Representative Smith's correspondent, should "abolish, rescind, delete most of, make impotent, or put in cold storage for five years all the bureaucracy and funding for: the Americans with Disabilities Act, the Endangered Species Act, the Clean Air Act, Wetlands Act, and any other anti-business act on the books. America can no longer afford these acts that have a sinister agenda."

There is nothing particularly new about such rhetoric. Similar passages can be found in the reactions to environmental protection legislation passed almost a hundred years ago. Here is one reported by Gifford Pinchot, the forester and conservation leader who almost singlehandedly founded the U.S. Forest Service; it comes from a speech by Senator Clarence Clark of Wyoming in the spring of 1897. Clark was responding to the proclamation by President Grover Cleveland on Washington's birthday that year which, following the advice of Cleveland's Forest Commission, had set aside more than 21 million acres of forest reserves in seven western states:

> The miner, said Clark, was compelled "to pause with pick in air, the settler shall not burn a stick of timber to light his hearth. . . . I honor them [Forest Commission members, including Pinchot]," said the Senator, with no little sarcasm, "I honor them for their knowledge; they are an ornament to the country; I read their reports with admiration; but they belong to that class of scientific gentlemen who think more of the forest tree than they do of the roof tree, and we have a whole lot of people in the West who think as much of their roof tree as the people of any other part of this nation."

Aside from its somewhat stilted nineteenth-century style, this passage could easily concern the current battle over spotted owl habitat in the Pacific Northwest, or over red-cockaded woodpecker habitat in Texas, or over clear-cutting in North Carolina, or over any environmental protection measure anywhere. There is nothing new in the argument that environmentalism causes economic disaster. What is new is that the disaster is actually taking place.

Or at least the economy is acting funny. There was, for example, a 68 percent rise in the price of lumber products during 1992, something Stone Forest Industries' Freeman seized gleefully upon as proof that "radicals" were destroying the American way of life. In fact, though, it proved no such thing. A study by the Congressional Research Service released on March 11, 1993 (one month to the day after Freeman entertained the free-enterprise faithful in Denver), concluded that the ongoing hyperinflation in lumber prices was primarily due, ironic as it may seem, to improvements in the economy. "Many factors have contributed to the recent price rise," the researchers wrote, "but the economic recovery is probably the most significant cause." The truth in the Congressional Research Service's suggestion was demonstrated quite conclusively a few months later when, with none of the fanfare that accompanied their rise, lumber prices quietly dropped again.

Does the concept of an economic "recovery" that leads to a nearly 70 percent price rise bother you? It bothers economists, too. Robust economies will always experience some inflation, but it is usually well under 10 percent annually. And it turns out that the presence of hyperinflation was not all that was wrong with the 1992–93 "recovery"; the relationship between economic health and jobs had apparently gone haywire, too.

Among the most basic assumptions that business leaders, economists, and politicians make about the world is that economic recoveries will always result in lower unemployment rates. That is supposed to be a given, along with the fact that clouds bring rain and stones do not fall up. But in February 1993, while the economy was hurtling along at a hefty 3.2 percent growth rate — the best in years — the number of people filing for first-time jobless benefits had actually climbed to over a million per month and was increasing by as many as 26,000 each week. In a "normal recovery," noted a frustrated President Bill Clinton, "three million more Americans would already be back at work by now." Such comments were small comfort to those, like Pratt & Whitney worker Dave Meikle, who were already facing job loss. "I don't see how things are recovering for people who have to pay bills," Meikle complained to Associated Press reporter Sharon Cohen. "I'd like to see how they come up with these numbers. It doesn't add up."

There are a lot of other things that don't add up. Despite tax increases big enough to have fueled a massive taxpayers' revolt across the country, the level of government services, especially local services such as schools and libraries, has actually declined significantly over the past decade. Our transportation infrastructure is aging and badly deteriorated, and there is no money available to replace it. The national debt has escalated out of control, and no amount of government penny-pinching seems able to contain it. The time-honored relationship between economic health and the balance of trade (a healthy economy requires a trade surplus) has apparently disintegrated, to the point where the same page of the newspaper can speak rapturously of an American economy that has "shifted into higher gear" and, in a separate article, report that the trade deficit for this "energized" economy is seventeen times higher than the deficit of the year before.

And the Phillips curve has failed. This probably bothers economists the most of all.

The Phillips curve failure is closely related to the failure of the relationship between job creation and economic growth, but it has been going on longer, and it operates at a more fundamental level of economic theory. Named after British economist A. W. Phillips, who first demonstrated it in a paper published in 1958, the Phillips curve is an empirically derived downward-sloping asymptote that shows an inverse relationship between inflation and unemployment: as inflation increases, unemployment goes down, and vice versa. This implies a tradeoff between jobs and inflation: you can lower the inflation rate, or you can lower the unemployment rate, but you cannot do both at the same time.

Phillips originally fit his curve only to one hundred years of data from Great Britain, but other economists (notably Paul Samuelson and Robert Solow) quickly broadened its application, and by the mid-1960s it had entered the lexicon of economic truisms — there didn't seem to be any data, historic or current, that the curve couldn't be made to fit. Until 1970. In that year, the data jumped backward off the Phillips curve it had been faithfully following, with near mathematical precision, for the previous decade; and over the next twenty years it proceeded to go totally bonkers. A plot of unemployment rates against inflation for the period since 1970 looks like a random walk by a drunken spider; despite some valiant attempts by Milton Friedman and others to create one, there is no perceivable relationship among the various data points at all.

And that is deeply disturbing. It takes away the neat predictability of the economist's universe, and does it in such a way as to leave the various tools of macroeconomic fiscal policy still potent but virtually uncontrollable, like a battery of howitzers with widely gyrating mountings. One can still fire them, but one has only a vague, general idea of what the results will be, and even the vague, general idea may turn out to be 180 degrees wrong.

The decoupling of joblessness from inflation represented by the disintegration of the Phillips curve, and the strikingly similar decouplings of jobs and trade deficits from economic growth, suggest strongly that the troubles facing the world economy today stem not from outside pressures, such as political realignments or increased environmental regulation, but from structural failure. The economy is not feeding off the environmental crisis, as environmentalists often suggest, but mirroring it. Earth First! and the Chamber of Commerce may disagree strongly with each other, but all the inflammatory rhetoric on both sides really amounts to is an ownership dispute over the *Titanic*.

The parallel states of the economy and the environment are telling us something that we all desperately need to hear. Market activities and environmental protection are not necessary enemies, fighting from skirmish to skirmish along a front composed of forests to be harvested or preserved, dams to be built or blocked, pollution to be tolerated or treated, jobs or species to be lost, market systems or ecosystems to prosper. Market activities and environmental protection are under attack together. Pollution, wildlands destruction, species extinction, and resource overuse — the whole shopping list of ecological turmoil — are not the result of market forces, but of forces *that also damage the market*. What hurts the ecology of the planet also hurts its economy. We are all in this thing together.

The Deer in the Mall

THE HIDDEN VALLEY housing development near Santa Clarita, California, recently achieved the dubious distinction of becoming the first residential area in the world to equip itself with a hydraulic bollard.

Strongly resembling a medieval antisiege device, Hidden Valley's $50,000 machine consists of two three-foot-long steel shafts concealed beneath the development's access road. Unauthorized use of the road triggers a pair of powerful hydraulic rams that shoot the steel shafts upward, impaling the offending vehicle. Twenty-eight cars had been damaged by the bollard by the end of its first ten months of operation, from mid-April 1992 to mid-January 1993. No lawsuits had yet been filed against the community, although several were threatened. Hidden Valley residents tended to shrug off the anger they had provoked among their neighbors by deploying antiterrorist weapons against them. "I'm sure you have a lock on your door," one homeowner remarked to the Associated Press.

A few days before the Hidden Valley story appeared in newspapers around the country, shoppers and employees at the Mountain View Mall in Bend, Oregon, watched in astonishment as two deer stepped hesitantly through the open doors of the Emporium department store and started up the aisle past the shoe department. Quickly panicking, the animals, both full-grown does, bolted through the women's wear section while humans leaped out of their way. One doe was herded through a stockroom and out a loading door by store personnel; the other, separated from its companion, was finally trapped in the ladies' room, where it destroyed one of the stalls with its hooves before local Fish and Wildlife Agency officials were able to subdue and remove it.

That same week, in a report datelined London, shipping experts were questioning the commitment of the world's seagoing nations to enforcement of tanker safety laws in the wake of the third major oil spill in less than three weeks. As these experts spoke with reporters, the supertanker *Maersk Navigator,* carrying 78 million gallons of crude oil, was ablaze and leaking off the coast of Indonesia following a collision with another, empty tanker earlier that same day. This was less than a week after the tanker *Kihnu* had split herself open on a reef in the Gulf of Finland, and just over two weeks following the widely publicized disaster in the Shetland Islands in which the tanker *Braer,* operated by a Connecticut shipping firm but registered in Liberia, was forced onto the rocks of Garths Ness by hurricane-force winds. On January 12, 1993, a week after grounding, the *Braer* broke into three pieces, scattering her entire 24.6-million-gallon cargo of light crude over one of the most productive fish and seabird grounds in the North Sea.

Meanwhile, back in the United States, professional mushroom pickers were preparing grimly for the coming spring season — preparation that included, out of necessity, the cleaning and conditioning of firearms and the purchase of bulletproof vests. This once bucolic profession has turned increasingly nasty over the past decade, with firefights over choice sites, and drive-by shootings, and kidnappings, and murders. Mushroom picking, says one Oregon law enforcement officer who deals regularly with the pickers, "has become a big-money, highly competitive business," so competitive that Forest Service employees patrolling national forest lands during mushroom season now must prepare the same way they do for hunting season, with loaded firearms and flak jackets.

A common thread runs through these four widely divergent reports. Each demonstrates the intricate intertwining of environmental and economic issues as they twist through the raveling fabric of society. On land ever more scarce and sea lanes ever more crowded, economic life must continue and humans and their wild companions on the planet must discover ways to adapt. As the brooding emptiness of the wilderness disappears, we find it increasingly replaced by a brooding emptiness in the human spirit. The deer in the mall are Everydeer, stand-ins for people as well as wildlife, wandering bewildered through the world that commerce has created and searching for the door back to the natural world that created us.

Just how lost we really are is perhaps best demonstrated by a recent incident in the spotted owl wars of the Pacific Northwest, an incident that seems to have passed virtually unnoticed by the media and the various players.

On May 22, 1992, in Eugene, Oregon, U.S. District Judge Michael Hogan ruled that critical-habitat designations for endangered species at the scale the U.S. Fish and Wildlife Agency was proposing for the spotted owl fell under the purview of the National Environmental Policy Act (NEPA), and thus required the preparation of an environmental impact statement. Those who had brought the suit were jubilant. "We hope this will open up the process," said one. "A whole range of alternatives have to be considered now." On the losing side, gloom prevailed. "We still believe no EIS was required here," one of the defeated attorneys remarked rather petulantly to the press.

Common stuff, these days, in environmental lawsuits. But one oddity set this one strongly apart. On the winning side, applauding the judge's ruling in favor of applying NEPA, was the business-oriented Board of Commissioners of the nation's single most heavily timber-dependent county — Douglas County, Oregon. And on the losing side, arguing strenuously against the application of the nation's premier environmental law, was the nation's premier environmental law firm — the Sierra Club Legal Defense Fund.

Two ❧

Thinking Like a Forest

Of Myths and Paradigms

THE RUNNING BATTLE between developers and environmental activists has escalated into a war that both sides are losing, along a front that has become increasingly irrelevant, between forces that only think they disagree with each other. Underneath the vehemence of the rhetoric and the violence of the confrontations over saving or preserving forests, using or halting pesticides, dumping wastes into our rivers or cleaning them up, and protecting or ignoring the ozone layer lies a series of shared myths, assumptions, and conventions, many of which are flat wrong. These shared myths, assumptions, and conventions are, in turn, built on a shared paradigm. The paradigm is wrong, too.

The word *paradigm* has a curious history in English. It appears to have been borrowed from scholarly Latin in late medieval or early Renaissance times: the editors of the *Oxford English Dictionary* have traced it at least as far back as William Caxton's *Golden Legende* of 1483, one of the first books published in the English language. Caxton spelled it *paradygme* and used it as a simple synonym for *example,* its meaning in Latin.

By the late seventeenth century, the word's meaning had gone in two different directions. Philosophers used it primarily to refer to large, overarching models that attempted to explain all of reality ("universal Exemplars"), while grammarians and linguists defined it specifically and narrowly as a list of all available forms of a sample word, used to show clearly how a particular class of words was to be conjugated. For a long time, the wordsmiths appeared to be winning. In fact, if you pick up almost any dictionary today, theirs is the meaning you will find listed first, with Caxton's simple synonym as number two. You are not likely to find the philosophers' definition at all.

Nor are you likely to find the most common meaning of the word in contemporary usage. Pioneered in the early twentieth century by an Austrian-born British citizen named Ludwig Wittgenstein, the modern sense of the term is that of a simple conceptual framework around which a complex system of thought or behavior can be organized. Paradigms are the scaffolding for ideas. Intuitive, universally known, and easily understood, they provide an unspoken central reference point for societies to judge themselves against. And in this modern sense, which combines the meanings of the linguists and the philosophers (Wittgenstein was both), the primary paradigm of American society is the frontier.

The frontier paradigm is a powerful intermingling of two distinct but closely related concepts. Frontiers are boundaries: they separate civilization from wilderness, the orderly from the disorderly, the known from the unknown, the tame from the wild. And frontiers advance. The sharp edge of progress moves forward into the great mass of tangled possibilities that exist beyond it, defining and clarifying those possibilities, converting them into actualities. Raw materials become manufactured goods. Prairie becomes range, which becomes farmstead, which becomes city. It is a continuous process, always growing, always reaching forward into new prairies, planting new cities, uncovering new raw materials. The frontier, stated Frederick Jackson Turner one hundred years ago, was "the outer edge of the wave — the meeting point between savagery and civilization." It was also, he postulated, the defining factor in American history:

> American social development has been continually beginning over again on the frontier. This perennial rebirth, this fluidity of American life, this expansion westward with its new opportunities, its continuous touch with the simplicity of primitive society, furnish [*sic*] the forces dominating American character.

So important was this pattern to America's self-image that when Turner, in the famous essay from which these quotes are taken, declared the actual physical frontier to be closed, a massive search was set off for substitute frontiers — a search that continues, unabated, to this day. Thus, Alaska is the "last frontier"; the ocean, or outer space, or the rural/suburban interface is the "next frontier"; Jack Kennedy's ambitious legislative agenda for his presidency was a "New Frontier." We speak of the "frontiers of science," the "frontiers of medicine," the "frontiers of art." In each case the underlying image is the same: Turner's "outer edge of the wave," moving rapidly forward into unexplored territory. Progressing. Continually, even urgently, becoming.

But here we must face an uncomfortable truth. The frontier as Americans have envisioned it never actually existed. The entire conceptual framework that we have used to define this country — the edge of civilization, man against the wilderness, the advancing tide of progress — is a cultural construct, a stack of mythical baggage not significantly different, in either truth or function, from the gods of Olympus or the great World Crocodile of the Nile.

It is easy enough to see where the idea came from. Pre-Columbian Europe was a tired land, a continent peopled to its summits and tilled to its weary bones. It was not thickly populated by today's standards, but it must have been running very close to capacity for the technological level at which the people lived. There was no new ground: a farmer cropped the fields his father cropped, or his neighbor's father, or the father of someone over in the next valley. Forests had fallen over much of the continent, and cities were rising. The enclosure movement (the legalized seizing of village commons and other communally held lands by private individuals, who then "enclosed" them with both deeds and fences) was nearing its zenith, and virtually all lands were now owned. It was a closed system, crisscrossed by boundaries; these boundaries could be shifted, but only at the expense of other boundaries. Lands could grow only if other lands shrank.

The discovery of the Americas opened the closed doors of Europe. Suddenly there *were* new lands, not only unowned but unknown. Huddling in their tiny, tossing ships off the coast of the continent, European settlers thought they saw a New World, a wilderness "full of wilde beastes and wilde men," untilled and unbounded. The ocean, which had formed the edge of civilization, was breached. The difficulty of the voyage, in small, wooden, ill-provisioned ships, underscored the magnitude of the leap they took.

The new lands seemed both hostile and endless. The colonists set about "taming" them, an acre at a time. Europe gained a foothold on the coast and moved slowly up the rivers toward their unknown springs. The myth was born of a people carving their way across the continent, converting the raw resources of an untouched land into the stuff of civilization. Somewhere there had to be a growing edge to that movement. That was the frontier.

Two accidents of North American geography helped form and perpetuate this idea. One was the north-south trend of virtually all the major American mountain systems; the other was the presence, just at the eastern edge of the vast open spaces of the Great Plains, of an immense and mythic river, trending, like the mountains, from north to south.

Moving westward beyond the Piedmont, Europeans encountered wave upon wave of mountains, like the waves of the ocean they had lately crossed. The strikingly parallel relationship of the mountain crests to the ocean's edge — the continental coastline — did not escape them. Crossing each crest became symbolically similar to crossing the ocean, a movement ever westward across physical boundaries that could be conquered, each conquest expanding the area under civilization, pushing the north-south edge (the frontier) farther across the continent. When Daniel Boone cut the Wilderness Road through Cumberland Gap in 1775, the breaching of this major mountain barrier became a symbolic opening of the "unpeopled" West to settlement. Leave aside, for the moment, what that statement assumes about the Native Americans; it also did not matter that St. Louis and Pittsburgh had each been founded more than ten years before, or that sails regularly plied the Great Lakes, or that, far to the west and south of the "advancing frontier," New Orleans was already a cosmopolitan city.

Beyond the last ridge of the eastern mountain systems there were wooded hills; the hills and the woods slowly dwindled and ran out as you moved west, finally stopping altogether. Where they stopped a great river flowed, a broad barrier of water moving from north to south, parallel to the coast of that other great water, the Atlantic Ocean; beyond this river a new ocean rose, an ocean this time of grass, as boundless as the woods of the East but of a totally different character. Beyond the grass, rumor had it, more mountains lay, range after range of them, taller and more rugged than anything in the East but still parallel and still trending from north to south. The pattern held. The image it evoked — that of an advancing tide, starting at the East Coast and slowly breaching each barrier in turn, its leading edge ragged but distinct along a north-south line — was natural and inevitable.

It was also false. The American landscape was neither unpeopled nor uncultivated before the Europeans got here. And European settlement did not move westward in the neat textbook patterns we are accustomed to. European settlement was nearly simultaneous all the way across the continent.

*   *   *

Take the second point first. If you stop to read historic markers as you travel around the United States, one thing that is likely to strike you is the close proximity of the dates appearing on nearly all of them. No matter where you are in the country, the "old" towns all seem to trace their founding events to the same fifty-year period, from roughly 1810 to the outbreak of the Civil War. There are exceptions, of course — places like Plymouth, Massachusetts (founded 1621); Santa Fe, New Mexico (founded 1610); St. Augustine, Florida (founded 1565); and Detroit, Michigan (founded 1701) — but these are scattered across the country nearly as evenly as the later towns are. The image that arises, from examining this data, is not so much that of a single advancing wave as it is of a bunch of pebbles thrown randomly into a pond, the circles that mark their entry expanding rapidly outward until they intersect one another. European settlement was not an orderly march from sea to shining sea; it was more like a fistful of seeds thrown up in a hurricane, scattering across the countryside, sprouting where they landed, and spreading rapidly and haphazardly outward from there. How many of us realize that San Diego, California, is more than 150 years older than Charlotte, North Carolina, or that the settlement of Cleveland, Ohio, preceded that of Astoria, Oregon, by barely fifteen years? To understand these things is to gain a view of American settlement totally different from what is generally taught in the schools. European settlement did not spread on this continent; European settlement exploded.

And it did so at the expense of settlements already present. There was no unbroken wilderness for the advancing tide of civilization to roll back. The unbroken wilderness had disappeared centuries before the Europeans got there.

Native American peoples have carried more than their fair share of the White Man's Burden. First there was the myth of the beast, the native as nonhuman, magically capable of transformation to human if he were willing to convert to Christianity, in which case he would take up clothing and tools and emulate his betters — part of the spread of the frontier, not the opposition to it. Next came the myth of the noble savage, the wiser race living in constant harmony with the earth, Adams and Eves in blissful pre-Fall ignorance from which they were rudely jolted by the arrival of the passenger train. In this vision the frontier is a destroyer rather than a redeemer, but it is still a frontier and it is still advancing. Related to this idea, but more recent, there has developed the myth of the downtrodden, the native as victim, hounded onto reservations, holding desperately to fading fragments of a wise and ancient culture in the face of a brutal, mechanistic society that is, again, surging over it. It is a pattern perhaps best symbolized by the famous photograph from Tiananmen Square of the lone civilian standing in front of the line of tanks, the kinder, gentler culture crushed under the relentless tread of the advancing machine.

Let us try to inject some reality into this picture.

First, the Native Americans have indeed been driven from their lands, but it was not the advancing tide of civilization that was responsible for this outrage, it was common white-collar thievery. The act was accomplished in a very deft manner, by redefining *property* so that those redefining it got it all. If land is declared as "beyond the frontier," by definition it belongs to nobody. As the frontier "advances," those in charge of this advancement can take what they wish from the "inexhaustible" pool of resources that is opened up. It was not just Native Americans who were victimized by this approach; any Europeans who happened to live on lands beyond the "frontier" were also fair game. The very first homestead claim recorded at the Nebraska Land Office — the claim celebrated today at Homestead National Monument — was filed on land that had already been settled and farmed for a number of years by an industrious but illiterate family of European descent who were unceremoniously evicted as "squatters" by a civic leader from the nearby town of Beatrice who had read the law, gone to the land office, and had a certificate of "ownership" in his vest pocket.

Second, there was no true wilderness out there. The appearance of America, with its vast, brooding woodlands and open, unfenced prairies where the grass grew tall and the buffalo roamed, was deceptive: the continent was no less managed than Europe was, it was simply managed differently. Much of it was farmed, although the crops were rarely monocultured and thus failed to look like crops to the Europeans. A fair amount of the farmland, especially in the dry Southwest, was irrigated. Farming requires permanent settlements — cities — and these existed, not only in the realms of the Aztec and Maya and Inca where we would like to keep them safely out of the way of the advancing United States, but within what are now U.S. boundaries as well: at Natchez, Mississippi; Macon, Georgia; East St. Louis, Illinois; The Dalles, Oregon; and hundreds of other places, large and small, scattered across the continent.

Where farms and cities were not established the people lived a nomadic life, but this did not mean simply following the game through the wilderness at the mercy of natural forces: the game was managed, and the land was managed to encourage game. A primary tool was fire. Native peoples set fire to the grasslands of the Great Plains to drive the buffalo; they set fire to forests, both in the East and in the West, to create improved browse for deer. When the landscape-preservation movement got its start in America in the late nineteenth century, among the prime motivators was the existence, beyond civilization, of open, "cathedral-like" stands of "virgin" forest. What the Johnny-come-lately Europeans failed to recognize was that these stands achieved their expansive, almost religious quality of openness through human manipulation. Generations of Native Americans had kept them that way by purposefully burning out the undergrowth. Europeans, in the name of "preserving nature," not only stopped this practice but actively suppressed natural fires in the woods as well. The resulting massive firetrap of tinder-dry, tangled undergrowth and fallen wood is not at all what the early preservationists thought they were setting out to protect.

The frontier paradigm has much to answer for. Frontier thinking has fueled our national obsession with "growth" and "progress," creating the impression that a people not constantly conquering new barriers and expanding their horizons are somehow ingrown and emasculated. It has caused us to seriously undervalue raw materials and undeveloped land: undeveloped things are by definition things beyond the frontier, things that belong to no one and are therefore "free," whatever their actual price. Restrictions on land development, on logging, on mining, and on all other extractive or destructive uses of the land are made more difficult to impose by the romantic mystique of the frontier. As long as undeveloped lands are perceived as places to continue to expand the frontier, land-use planning, forest protection, zoning, and even property taxes will continue to be seen as impositions on the rights of the people to go out, as their ancestors did, and wrest productive uses from the raw, relentless wild.

But it is not only developers who are caught by the old paradigm. We environmentalists are fond of castigating our opponents as people whose outlook has not grown beyond the frontier, but our own thinking suffers from the same delusion. Through the creation of wilderness areas, parks, and other protective categories, we seek to preserve as much as possible of the mythical frontier experience of untouched, raw land. By regulating the contents of industrial and municipal waste outfalls we attempt to re-create the conditions found on pristine, unsettled rivers. Ours is a mirror world to that of the developers, the flip side of unregulated, unrestricted, frontier-style resource exploitation. It is prettier, tidier, and cleaner than the other face of the coin; but it is every bit as unrealistic.

The war between preservationists and developers is, at heart, a conflict between two opposing types of preservation: one that attempts to preserve the direct experience of the untouched frontier, and one that attempts to preserve the unfettered opportunity to exploit it. It is time to move beyond both of these ancient and indefensible positions. A new outlook must be developed, one that defines its success in terms of ecosystem health rather than in acreage preserved or resources removed, one in which environmental protection and development guide and renew each other, fitting human society to the land rather than ignoring or scorning either. A new agenda must be formulated. A new paradigm is needed.

Those who cling desperately to either side of the old paradigm would do well to consider the position in which the defenders of the Cumberland Gap found themselves during the Civil War. Though fewer than ninety years had passed from the "breaching of the frontier" by Boone's Wilderness Road to the secession of the South, this "American Gibraltar" (so called because of its perceived strategic position on the route from Civilization to the Great West) had already become irrelevant. Caught in the magnified sense of importance of the frontier paradigm, the Confederacy massively fortified the gap. Caught in the same mode of thinking, the Union threw armies at it, conquering it, and losing it again, numerous times in the brief four-year span of open warfare. Absolutely none of this, historians agree today, had more than a marginal effect on the outcome of the greater conflict. There was little need for either side to worry about whether the troops at the Cumberland frontier were friend or foe; as the National Park Service has written, on a sign posted today at the crumbling remains of the gap's once proud fortifications, "It was easier for the war to go around them."

Spaceship Gaia

W HAT NEW MODEL shall we choose to replace the
    failed paradigm of the frontier? Three possibilities have
been floated over the past several decades: the spaceship, the
organism, and the household. None is fully satisfactory. I am
about to propose a fourth; but first, let us take a close, critical
look at the failed ones.

Credit for first conceiving of the Earth as a spaceship usually
goes to the inventor and philosopher Buckminster Fuller, a tire-
less and enthusiastic proponent of what is now called "alternate technology," who began using the paradigm in speeches
at least as early as 1964. "I wish to point out vigorously to
you that we are indeed aboard an 8,000-mile-diameter spheri-
cal space vehicle," Fuller remarked to a Senate subcommittee
in 1969.

> Earth is a beautifully designed spaceship, equipped and pro-
> visioned to support and regenerate life aboard it for hundreds
> of millions of years. . . . [But] we are not going to be able to
> operate our spaceship Earth successfully nor for much longer
> unless we see it as a whole spaceship and our fate as common.
> It has to be everybody or nobody.

The spaceship image is powerful. It suggests at once vulnerability, interdependence, and closure. Spaceships are small and
fragile in the depths of space, prey to meteorites and radiation
and able to support life only so long as they remain intact.
They are thoroughly and completely interconnected systems,

with every part necessary and every part dependent on the other parts to function properly, from the human pilots and their oxygen supply right down to the clips that hold the control consoles in their brackets. And they are also thoroughly and completely closed systems. There is no running down to the corner store for something that has been forgotten: all you have is what you have carried with you from the launching pad. Everything must be either used over or used up. Crew members of a spacecraft do not recycle because it is politically correct to do so; they recycle because if they do not they will die.

All these qualities make the spaceship a far better paradigm than the frontier has ever been for modeling a dynamic society on a finite planet. It is, nonetheless, not entirely satisfactory. The primary problem lies in its technological, human-constructed nature, which suggests that technology is the answer to environmental problems as well. Worse: it suggests that when things begin to go wrong, the proper course of action is to tinker with them. Both of these assumptions are correct for machines but dangerously misleading for the planet. Life is an evolved system, not a designed one, and it cannot be treated as though a quick look at the blueprints and a couple of bobby pins can cobble it up and make it run right again. There are too many connections, and they lead off in too many different directions, for us ever to be able to anticipate completely the results of what we do. In such a situation, tinkering is ill advised. Attempting to fix ecosystem problems with technology, the English biologist Charles Elton remarked a half century ago, is equivalent to attempting to fix a complex and delicately adjusted piece of machinery by flinging a crowbar into it. The vast leaps in technology since Elton's day have not really changed that assessment. The problem is not the limits of human ingenuity; it is the limits of human perceptions, especially our perceptions of time. A species geared to think of one hundred years as a long time simply cannot grasp the dynamics of a system geared to eons, a system for which a millennium is merely an eyeblink. Technology is a human creation, and it cannot escape human time. The spaceship paradigm is powerful and effective, but it is also fundamentally flawed. We must look elsewhere.

The second paradigm, that of the organism, is a very ancient one, reaching back to before the dawn of history, to a time when rocks had souls and the Earth was our mother. The scientific formulation of the paradigm begins with the eighteenth-century Scottish naturalist James Hutton, the "father of geology," who wrote of the planet as a "superorganism" that was best studied as a whole rather than as a collection of parts. In recent years the earth-as-organism idea has been stated as a formal hypothesis by the British ecologist James Lovelock, both in scientific papers and in a pair of popular books, *Gaia* (Oxford University Press, 1979) and *The Ages of Gaia* (Norton, 1988). Lovelock and his followers teach that life itself creates the conditions necessary to maintain life; that the composition and stability of the atmosphere, the narrow temperature range at the surface of the Earth (compared with other planets in the solar system), the presence of sufficient stores of free water, and most other aspects of our planet's uniquely life-friendly environment have been developed and maintained through self-correcting negative-feedback loops that have evolved along with, and as a result of, the evolution of life, and function in the same way as the metabolic cycles and self-healing abilities of living things.

The organism paradigm shares with the spacecraft paradigm an emphasis on interconnectedness and closure: living things are comprehensively interconnected, interdependent systems, and they are strongly self-contained, each within its own wall of skin, bark, or cell membrane. Organisms are vulnerable to harm — they can in fact be killed — an attribute that, like the fragility of spacecraft, encourages careful use and preservation. And because they are evolved rather than constructed systems, they avoid the spacecraft analogy's almost compulsive encouragement of technological fixes and tinkering. When living things are malfunctioning — that is, ill — the first impulse is to adjust the inputs rather than tinker with the mechanism. Surgery is reserved for extreme cases.

This emphasis on evolutionary rather than technological solutions makes the organism paradigm a considerable improvement over that of the spacecraft as a model for humans' interactions with one another and with the planet. But the improvement brings its own set of problems.

Evolution works because organisms react to stimuli, altering their behaviors and even their structures to conform to changes in the conditions around them. This gives life the ability both to heal itself and to adjust to pathological conditions. And this, in turn, allows — even encourages — a relaxation of vigilance. If the planet can heal itself, why should we worry about it? It is a telling commentary on the usefulness of the Gaia hypothesis as an environmental tool that among its strongest proponents are industrialists, developers, and others for whom life's capacity to adjust has become an excuse to avoid making any adjustments themselves — and who remain blissfully oblivious to the fact that life's adjustment to the irritation provided by the human race may simply be to get rid of the irritant. The easiest way for the planet to address the imbalance caused by one particular species running amok is to eliminate that one particular species. Gaia will almost certainly survive, but there is nothing in the process that guarantees that humanity is going to survive along with her.

The third alternate paradigm, that of the household, has one emphatic advantage over the spaceship and organism models: it is already in widespread use. The metaphors that allow us to speak of it have not required invention by a Fuller or a Lovelock: they are already deeply embedded in the language. The terms *ecology* and *economics,* with their derivation from the Greek word meaning "household," are only one example of this; we also speak regularly of the "family of man," of "homelands" and the "home planet," of the "foundations of society," of "brotherhood," of "our animal kin." We slip easily into these images, we are comfortable with them. Few, if any, will deny their validity — a situation that is simply not true of either Gaia or Spaceship Earth.

To use the word *household* in this manner is to imply relationships. People in a household interact regularly. They talk to one another; they provide for one another. They affect one another's actions. There may be cooperation or there may be conflict; there may be love or there may be hate; there may be ties of blood or ties of affection or merely ties of pragmatism, two people living as roommates because it is cheaper and easier to live that way. What there is not is atomistic individuality. People living together, like planets, affect one another's orbits. You cannot live alone and as a member of a household at the same time.

Thus the household paradigm, like the spacecraft and organism models, implies connections. It also implies closure (the four walls of the house) and vulnerability to tampering (burglary, fire, electrical malfunctions). At the same time, it avoids most of the pitfalls of the other two frameworks. No one has ever suggested that a household is a self-correcting entity that will run itself without attention, or that it is all right not to worry about burning the place down if someone insists on playing with matches. And while there must always be access to a good plumber, no one counts on technology and tinkering to keep the human relationships the household depends upon functioning properly. We understand that these require, not the attentions of a mechanic or a handyman, but nurturing and care and love.

But this great strength of the household paradigm is also its principal weakness. It is human centered; it places the other parts of the household in supporting roles. And we simply cannot afford to do that anymore.

Copernicus took us out of the center of the solar system; we now need to take ourselves out of the center of the biosphere as well. We are not the focus of a spacecraft's support systems, or the brain and nervous system of a world being, or even the head of the planetary family. We are a functioning part of an ecosystem, one out of many, neither above nor below any of the others. And that is precisely the way we must begin thinking of ourselves. The paradigm we must now adopt is that of the ecosystem. We need to learn to think not like a household but like a forest.

Thinking Like a Forest

To think like a forest is to think in circles rather than in lines; to think of webs rather than of chains; to think, in Wisconsin environmental official DuWayne Gebken's excellent analogy, "sideways." Where the frontier view sees throughput — resource to manufacture to use to scrap heap — the ecosystem view sees what we might call "aroundput," where everything is both a beginning and an end, both a waste and a resource, the side effects spinning off indefinitely in all directions. Living, a tree takes minerals from the soil; dying, it puts them back. In sunlight, a tree inhales carbon dioxide and exhales oxygen, balancing the atmospheric effects of its animal neighbors, which inhale oxygen and exhale carbon dioxide. The grass is food for the deer, which is food for the coyote, which — dying — is food for the grass. There is no beginning to these cycles, and no end. Things can be ejected from one cycle, but they only end up going round and round another.

Economics fits quite neatly and comfortably into this conceptual framework. Economics, like ecology, concentrates strongly on webs of relationships and interactions. The picture is already focused and well composed; all that needs to be done is to get rid of the frame.

In economics the primary model is the market, the complex of whims and needs and costs and abilities that is summed up so neatly by the intersecting lines of supply and demand in textbook graphs. Ecosystems also deal with whims and needs and costs and abilities, but there is this difference: where economics concerns itself primarily with the human members of the household, ecology considers all the residents equally. Nature enters into economics, but only as factors in the shape of the human curves of supply and demand. In ecology, nature has its own curves of supply and demand, and the science is interested not in the location of a single point of intersection but in the pattern made by thousands and thousands of intersections.

"When we try to pick out anything by itself," wrote John Muir a hundred years ago, "we find it hitched to everything else in the Universe." Barry Commoner, in his 1971 classic *The Closing Circle,* put it somewhat more succinctly: "Everything is connected to everything else." We will put it more succinctly yet: *Everything is connected.* No qualifications; no exceptions. All deeds have antecedents; all deeds have consequences. Every effect is also a cause, and every cause is also an effect. The actions that we take are like pebbles dropped in a pool: the ripples spread out and away, and no one can know what their effects will be on the far bank.

"Who knows?" says a devout but earthy Martin Luther in John Osborne's 1961 stage hit, *Luther.* "If I break wind in Wittenberg, they might smell it in Rome."

As an average person, you will draw in a breath and expel it again around 18,000 times between now and this time tomorrow. You will consume a little over five pounds of food and water, and will eliminate roughly three-fifths of that amount, primarily as urine. You will earn, or receive from a variety of non–wage and salary sources, approximately $45, and spend $36 of it. Four people will call you on the telephone; you will call about the same number. The mail carrier will drop at least one letter (or package, or magazine, or bill, or yellow envelope with Ed McMahon's picture on it) at your door. And you will watch (or at least be exposed to) a mind-numbing thirty-four minutes of television commercials.

All these activities have at least one thing in common: they connect you to the outside world. The air you breathe comes from the room around you, and from the outdoor air around that; it may have been down the block ten minutes ago and on the other side of the world last week. In fact, since oxygen and nitrogen, the two principal components of air, can be neither created nor destroyed by any force outside the center of a star, the molecules of air you breathe may well once have filled the lungs of dinosaurs or coursed through the bloodstreams of trilobites.

Letters and telephone calls come to you from someone; someone else created the television commercials, and several million other people are seeing them at the same time you do. Your food came from the store, and before that from the truck that delivered it, and before that from the plant that packed it, and ultimately from the seed, the sun, and the rich dark loam of the earth. Every dollar you receive has passed through the hands of an average of five other people during the past year; every dollar you spend will change hands another five times before the next year is out. Everything is connected. Even if you choose not to spend your money, even if you hide it under your mattress or bury it in a fruit jar in the back yard, you are connecting with other people. You have taken money out of circulation, decreasing the total money supply and ultimately lowering, even if only by an infinitesimally small amount, the nation's gross national product.

When everything is connected, certain corollaries necessarily follow. One is a line that both ecologists and economists are fond of quoting: *there is no such thing as a free lunch.* Someone — or something — must ultimately pay for everything. The costs may not be measurable in money, and they may not be paid by the same person who receives the benefits. But everything is connected. No action can ever be completely severed from its causes or its consequences.

A second corollary is that *nothing can be thrown away.* When you put something in the garbage or flush it down the sewer, you are not causing it to disappear; you are merely placing it where you don't have to think about it anymore. Jane Elder, the Sierra Club's staffer in charge of Great Lakes pollution issues, is fond of saying that "pollution never goes away, it just goes someplace else." In fact, though, it doesn't even do that. If everything is connected, there is no someplace else.

Finally, the fact that everything is connected means that we cannot ignore anything. Knowledge of connections brings with it an obligation to consider the effects of our actions on the things we are connected to. Recall Cain asking plaintively, "Am I my brother's keeper?" All the world's religions answer that question, Yes. Connections are relationships, and relationships bring with them responsibilities. We are not only our brothers' keepers, but keepers of the grass and trees and oceans and stones and microbes.

Earlier in this book I stated very strongly that ethics are not sufficient to achieve environmental protection. People will not do things because they "ought" to; people require more concrete motivations. This is especially true in those cases where what they "ought" to do appears to be costly or painful. The land-ethic approach preached by Aldo Leopold and others — the "extension of the social conscience from people to land," to quote Leopold himself — is not now sufficient, never was sufficient, and never will be sufficient to save the land.

I continue to stand by these statements. I think it is necessary to emphasize here, however, that the practical failure of the land-ethic concept in no way compromises its validity.

The moral obligation to the land is real. But it is not going to be felt by everyone until everyone feels the connections that make it so. The morality flows from the connections, not the other way around. When we feel those connections — really *feel* them, not merely grasp them intellectually or have them shoved down our throats by the regulatory apparatus of governments — the land ethic will happen. Until then we are, like Martin Luther, merely breaking wind in Wittenberg.

Leopold himself understood this clearly. This is how he put it near the end of "The Round River":

> Considering the prodigious achievements of the profit motive in wrecking land, one hesitates to reject it as a vehicle for restoring land. I incline to believe we have overestimated the scope of the profit motive. Is it profitable for the individual to build a beautiful home? To give his children a higher education? No, it is seldom profitable, yet we do both. There are, in fact, ethical and aesthetic premises which underlie the economic system. Once accepted, economic forces tend to align the smaller details of social organization into harmony with them. . . .
>
> I think we have here the root of the problem. What conservation education must build is an ethical underpinning for land economics and a universal economic curiosity to understand the land mechanism. Conservation may then follow.

Three ≈

Limits

Scarcity

A T 1:23 A.M. ON APRIL 26, 1986, in the middle of a botched experiment in low-power operation, the number four reactor at the Chernobyl nuclear plant in the northern Ukraine went critical, causing a core meltdown and an enormous outburst of intense heat. All the water in the reactor pool flashed into steam within a space of approximately four seconds. The pressure of the steam blew apart the containment building, scattering pieces of the massive concrete walls hundreds of yards away in all directions and sending a plume of radioactive water vapor and debris nearly into the stratosphere. Crops in Wales, two thousand miles and four countries away, had to be destroyed: Chernobyl fallout had shoved radioactivity levels twice as high as British health standards allowed for human consumption. Two people were killed outright by the blast, and 28 others died shortly afterward. The 135,000 people unfortunate enough to live within eighteen miles of the plant were evacuated from their homes. Soviet authorities suggested that the evacuation would probably have to be permanent. They also estimated the total cost of the accident: translated into American currency, the figure came in at right around $4 billion.

In late 1991 the Soviet Union fell, and the Ukraine became an independent nation. Along with this political realignment came a concurrent realignment of the Eastern European power grid. Electric transmission lines, generating stations, and transformer sites that had been safely within the purview of a single central authority were suddenly scattered across several international borders. Tariffs on electricity developed. Russian authorities, trying desperately to exert some control over their former satellites, shut off many cross-border power transmissions altogether. The brand-new Republic of the Ukraine found itself suffering from a severe scarcity of electricity.

Any economist (and probably most noneconomists as well) could easily have predicted the next move. On December 13, 1992 — quietly, with as little fanfare as possible — the least-damaged reactor at Chernobyl was started up again.

When we discuss either economics or ecology, what we are really talking about is scarcity and how it affects living things. Much of the time we may appear to be examining other topics: markets, for example, or ecosystems, or pollution, or private-property rights. The arguments will occasionally seem to range quite far afield. But at every point in the discussion, pulling back the surface layer of language will reveal the concept of scarcity lurking just underneath.

We are used to thinking of scarcity as a lack of something, so it is important to emphasize right away that the sense in which both economists and ecologists use this term is subtly but significantly different from the way we use it in everyday conversation. Scarcity, as these two disciplines define it, is a state in which the supply of an item is insufficient to meet all the demand for that item. The absolute amount of the item does not matter; what we are looking at is the amount *available for use,* compared with the amount that we *want to use.* If the second amount is greater than the first, scarcity exists.

A simple example from ecology may help show what this means. If you stand on the edge of a bluff or at the top of an observation tower and look out over the canopy of an unbroken forest, one of the things likely to strike you immediately is that nearly all the trees, whatever their species or variety, are almost the same height. The reason for this is competition for a scarce resource — sunlight.

Sunlight, of course, is in no *absolute* sense a scarce resource; it falls on the Earth's outer atmosphere at the rate of more than a million Btu's per square meter per day. Even filtered down several orders of magnitude by the atmosphere, sunlight remains abundant (as you will recall from the last time you went to the beach while the summer sun was shining). But if one tree grows taller than its neighbors, it casts shade on them; and *in the shade* sunlight is scarce. The shaded trees overcome this scarcity by putting on a little extra growth spurt to raise their heads back into the sun. The effect ripples out through the forest until all the trees are once again the same height.

The important thing to note here is that a good that seems abundant, like sunlight, may still be scarce in an economic or ecological sense. In fact, we can consider this a general law of nature: *everything is scarce.* The planet is finite. Life is continually pressing against those finite limits. That is the chief means by which we can tell that life is alive.

Neither economics nor ecology would exist without scarcity. There would be no point to them. If all our wants were satisfied, we would feel no scarcity of goods, so we would not need to buy or trade anything. The economy would disappear. If living things did not grow, eat, and reproduce, there would be no scarcity of food or living space, but there would also be nothing for ecologists to study.

Scarcity drives variety and innovation. If the supply of a substance is limitless, there is no need to find substitutes for it. If hunting and gathering peoples did not suffer through cycles of scarcity, there would have been no reason for anyone to think of saving seed and planting it. Agriculture would never have developed. If firewood had not become scarce in Europe in the Middle Ages, it is unlikely that people would have turned to burning coal. If nutrients were not scarce, living things would not have had to come up with so many different ways of obtaining them, and the great wealth of species the earth enjoys would never have developed.

Scarcity is subjective; since the scarcity of an item can only be measured by comparing the existing amount of the item to the amount we think we need, our perception of it can change radically depending upon who we are and what we are using to make the comparison. A human in a house with five clean bathrooms, for example, may not recognize a scarcity of anything important. A cat in the same house will easily recognize a desperate scarcity of sand.

The subjective nature of scarcity makes it difficult to talk about. Our perceptions become involved, and perceptions are notoriously undependable. Is there an abundance or scarcity of drugs on the streets of New York? Your answer may depend on whether you are trying to rid the city of drug dealers or trying to score a line of coke. Is there an abundance or scarcity of old-growth timber in the Pacific Northwest? Our perception of the answer is strongly colored by whether we come at the question as loggers or as environmentalists. Is there an abundance or scarcity of water during a flood? Most of us would immediately say an abundance. Now add the condition that the flood has knocked out your municipal water-treatment plant — as happened in Des Moines, Iowa, in the summer of 1993, and in my own city of Ashland, Oregon, a few years before. I can assure you that at such a time there is no sense whatever of water being abundant, despite the rivers in the streets and the record downpour going on just outside the door.

Here is a mental experiment that will help demonstrate the very subjective nature of our perceptions about scarcity. First, imagine yourself on the bank of one of our great rivers — the Mississippi, say, or the Columbia, or the Hudson. As you watch that immense amount of water surge past you, think of all the other great rivers of the planet — the Nile, the Rhine, the Mekong, the Yellow, the Amazon, the Zambezi. Think of all the small rivers, the streams and brooks, the lakes and ponds. Think of the Great Lakes, Great Slave Lake, Lake Winnipeg, Lake Victoria, Lake Baikal. Is fresh water a scarce resource? It would certainly not seem so.

Now get a basketball, go to your kitchen, and set the basketball on the kitchen table. Open the cupboard, get out a bottle of sesame seeds, and place a single seed beside the basketball. If you were to reduce the Earth to the size of a basketball, all the fresh surface water on the planet — all those rivers and lakes and ponds and streams — would fit inside that one tiny sesame seed. Add a second sesame seed: now you have all the usable underground water as well. Is fresh water a scarce resource? What do you think now?

Value

OVER TWO HUNDRED years ago Adam Smith pointed to a strange paradox in human value systems. Water, which is absolutely essential to human life, is treated as a free good with little or no economic value, while diamonds — in Smith's day, useless for anything but decoration (we know a few more uses for them now) — are among the highest-valued commodities in commerce. What are we to make of this odd state of affairs?

Smith provided part of the answer. Diamonds, he pointed out, are scarce; it takes a great deal of effort to locate them, mine them, process them, and transfer them to the marketplace. Water is abundant, and anyone can get it just by going down to the creek or the river or the well. So the diamond, as a product, represents considerably more labor than the water does. Thus the diamonds-and-water paradox becomes one of the cornerstones of the labor theory of value. If the value of a good is strictly dependent on the amount of labor that goes into producing it, diamonds are by definition of greater value than water, and there is no paradox.

Smith was right, but he was only partly right. The labor content of a diamond brought to market is one reason we price it as we do, but it is not the only reason. Scarcity itself has a great deal to do with it.

One of the few places in North America where diamonds can be found is a small area in Pike County, Arkansas, not far from Bill Clinton's childhood home, where the core of kimberlite at the heart of an extremely ancient volcano has become exposed on the surface of the earth. The diamonds are too few, and of too low quality, to make mining profitable, and for a number of years now the deposit has been operated as a state park named Crater of Diamonds. An entrance fee is charged; visitors can poke around the deposit as long as they like and can keep any diamonds they find. Hunting is best after a rainstorm, when the weather has been moving the earth.

Suppose now that two people enter the Crater of Diamonds at the same time. One is a long veteran of the search who lives nearby and has visited the park every day for twenty years without finding a single gem. The other is a green tourist from California. In the center of the deposit a diamond lies on the surface, exposed by last night's rain. The two diamond hunters walk toward it together. The tourist sees it first, and picks it up. He has spent twenty minutes searching. Is the find therefore less valuable than it would have been if the native had found it after her fruitless search of twenty years?

There are actually two answers to that question.

From the standpoint of the tourist and the native, the answer is yes, the diamond is less valuable. The tourist, from the perspective of his twenty minutes on the ground, has a skewed view of just how lucky he has been, and that view will depress the gem's value in his mind. The native, from the perspective of her long search, knows how rare the find is, and she would almost certainly prize it more highly for that.

But from the standpoint of the market, *there is no difference at all*. The diamond will assay at the same value no matter who brings it into the assayer's office. The much longer labor of the native will not matter one bit.

Is the market right? Is the tourist right? Or is it the native whose assessment of the value is the most trustworthy? A modern economist would answer all three of those questions the same way: yes.

Economists today recognize two types of value, which may differ widely for any given commodity. The first is *value in use:* it is the "value" the diamond would have for someone who wanted to employ it to do something. Under this meaning of the term, the diamond is almost valueless; aside from certain industrial applications (cutting, grinding, electrical current modulation) for which there exist adequate if not perfect substitutes, the only use the diamond has is as an item of display.

Value in use has little to do with the length of the search or the effort involved in it. When we use an object, we are primarily concerned not with the amount of labor that went into finding or creating the object but with how well it fits the use — how well it does the task we are putting it to.

The second type of value is *value in exchange.* This is the "value" the market places on a good, and it does depend on the labor put into the search — but not quite in the way we think. The difference in the amount of labor the tourist and the native have expended in our diamond example is not what the market looks at. Twenty minutes, twenty years, twenty centuries — it is all the same to the market *as regards that particular diamond.* The market is concerned with the general case. How hard is it to find diamonds *generally?* How easy would it be to replace this one if it were lost? Note that these questions may be answered differently by different people. The tourist values the diamond less highly than the native would, because he exchanged less for it than she would have; the value of twenty minutes of a vacation morning while passing through southwest Arkansas is demonstrably less than that of twenty years of unremitting effort. The genius of the market is that it smooths out these individual differences. In the field the value in exchange can be quite different for different people at any given instant; in the market, it is always the same.

Which is the "right" type of value to assign to something? There is no correct answer to that question, but there are some observations that can be made about it.

First, we should observe that things can have either utility (water, reading, trees) or disutility (pollution, distractions, parasites). Things that have utility are goods and become generally more valuable as they increase. Things that have disutility are "bads" and become generally more valuable as they *decrease*. Any "correct" definition of value has to take this fundamental dichotomy into account.

Second, we need to note that all things are scarce, but some are scarcer than others. The scarcer a good is, the worse off we are; the scarcer a "bad" is, the better off we are. So scarcity may increase or decrease total value, depending upon whether the scarce item is useful or not.

Third, we observe that, given two items of equal scarcity, the one with more utility has the higher value. This is easiest to see by assigning one of the items utility and the other disutility; to someone who is thirsty, for instance, a quart of water obviously has higher value than a quart of toxic waste does. Less obvious, but still apparent when you think about it, is the case where both items have utility; if a person dying of thirst is given a choice between a quart of water and a quart of diamonds — neither of which will be replaced for the next forty-eight hours — he or she will choose the water nearly every time. (Those who do not choose the water are, for the purposes of our analysis, a self-correcting problem because they effectively remove themselves from the data set.)

So value is set partly by utility and partly by scarcity. But here a seeming paradox begins to emerge: *the scarcer an item is, the more its value will be determined by utility.*

The scarcer clean water becomes, the more valuable it appears in relation to other scarce things of equal or lesser utility.

The scarcer wild places become, the more valuable they appear in relation to other places of equal or lesser utility.

It is possible to quantify, to some extent, the relationship between scarcity and value. To do this, economists turn to a pair of separate but closely related concepts: diminishing marginal returns and opportunity costs.

Margins and Opportunities

I ONCE KNEW a professor of economics who, at a certain point in each term, would hide a number of chocolate bars about his person before going in to face his beginning economics class. Standing at the lectern, he would begin describing the qualities of fine chocolate: the smooth, sensual feel in one's mouth, the rich, dark appearance, the quiet but compelling aroma, the blissfully full, warm, bittersweet taste. When a sufficient number of students were slavering, he would reach into the inner pocket of his jacket, pull out a single bar, and offer to auction it off to the highest bidder. Inevitably someone would purchase the bar at approximately twice the going retail price.

The professor would smile and collect the money, and continue to lecture about chocolate. Soon a second bar would make its appearance, perhaps from a side pocket. This bar, too, would be auctioned off. The price the professor received for the second bar, however, would be somewhat less than what he had obtained for the first one.

By the time the fifth or sixth bar made its appearance, the price would have dropped to below retail, the first few purchasers would be feeling silly, and the class would have begun to get the idea: each additional unit of a good has less market value than the unit preceding it. Economists call this the *law of diminishing marginal returns*, and it has an important corollary: since the value of a homogenous good is homogenous as well — chocolate bars of the same size and brand are completely interchangeable with one another, so they must all be of equal (or equivalent) value — the value of every good in a homogenous group is equal to the value of the last good added to the group. As an economist would put it, *value is determined at the margin.* That is why the first few chocolate bar purchasers in my professor friend's class always felt so silly. They had paid more for the good than it had turned out, in the long run, to be worth.

There is a common belief that economics is about money. This is false. Economists talk a lot about money, but it is only a side issue to the real business of the discipline, which is the study of choice. Humans are constantly choosing among a wide range of alternative actions. Some of these choices are large and important — what career to enter, what college to attend, what person to marry. Others are trivial — which brand of toothpaste to buy, whether or not to finish this chapter before turning out the light. Economics studies our methods of making these choices and the effects of the choices after they are made, both on our individual lives and on the collective life of our society.

In order to talk rationally about choices, you need some way of measuring them — some yardstick by which to measure both the criteria used in making the choice and the effects that follow from it. That is where money comes in. It makes a convenient tool for determining the size of the values we are considering in our choices — so convenient that it is easy to forget that it is only a tool, and not the value itself.

Shortly after seven o'clock this morning I was lying on the couch in my living room, propped on my elbow, watching the weather out the front window. A high overcast, lit from behind by the low morning sun, colored the sky a bright translucent gray; the dark, blue-black pyramid of Greensprings Mountain across the valley from my house stood out sharply against the glowing sky, above low, slowly moving clouds that sniffed their way cautiously across its middle slopes, obscuring some ridges, highlighting others. Rain fell gently. I recalled similar mornings seen from the other side, boots on my feet and a walking staff in my hand, crossing through wide, rain-soaked meadows from which I could look down the long sweep of the timbered mountain to a valley and a town alternately hidden and highlighted by the shifting clouds lying across the mountainside. Later, coffee finished, I walked in the rain, smelling the fresh, wet spring smells, the green scent of grass and the perfume of almond and plum blossoms mixed with the faint breath of evergreens blown in from the mountains, understanding clearly why bears, whose noses are so much keener than ours, appear to like inclement weather so much. Who can tack a dollar value onto such things? How can we put a price on morning?

The answer is that we cannot. But this does not mean that such experiences have no value, or that they cannot enter into the calculations of economics. Price is a convenient measuring tool for market values. For unmarketable things like scenery and the scent of rain-dappled blossoms it falls far short. But other measuring tools can take its place. One that economists use regularly is *opportunity costs.*

When you use resources to accomplish an action, you always preclude their use in some other way. Machinery being used to make toasters cannot simultaneously be used to make baby carriages. Petroleum burned in automobile engines can no longer serve as a raw material source for pharmaceuticals and plastics. You can harvest a tract of timber for building materials, or you can preserve it for wildlife habitat, but you cannot do both at the same time.

Thus, faced with a resource, you must always make a choice — and whatever activity you choose to employ that resource for means forgoing the opportunity to use it in some other manner. These forgone opportunities are the real cost of using the resource. Financial costs may or may not reflect them.

Economists refer to the costs of actions in terms of forgone opportunities as the actions' "opportunity costs." They are of extraordinary importance to economic theory, because it is they, not financial costs, that usually determine the course of economic events. If there is one single idea that economists of all ideological stripes can agree on, that is the one. So broadly is its importance recognized, in fact, that when an economist refers to "costs" without quantifying the term in some manner you can be virtually certain that what he or she means is opportunity costs.

Consider a simple example. You have five dollars that you plan to spend on apples and oranges. How do you decide how many of each to buy?

The answer is straightforward: you compare opportunity costs. Every time you spend a penny on apples, you forgo the opportunity to buy a penny's worth of oranges; every time you spend a penny on oranges, you forgo the opportunity to buy apples. If you like oranges better than apples, you will value the opportunity to buy oranges more highly than someone would who likes apples better than oranges. Your mix of purchases will reflect that preference.

Note that even in this simple fruit stand example we could not talk about opportunity costs without bringing subjective values — your preference for apples over oranges, or vice versa — into the discussion. This may give you some idea why it is so difficult to reach agreement on economic problems. It is simply not possible, through pricing alone, to get a handle on opportunity costs, which always include some subjective elements. My mix of apples and oranges will differ from yours. That does not mean that one of us is right and the other wrong; it only means that, while we measure the prices the same way, we measure the opportunity costs differently.

Now let us leave the fruit stand and go out into the environmental realm, where we will ask a question similar to that of the apples and oranges. We have a hundred-acre woodlot. Do we cut down the trees or do we leave them standing?

There is no way to answer this question without considering opportunity costs. If we leave them standing, we lose the opportunity to sell them, which can add to our money supply;

we also lose the opportunity to build our own house out of them. If we cut them down, we lose the opportunity to walk through them for pleasure, and to use their ability to anchor the soil and to keep fish spawning habitat the proper temperature and to provide homes for wildlife and all the other things that forests do when they are left intact. And our decision is not going to be based solely, or even largely, on the price of lumber. What we are going to do is attempt to balance the opportunities the intact trees would provide against the opportunities the money obtained by cutting down the trees and selling them would provide. The price of lumber helps us judge those opportunities, but it does not determine them. The determining factor is which set of opportunities means less to us, and which we want to keep intact, and which we are willing to forgo. Everything else — ethics, lumber prices, the state of our bank account, empathy with the earth, love of scenery, druidism, what have you — is important only insofar as it helps determine which set of opportunities we are more likely to decide to preserve.

And this brings us back, full circle, to the law of diminishing marginal returns. It should be obvious by this time why the law holds. The less of an item we have, the less opportunity we have to use it. The less opportunity for use, the higher the opportunity cost should we lose it, or use it up. When the amount declines all the way to zero, the opportunity cost becomes infinite: we cannot buy the opportunity to use a nonexistent good for any amount of money in the universe.

Before we leave the topics of diminishing marginal returns and opportunity costs, there are three more lessons we need to draw from them. The first lesson is about landscapes. The law of diminishing returns states quite clearly that, as the quantity of a good is increased, the value of each additional unit becomes lower and lower. But the reverse is also true: as the quantity of a good is *decreased,* the value of each unit *removed* becomes *higher and higher.* And since value is determined at the margin, when you remove any unit of a good you cause all the remaining units to become more valuable. Every acre of natural landscape lost to development causes all acres of untouched land remaining to increase in value. Conversely, every added acre of development causes all acres of developed land to decrease in value. At some point, the rising value curve of undeveloped land is going to cross the falling value curve of developed land. That is the point at which good economics says that development of additional land should stop.

Notice that we have used the term *value* here — not *price.* As anyone who follows the real estate market knows, the price of real estate rarely goes anywhere but up. Real estate prices, however, are not determined by the quantity of developed land compared with the quantity of undeveloped land; they are determined by the quantity of developed land *compared to the demand for developed land.* This point is often missed, but it is of vital importance. The fact that real estate prices are going up is a valid excuse to develop more land only when the value of undeveloped land is less than the value of the same land, developed. And that is primarily determined not by price but by the relative amounts of land in the developed and undeveloped states. Undeveloped land has its own demand curve, and its price is determined by that curve, not by the curve for developed acreage. It is not only theoretically possible but probably inevitable that as the amount of landscape we have devoted to development increases at the expense of natural areas, at some point the market price of developed land is going to fall below that of undeveloped land. At that point profit-making landowners will be razing subdivisions to create wildlands, not the other way around.

The second lesson deals with a subject that is often extremely uncomfortable to environmentalists. That topic is profits. Economists recognize two types of profits, usually referred to by the terms *normal* and *excess*. The difference between the two is very clear and specific. If profits equal opportunity costs, they are normal; if they are above opportunity costs, they are excess.

It is important to comprehend this difference, because the two types of profits have significantly different social and environmental effects. There is absolutely nothing inherently wrong with earning normal profits — on the contrary, there is something wrong with *not* earning them. A firm that cannot earn normal profits will either change its production over to some other type of good, or go out of business. Sometimes this result is what we want; sometimes it is not. Environmentalists might cheer if a firm producing DDT could not make normal profits on its operation, forcing it to close; their feelings would be quite different if the firm forced to close was one recycling paper products. Since the profits of the two firms are functionally identical (assuming both are normal), it is clear that profits themselves are not the problem. The terrorists who blew a Ryder truck to bits in the parking garage of the World Trade Center in the spring of 1993 undoubtedly assembled their bomb with the assistance of a screwdriver. No rational person would argue that this makes all screwdrivers inherently evil.

The situation is quite different with regard to excess profits. This type of profit always results from some kind of distortion in the marketplace. Usually the distortion is some form of monopoly (excess profits are often referred to as "monopoly profits" for precisely this reason). At other times, another variety of distortion may be involved: informational flaws, perhaps, or excessive decision costs. ("Decision costs" are those involved in deciding to do something — the costs, for example, of altering sawmill machinery so it will handle second-growth timber instead of old-growth. Since high decision costs create barriers to the entry of firms into markets, they are almost always associated with monopolies; but it is at least theoretically possible to disassociate the two.) Whatever the distortion, it always moves the economy away from its peak efficiency, thus reducing the amount of goods that the economy can produce with a given set of resources. Excess profits therefore cause an economy to operate inefficiently. And inefficiency always wastes resources. Wherever excess profits exist, society can produce the same amount of goods with less use of resources, and thus with less impact on the environment. Normal profits are environmentally neutral. Excess profits are always environmentally bad.

The third lesson to be learned from opportunity costs and the law of diminishing returns may be even more uncomfortable for environmentalists than the lesson about profits was, but it is equally important. It has to do with pollution. As you decrease the amount of pollutants spewing into a river, or an airshed, the law of diminishing returns states that the value of each additional unit of pollution will go up. At the same time, the value of each additional unit of clean water, or clean air, will come down. At some point these two curves, like the curves for undeveloped and developed landscapes, are going to cross each other. Where that crossing occurs is the point at which pollution-control efforts should stop. The goal of zero discharge is ethically attractive, but it is as impractical and illogical as the goal of zero wilderness.

Market Ecology

A S ADAM SMITH understood long ago, no voluntary exchange can take place unless both parties to the exchange believe they are improving their lots. A person selling pins (to use Smith's favorite example) will not part with them unless and until the money she receives is worth more to her than the pins are; a person buying pins will not pay for them unless and until the pins are worth more to him than the money he pays for them. There are no exceptions to this: analysis that sees apparent discrepancies (purchasing a dime's worth of pins for ten dollars at a charity auction) is focusing on the wrong exchange (the buyer at the charity auction is not purchasing pins; he or she is purchasing the charity).

But exchanges looked at individually are meaningless. You cannot learn anything significant about them from studying any individual exchange; you must study groups of exchanges, the composite structures economists refer to as *markets*.

Markets do not have a good name among environmentalists. They are viewed much as cats are by mice, with deep suspicion and a nagging fear that they may be about to turn upon us and swallow us whole. Andrew Bard Schmookler, who has written several works on the evils done by the market system to society in general and to the environment in particular, sums up the argument well toward the end of his 1993 book *Fool's Gold*:

> In the grip of a system that breaks everything down into commodity form, the earth is violated. The living planet is

dismembered, as land becomes real estate, forests become lumber, oceans become fisheries and sinks. . . . Separation is the essence of sin; thus the economy that separates man from nature is an economy of sin. And the wage of sin is death.

But this argument misses an important point. Markets are not arbitrarily created systems: they are evolved ones, based firmly on the laws of supply and demand, *which are natural laws*. And we cannot pick and choose which natural laws to support. We cannot demand that society learn "lessons from nature" (the title of a book by environmentalist Daniel D. Chiras) and then insist that those lessons include only those parts of nature (the "natural" parts) that we approve of. Natural law is a single piece: the strands of it are inseparable from one another. Market systems are one result of those laws. We cannot logically condemn them without condemning the rest of the laws' results as well.

The great nineteenth-century British essayist and skeptic Thomas Carlyle was once said to have remarked to a friend that the best way to train an economist was to purchase a parrot and teach it to repeat the phrase *supply and demand* over and over. Anyone who follows business news for a few days will tell you that there is more than a grain of truth in that statement. What most people fail to realize, however, is that the laws of supply and demand are at least as important in ecology as they are in economics. This is true not only of cases, such as the Ukraine's decision to restart Chernobyl, where scarcity couples with economic supply-and-demand curves to compel the undertaking of actions that are extremely questionable from an ecological standpoint. In fact, supply and demand are ecological as well as economic forces. Ecosystems and economies can both be thought of as massive engines. Scarcity is the driving force, the fuel. Supply and demand are the pistons and connecting rods and crankshafts.

The laws governing these forces are so simple as to be

almost intuitive. What economists call the *law of supply* states merely that, all other things being equal, as the price of something rises, suppliers will supply more of it. The *law of demand* is similar but reversed: as the price rises, consumers will demand less. All markets do — *all* they do — is establish a balance between these two opposing tendencies.

Take a piece of paper and draw a vertical line someplace near the left-hand edge. That line represents prices: the higher up the page, the higher the price. Now draw a horizontal line starting at the bottom of the price line and extending to the right. This line represents quantity: the farther to the right, the larger the amount. Within this framework, a line representing demand will always start high on the left and slope down to the right (as price falls, the quantity buyers demand rises), and a line representing supply will always start low on the left and slope up to the right (as price rises, the quantity sellers are willing to supply will rise with it).

Pay particular attention to the point in the middle of the page where the lines cross. At that point, the quantity buyers demand is exactly equal to the quantity that sellers are willing to supply. Economists call this the *equilibrium point* (or *market equilibrium*), because it is the point at which the economy tends to settle down.

Exactly the same truth holds in ecosystems as in economies. When grass is plentiful in the spring, deer eat little else; when it becomes scarce, in the fall, the deer switch to eating other things rather than pay the increased price in time and energy necessary to locate and travel between the last few decrepit grass blades. The price of grass has increased, so the demand for grass has gone down. The next time you pass a meadow in the early spring where a deer herd has been overwintering, take a close look at the lower branches of the trees at the meadow's edge. The bottom twigs are likely to have been chewed off in a remarkably straight line parallel to the ground all around the meadow as high as a deer can conveniently reach. That is supply and demand in action. Twigs are not the most palatable of foods, even for a deer; this squared-off line, known as a "browse line," develops only when the supply of food has become so limited that the price of eating twigs — in unpalatability — is lower than the price of eating anything else.

Because they are natural laws, the laws of supply and demand are immune to ideological tampering. They are not something that can be altered by changing economic systems. Capitalists, communists, socialists, mercantilists, and feudal lords all have to deal with them. We cannot evade them or wish them away. We can ignore them, but we cannot suppress them; they will continue to operate in the background, skewing the results of our activities, which then become unpredictable.

And if supply and demand are natural laws, then markets — based on supply and demand — must be natural, too. Schmookler and others who decry our dependence upon markets may want to take another look at them. If markets are natural, regulations and ethical systems that attempt to do away with markets are in for the same serious problems as those that would attempt to do away with inertia or gravity.

None of this should be taken to imply that market excesses do not exist. They not only exist, they are a very serious problem. But we must recognize them for what they are, and what they are is precisely what we have just called them: market *excesses*. They are not legitimate fruits of the market system; they are the result of flaws in the way we have allowed that system to be distorted by taking it outside the realm of natural law. Environmentalists' insistence on condemning markets out of hand contributes to the delusion of their separation from nature, and hence increases the distortions. We feed the very monster we despise.

Markets do not damage the environment; market imperfections do. We need to learn to make the distinction. Markets are not our enemies. Under the proper conditions, markets can help us solve the very excesses we have been falsely attributing to them.

The kicker here, of course, is that qualifying phrase: *under the proper conditions.* As Adam Smith himself recognized, those conditions are often the exception rather than the rule. And the problem is much worse in our day than it was in Adam Smith's.

Classical economic theory is based on what economists have since come to call a *perfect market.* A perfect market exists if, and only if, four basic conditions are met.

The first condition is *homogeneity.* Products from different vendors must be enough alike that price becomes the principal factor guiding choice. If there are two hot dog stands side by side on a city street, you are free to choose which one to patronize according to the prices they post. If the choice is between hot dogs from one stand and pretzels from the other, price is still going to be important, but it is going to become secondary to whether you prefer hot dogs or pretzels.

The second condition is *complete information.* Buyers and sellers must have complete information about each other because incomplete information leads to wrong choices. One does not knowingly buy stale bread or sour milk or a damaged ozone layer — at least not at the same price as fresh goods or undamaged ozone. Knowledge alters the way these goods behave in the marketplace.

Consumers must know what each vendor's price is; otherwise, they cannot choose the one with the lowest price. Vendors must also know what each vendor's price is, or they will not be able to respond to consumer movement to their competitors. If those two hot dog carts do not post their prices, you will not be able to tell whether one is cheaper than the other. If the carts are positioned so that neither vendor is able to see the other's prices, they will have no idea where to set their own prices in order to compete adequately. In either case, price will no longer reflect supply and demand, and the market will fail.

The third condition is *lack of friction*. Transactions must be frictionless — that is, devoid of what economists call decision costs and transaction costs — because exchanges must be based on the values of the goods exchanged, not on the costs of making the exchanges happen. Costly transactions skew prices, because the price of a transaction is a cost to both the buyer and the seller, whereas the actual price of the goods exchanged is a cost only to the buyer; it is a *benefit* to the seller. If the balance point of costs and benefits is to be our criterion for making choices, we do not want to have anything enter the equation that will move that point off the cost and benefit curves.

The fourth condition is *adequate size*. For a market to function properly, the numbers of consumers and vendors must both be high enough that no one transaction is able to alter the price. No single individual can be allowed to affect the market, because when that happens the effects are almost always benefits to the market-affector at the expense of everyone else.

When one person holds a monopoly on a product or a service, he or she can control the amount supplied, artificially raising the price by holding goods back or lowering it by flooding the market — whichever will benefit the monopoly-holder more. The laws of supply and demand do the rest. Under these conditions, the market is being manipulated to the benefit of the monopolist and against the customer — and, not incidentally, against the welfare of society as a whole. Gifford Pinchot, the idealistic conservationist who founded the U.S. Forest Service, was an ardent campaigner against monopolies, because, he said, monopolies and conservation were natural enemies. Conservation benefited everyone; monopoly benefited only a few. The two could not possibly work together.

* * *

Before going further, we need to clear up a common and extremely dangerous misconception having to do with supply. The supply of a good and its availability are not the same thing. Availability is *the amount of a good that is readily obtainable;* supply is *the amount of a good that sellers are willing to bring to market.* The two concepts sound much alike, but they are actually polar opposites.

The relationship between supply and price is price-driven: as price rises, supply will rise as well. As sellers are rewarded more for bringing a good to market, the amount they are willing to bring will increase. But the relationship between availability and price is availability-driven: as availability goes up, price goes down. As goods become more common, the price drops. We will refer to this relationship as the *rule of availability.*

As with supply and demand, all living things (not just humans) are subject to the rule of availability. Define price in monetary terms, and the rule explains why pocket calculators, personal computers, VCRs, and similar consumer goods are far cheaper today than they were when first introduced onto the market: there are simply many more of them today than there were then. Availability has increased, so price has gone down. Define price as the effort necessary to locate game, and you can watch the rule of availability play out among lions and wildebeests on the Serengeti: as wildebeest herd sizes increase, lions find hunting easier. The higher the availability, the lower the price. Or define price as leaf size, and the rule of availability shows up in the structure of the forest: the higher the availability of sunlight, the smaller the leaf. Overstory trees have small leaves. Understory plants uniformly have large ones, the price they pay for scarce sunlight beneath the canopy. In fact, if you look closely at most hardwoods, you will often see the rule of availability played out on each tree: the leaves on the bottom branches tend to be larger than those on the upper ones. The tree is willing to "pay" more for sunlight on its lower branches, where the good is scarce, than it is on its crown, where the good is abundant.

The law of supply is a seller's function; it is not directly affected by buyers' decisions. Only the price affects it. If the price of a good rises, supply will increase. If it falls, supply will decrease. Whatever determines the price, therefore, also determines the supply.

It is important to emphasize this connection, if only because it is so often overlooked. How do you make a good more widely available to the public? The easy answer is to hold the price down, because then more people will be able to buy it. But the easy answer is wrong. The lower price will drive the supply down, too: sellers will simply bring less of the good to market. You will end up with less of the good available to society, not more. Expanding supply while lowering price can be done, but only if you can find a way to shift the entire supply function. Merely legislating price ceilings will not, and cannot, do it.

The law of demand is a buyer's function; like the law of supply, it is price-driven, but its relationship to price is the inverse of that of supply. As price rises, supply rises with it; but as price rises, demand falls. The higher the price a seller asks for a good, the less of the good he will be able to sell. As with the law of supply, the actual amount available for sale has no bearing on this relationship. It doesn't matter whether you have one item, or 1 million, for sale. Raise the price, and buyers' demand will drop; lower it, and demand will come back up again.

The rule of availability, however, is neither a buyer's nor a seller's function. It is a *resource* function, driven from the availability end rather than the supply end. And this makes it fundamentally different from the other two. It is especially important for economists to avoid confusion on this point. Availability cannot be treated in the same way as supply: if you do so, you are likely to come out with results that are both personally embarrassing and economically disastrous.

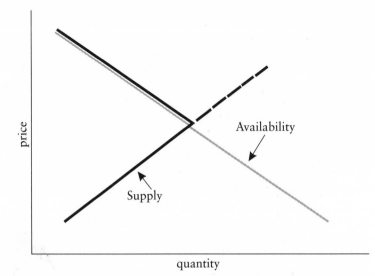

price

quantity

Supply cannot exceed availability, because above the availability function there are no goods to be had. Above this point, no matter how high you raise price, quantity is still going to fall.

The law of supply is a direct relationship; if you graph it on a price/quantity axis, the line you get will slope upward toward the right (higher prices are associated with higher quantities). Compare this with the rule of availability, which is an inverse relationship (higher prices are associated with lower quantities; the line slopes downward to the right). The two lines are not identical, or even parallel. Placed on the same graph, they tend to converge. At some point they will meet. *But they will never cross.* They cannot: supply can never exceed availability. Above the point where it intersects the availability curve, the supply curve has to follow the availability curve.

Economists rarely consider this part of the graph, but it is extremely important. All standard analysis of market behavior deals with rising supply functions and descending demand functions. If the supply function is falling, the relationships this analysis reveals will no longer hold true.

And so it is relevant to ask, how close are we to the supply/availability intersection? This is functionally equivalent to asking how close we are to what ecologists call *carrying capacity.* Once we hit that point, it no longer matters how high the price is pushed. The supply is still going to go down.

Limitless resources are a frontier myth. The real world has limits. Economists must recognize this truth just as environmentalists must heed the uncomfortable truth about the reality of markets.

Limits

THE EARTH is a finite planet. Therefore, the amount of resources it can provide for us is finite as well.

These statements may seem self-evident, but there are few ideas in all of human history that have generated more fervent debate. A little over twenty years ago, an international research group headed by a pair of systems analysts from the Massachusetts Institute of Technology, Dennis and Donella Meadows, published a small volume called *The Limits to Growth* in which they argued that worldwide growth rates of a number of parameters — population, energy use, strategic minerals, agriculture, and others — were such that the planet would begin running out of virtually everything within fifty to one hundred years. The level of shrillness to which the discussion of this book immediately climbed — with economists primarily arrayed against it and ecologists lined up for it — does not suggest that limits are a subject that these two disciplines can agree on at all.

And yet the agreement is there. In fact, the study of limits is a central part of both economics and ecology. It is the way they view them that is different. And this, in turn, derives from a fundamental difference in the way the two disciplines study the world.

Economics is principally about open systems. It focuses on the point of exchange of goods, and how the things that happen at that point of exchange affect society as a whole. In this view, where goods come from before the exchange and where they go to afterward is largely irrelevant, except as inputs and outputs for other exchanges. A phrase you will hear constantly from economists is *ceteris paribus,* a Latin term meaning "other things being equal." Like other scientists, economists attempt to isolate the effects of one variable by holding all others constant. When an economist studies the effect of supply and demand on price, he or she must assume that supply can always be provided if the price is high enough. If supply is conditional on something other than price — availability, say — it violates the conditions of *ceteris paribus,* and the analysis of price becomes far more complex and haphazard, if not downright meaningless.

One of the ways in which economists match *ceteris paribus* to the real world is to assume substitutes. If the price of a good becomes high enough, they argue, a lower-priced good will be substituted for it, and the transaction process will continue as before. This is the assumption at the heart of economists' disagreement with Dennis and Donella Meadows. We will not run out of all those things *The Limits to Growth* predicts we will, economists say, because long before this happens the laws of supply and demand will have priced these things so high that they price themselves right out of the market and substitutes will be employed in their stead. To ask what these substitutes will be misses the point. The economist is not interested in what the substitute will be, only in the process of substitution itself. Something will turn up. Something always has.

Note that this reasoning does not state that limits do not exist; it merely states that they cannot be reached. This is the major point where economists' views of limits differ from those of ecologists. Ecologists almost universally believe that limits can not only be reached but exceeded, at least on a short-term basis. It is just that if this happens the results are likely to be catastrophic.

Ecologists study the behavior of closed systems. This leads to a view of inputs and outputs radically different from the open-system view of the economists. Open systems imply throughput — substances coming from one place, flowing through the system, and then going out to someplace different. Closed systems imply cycles. To an ecologist (or to anyone who studies closed systems) the someplace that substances come from and the someplace they go to are ultimately the same place.

When things affect each other in more than one way, the condition of *ceteris paribus* no longer exists. With *ceteris paribus* out of the way, limits can be exceeded. And when the limit involved is carrying capacity, exceeding it can be extremely hazardous to environmental health.

Ecologists define the carrying capacity of a piece of land as *the number of individuals of a given species that the land is able to support in a sustainable manner.* When species numbers are beneath the carrying capacity, there is room to expand the population without degrading the environment. When numbers exceed the carrying capacity, the environment begins to go.

Two principal factors determine carrying capacity: assimilative capacity and land capability.

Assimilative capacity is the total amount of pollution that a local environment can absorb without being damaged. *Absorb* here generally means one of four things: the pollution is either used by the biota, broken down into harmless components, buried, or carried away. All of these methods of assimilation have a time component, so assimilative capacity is usually stated as a rate of flow: so many gallons per day, tons per year, milligrams per hour. Acceptable rates can vary dramatically depending upon the type of pollutant involved; the size of the receiving body (the Ohio River has considerably more assimilative capacity than does, say, Town Brook in Plymouth, Massachusetts); and a variety of environmental factors such as soil chemistry, prevailing wind, and average ambient temperature. For some substances in some places (Mirex, a pesticide, in the Great Lakes), assimilative capacity is essentially zero. For other substances in other places (sewage in the lower Mississippi), assimilative capacity may be extremely high.

Only when the assimilative capacity for a given substance is negligible to nonexistent are we justified in seeking a total ban on that substance. For other substances, the proper goal is control to within the environment's assimilative limits.

Land capability is the total amount of biomass that a piece of land is able to produce each year. Capability, in turn, depends on a variety of subfactors, including soil fertility, ambient temperature, and the availability of water and sunlight. When all these factors are present in large amounts, capability is high, and the carrying capacity of any given species is likely to be high as well. This is just another way of pointing out that life is easier in a rain forest than on the top of a mountain. In the verdant coastal forests of Alaska there are far more bears than there are on the tundra of the Brooks Range. That is not because bears cannot live well on tundra; it is because it takes more square miles of tundra to support each bear. Bear densities — and hence, bear numbers — reflect this.

The bear numbers example reflects another truth about carrying capacity: if all other factors are held equal, a species will tend to match its numbers to the carrying capacity of the environment. As long as there is room for more blackbirds in a cattail marsh, the number of blackbirds in the marsh will continue to expand. When blackbird numbers reach the carrying capacity (for blackbirds) of the marsh, population growth will stop.

Economists should note the manner in which *ceteris paribus* conditions show up in that last paragraph. The tendency of species to stop expanding at their carrying capacity is not innate in the species; it is a result of environmental pressures, the complex sum of forces that ecologists refer to as *environmental resistance*. These forces are what give rise, in this case, to *ceteris paribus*. If they are disturbed, *ceteris paribus* no longer holds, and the relationship between carrying capacity and population size is no longer trustworthy. One imagines an ecologist saying patiently to an economist, "Yes, but other things are *not* equal."

The classic example of what happens to the population/ carrying capacity relationship when environmental resistance is disturbed is the now famous incident on Arizona's Kaibab Plateau in the early twentieth century. On the north rim of the Grand Canyon, encircled almost completely by the tawny immensity of the great gorge, the Kaibab is essentially a biotic island. Prior to European arrival, it supported a herd of roughly 30,000 deer, stabilized against the combined resistance of a limited food supply, a climate that tended to extremes, and a broad array of predators which included wolves, coyotes, bear, cougars, and Native Americans.

Beginning about 1885, livestock were moved onto the plateau. The livestock competed with the deer for the food supply, and deer numbers began to decline, reaching a low of about 6,000 animals in 1906. Predator control also began during this period, and Native American hunting declined. This reduction in predation relaxed environmental resistance, allowing the combined grazing by deer and livestock to exceed the plateau's carrying capacity for grazing animals. Degradation began to set in.

In 1906, the Kaibab came under the care of the newly created U.S. Forest Service, which decided to restore the deer herds. The livestock were moved out, and predator control efforts were stepped up. The environmental brakes were suddenly completely removed from the deer herd, which rebounded rapidly toward carrying capacity — and overshot it. By the winter of 1924, the deer population of the Kaibab had reached more than 100,000, and massive resource degradation had set in — the inevitable result when carrying capacity is exceeded. Foodstocks plummeted. That winter 60,000 deer died.

The population decrease continued, though more slowly, over the next decade. In 1931, with deer numbers down to about 20,000, the predator control program was finally suspended. By this time, what was left of the Kaibab could only support about 10,000 animals — the result of habitat alteration caused by overgrazing. Overshooting the carrying capacity had not only killed those that overshot it, it had caused the carrying capacity itself to decline.

Economists have a concept similar to carrying capacity, known as the *production possibilities frontier* — PPF, for short. PPF is essentially a tradeoff. The standard example is that of butter and guns: an economy can produce x number of guns if it produces no butter, and y amount of butter if it produces no guns. If it attempts to produce butter along with the guns, the number of guns produced will have to shrink because some resources will have to be diverted from the production of guns to the production of butter. Given perfect transferability of production resources — that is, assuming that factories that make guns can make butter equally well with no changes in equipment (a *ceteris paribus* condition that never holds in the real world) — one can plot a graph of the relationship between gun production and butter production rather simply. Draw a pair of x and y axes, mark off units of guns on one and units of butter on the other, and place a mark on each axis at the amount of production that would be possible for that axis's good if production of the other good were zero. Connect the two points with a straight line. You can now read the tradeoff between guns and butter directly from the line. If maximum butter production is y units, and you want to know how many guns can be produced if you reduce butter production by 50 percent, simply start at the $y/2$ point on the y axis and draw a line parallel to the x axis out to the right until it intersects the guns-and-butter tradeoff line. Drop a line vertically from there to the x axis to find out how far out you have come. That is the number of guns you can produce at 50 percent butter production. The tradeoff line is a production possibilities frontier.

Production possibilities frontiers have two characteristics

that are particularly important for our discussion. First, they define a society's level of maximum efficiency; as long as the economy is operating on its production possibilities frontier, no member of society can be made better off without some other member of society being made worse off, a condition known to economists as *maximum social welfare* (MSW, or MXSW). And second, in real life, PPF curves are almost always convex. This is because our simple *ceteris paribus* condition of perfect transferability of production facilities rarely or never exists in the real world. Some types of facilities can produce butter far better than they can guns (cows, for instance). Other types of facilities (machine shops) can produce guns better than they can butter. The closer you come to full production of a single resource at the expense of all others, the less marginal production you get out of each added unit. So the curve tends to straighten out as it approaches each axis, and to bow outward in the middle between the two. What this means, practically speaking, is that the actual production capability of a society is always above the point represented by a one-to-one tradeoff between the different items being produced: if a society can produce x guns or y butter, the amount of guns *and* butter that can be produced is always going to be greater than $(x + y)/2$. A mixed economy outproduces a specialized one every time; in fact, maximum absolute production comes at the point where the economy is most thoroughly mixed — the point where the convex curve bows the farthest outward from the straight tradeoff line. Economists, honoring Vilfredo Pareto, the Italian sociologist who was the first to study the problem, call this point the *Pareto optimum.*

The significance of Pareto optimality for everyone, from the most rabid Earth First!er to the most shameless "wise-use" booster, cannot be overstated. Logging *and* wildlands are always a more productive mix than logging *or* wildlands. Mixed crops are always more productive than monocultures. A country with a mix of regional cultures, including indigenous cultures, is always more productive than one that insists on becoming the same indistinguishable strip of freeways, malls, and fast-food joints from coast to coast.

But there is a third thing we must bear in mind here as well. Maximum production, as used here, does mean *maximum* production. An economy can operate outside its production possibilities frontier, but only at the expense of the integrity of its production facilities. For sustained production, one must stay at or below the line. In this way, the PPF is exactly equivalent to the ecological concept of carrying capacity. Go outside the PPF — operate above carrying capacity — and you will pay by losing some of your capability to produce over the long term. The PPF will shift leftward and downward, toward the origin. That is what happened to the deer on the Kaibab Plateau.

And there is a fourth (and final) thing we must note about the production possibilities frontier: its name. Too often, the name makes the reality. In calling the production possibilities curve a frontier, economists connect it far too thoroughly with the frontier paradigm. The area beneath the curve becomes civilization, where productive activity is taking place. The area outside the curve represents the lands beyond — resources unused, countries to be tamed and conquered. The fact that the curve can be moved through the exercise of technology enforces this idea. It is too easy to drift into the idea that this movement can continue forever, when in fact there are limits. Those limits exist *at that point where the production possibilities frontier coincides with the carrying capacity of the planet* — the point, in other words, where the law of supply runs up against the rule of availability.

The rule of availability, like most economic laws, is very sensitive to whether or not *ceteris paribus* conditions exist. If all things except availability and price are held constant, the rule of availability holds strictly. If other things are allowed to change, the rule remains in effect but may be weakened to meaninglessness. Unfortunately — and confusingly — the principal weakening mechanism for the rule of availability is precisely the factor that allows *ceteris paribus* to remain true for supply and demand: substitution.

If orange juice is the only juice available, a late frost in Florida will have a strong impact on juice prices. If buyers can get apple juice or grape juice instead, the price of orange juice will only have to climb a short distance before sales begin to fall off as buyers desert the good for its substitutes. At that point the price will stop rising.

How this will affect things depends very much on how you view it. Looked at from the standpoint of the ecosystem paradigm, substitution is a very healthy thing. It promotes diversity and stability. As a good gets scarce in a diverse ecosystem, its price rises according to the rule of availability; but as the price rises, organisms that would normally consume the good switch to something else. This takes the pressure off the scarce good, and it stops getting scarcer (this is equivalent to saying that the price stops rising). If the "good" is itself an organism, the relaxation of pressure will probably allow it to reproduce, sending its numbers back up to where its consumers will again consider its price payable, and they will switch back to it. In this way, in a diverse ecosystem, numbers of all species remain relatively constant. If there is plenty of grass, deer eat the grass; as grass becomes scarce, its price rises (in effort needed to locate new clumps), and the deer switch to tree leaves, allowing the grass to recover. If the deer themselves are abundant, predators such as coyotes or cougar will take them; if the deer become scarce, their price will rise (in hunting effort), and the predators will switch to rodents or lagomorphs, allowing the deer a chance to breed their numbers back up. The more substitutes there are available, the less the price has to rise before substitution takes place, so the less the availability will fall before the pressure that is causing the availability to fall switches its attention to something else. Diversity breeds stability. The mechanism it breeds it through is substitution and the rule of availability.

But look what happens to this mechanism when you switch to a frontier paradigm. The basic tenet of the frontier model, remember, is inexhaustibility of resources: it is always assumed that there is plenty of the good available over the next hill. Scarcity thus becomes a strictly local phenomenon; the overall quantity of the good is assumed to remain, for practical purposes, infinite. So when scarcity drives the price up and substitution begins, what tends to be substituted under the frontier paradigm is not another good: *it is the same good, taken from more distant supplies.* When you have cut down all the local timber, you don't substitute building stone; you substitute the timber over the next hill, and the next, and the next, and the next.

This substitution of distant goods instead of different goods has extremely important consequences. The effect of the substitution on the rule of availability remains the same: prices level out. But since no real substitution of goods has taken place, *the local good continues to be used.* Pressure does not relax, and no recovery happens. The possibility of substituting distant resources keeps the price down; the actuality of having to pay transportation prices for those distant resources keeps the impact of those low prices local. The resource is stripped from the immediate area. When it is gone, the stripping proceeds outward. Because there is always more over the next hill, other resources are not substituted. One continues stripping hills one after another until the whole world is bald as a nut.

Pursuing these lines of thought, it is interesting to note a couple of recent news stories concerning events in the forest products industry. The first, which hit my local newspaper on March 30, 1993, concerned experiments by two major U.S. forest products companies, Boise Cascade and Potlatch Corporation, to grow and harvest cottonwoods as a replacement for Douglas firs in paper production. The cottonwoods require a set of environmental conditions completely different from those of the firs and so would not be grown on the same lands; they also produce a different type of fiber, making some adjustments necessary in paper mills. This is, in short, a case of substituting a different good instead of a distant one. The ecosystem paradigm is beginning to make some headway in those boardrooms.

The second article hit the same newspaper four days later, on April 3, and it is not nearly so heartening. It concerns efforts by some segments of the forest products industry to shift their harvests abroad. Louisiana Pacific, the article stated, had "recently signed a deal for a million acres of Venezuelan timber." Chile, New Zealand, Norway, Sweden, Indonesia, and Malaysia were also mentioned as potential sources; the Agriculture Department had "just issued standards for New Zealand logs and in the next month expects to release proposed regulations covering imports of wood from all foreign nations." The area most strongly coveted was Siberia, with "the planet's largest and least-touched stands of trees, making up 58 percent of the world's softwood timber — compared to 27 percent held in all of North America."

The frontier paradigm obviously is not going to die easily. As long as forests stand in Siberia and substitution-by-distance remains a viable fiction, there is not a stick of timber in America that is completely safe.

Four 🎗

What Does It Cost
to Run a Country?

The Whole Is Not the Total

I N T H E L A T E F A L L O F 1967 my wife and I, newly
married, were living in the north end of Seattle while I at-
tended the University of Washington and she worked for the
Washington State Fisheries Department in a small brick building just south of the university campus. The logical route
from our tiny garage apartment to the university led down
the newly completed Interstate 5 freeway, which featured central "express lanes" — extra traffic lanes whose direction was
reversed daily, doubling the traffic capacity into the city center in the morning and out to the suburbs in the evening.
People had quickly become used to using these extra lanes,
and the whole procedure worked very smoothly — until one
morning when the lanes failed to reverse. Suddenly, the in-
bound rush-hour traffic load was squeezed into half its normal number of lanes. Gridlock quickly developed, slowing
the average vehicular speed to approximately five miles an
hour.

Paralleling the freeway all the way to the University District was a large arterial, Roosevelt Way, on which the posted
speed limit in those days was 50 miles per hour. Sizing up the
situation as we crept up the freeway on-ramp, we made a
quick decision to get off at the next exit and slip over to
Roosevelt Way. Traffic there was nearly nonexistent, and we
were easily able to keep our Volkswagen's speedometer at 50
the entire eight miles down to the university. At every intersection we could look west and watch much of the rest of

north Seattle creeping down the almost completely clogged freeway at approximately one-tenth our speed.

Somewhere in the course of each of the many lectures he gave each year, the late R. Buckminster Fuller would usually poll his audience: how many of them, he would inquire, were acquainted with the concept of synergy? The results were always disappointingly the same. "I can say authoritatively," Fuller told a U.S. Senate subcommittee toward the end of his long life,

> that less than 10 percent of university audiences and less than 1 percent of nonuniversity audiences are familiar with the word and meaning of synergy. Synergy is not a popular word. . . . The word "synergy" means "Behavior of whole systems unpredicted by behavior of any of the systems' parts." Nature is comprehensively synergetic. Since synergy is the only word having that meaning and we have proven experimentally that it is not used by the public, we may conclude that society does not understand nature.

To which we may add that society doesn't understand society, either. Societies, like nature, are comprehensively synergetic, and their economic structures show it. The whole is not the total: nothing adds up the way you think it is going to. You cannot predict the characteristics of a machine, an organism, an ecosystem, or an economy by summing up the characteristics of its parts.

Fuller's favorite example was that of the human body. You can describe in minute detail the bone structure, the digestive and circulatory and nervous systems, and the intricate levers and pulleys of the muscles, he would point out, but you cannot explain from that why looking at an attractive member of the opposite sex causes you to want to make love. Most ecologists are more mundane. They ask you to look at something you think you know something about, something like — oh, let us say, dirt.

Consider a spadeful of soil from your back yard. It is relatively easy to analyze the contents of that soil — to count the number of earthworms and sow bugs and soil microbes, to determine the amount of hygroscopic water, to describe the soil structure (blocky, platy, puddled, or prismatic), to list the percentages of calcium, phosphorus, iron, and organic molecules, and to describe and quantify anything else that happens to be present. But you cannot take such an analysis, even a thoroughly comprehensive one, and use it as a recipe to construct a cubic yard of soil. The whole is not the total. Soil does what it does because of the way its components interact with one another and because of the way the various interactions build on one another's results, not because, say, the soil moisture tension is 0.26 atmospheres and the argillic clay content is 19.8 percent. And these interactions cannot be constructed. They can only be evolved, bit by bit, as the various parts of the soil adjust to one another.

The concept of synergy is at least as important in economics as it is in ecology, although economists give it a different name. They refer to it as the *fallacy of composition,* and define it as the belief that what makes sense for the individual necessarily makes sense for society as a whole. This belief, they state, is thoroughly fallacious. It ignores the far-reaching synergy of the economy. The whole is not the total; if you add up a large number of completely and impeccably logical individual decisions, each carefully aimed at improving the welfare of the decider, you will end up with a social disaster as often as you will a social good.

Economist Roger Arnold likes to use crowd behavior at football games as an example of the fallacy of composition in action. Suppose you are in such a crowd, he points out, and you decide to stand up to see better. Are you better off? Of course. Now suppose the rest of the crowd stands up to see better. Are they better off? Not likely. In fact, the chances are that they are now worse off: they can see no better than before, and their legs are getting tired.

A problem similar to that faced by Arnold's football crowd shows up in popular vacation-home areas. The piecemeal nature of private lands in these areas creates a fallacy of composition type of phenomenon that might best be called the "incremental effect." Stated simply, the incremental effect is this: *things you want add up to things you don't want.* It is the sum of actions that we need to worry about, not each action individually. One person may do something environmentally damaging and still cause little harm, because it is only one person doing one thing. But if one hundred other people in the same vicinity copy the action, the damage is likely to become severe. Each action may be insignificant in itself, but it becomes an increment of a larger collective action that is potentially devastating.

And thus we lose our lakeshores. One vacation home in the woods on the edge of a 100-acre lake is no trouble; 100 homes on little one-acre parcels, each with its 200 feet of waterfront, will probably destroy the lake. Or we lose our farmland: one farmer may get away with subdividing the south forty, but all farmers cannot, because then there will be no land left to grow food. We lose our rivers pipe by thirsty pipe into swimming pools and cotton fields and bathtubs, each taking only a tiny, insignificant amount of water, the sum of them sucking the river dry. We lose our forests, one tree at a time.

Virtually all of the Atlantic and Gulf coasts of the United States, from Cape Cod right down around Florida, to Brownsville, Texas, are rimmed by barrier islands — long, linear stretches of hilly sand, sand dunes really, separated from the shore by broad lagoons and facing the restless wilderness of the open sea. Breakers crash on hundreds of miles of smooth, mirror-wet beach, scattering sanderlings; gulls wheel in the winds that shake the sawgrass. Back from the beach, on the larger islands, forests have established footholds: beech/maple woodlands in the north, live oaks draped with vines and Spanish moss in the south. Barrier islands are fascinating, exhilarating places to spend a life. The incremental effect is killing them.

The island system's own intrinsic attractiveness is primarily to blame. Visitors have a strong urge to settle down. A few follow that urge, building simple homes in the woods or on the summits of lonely, windswept dunes. No harm comes. Others think: we can do that, too. More homes are built. Speculators get into the act: subdivisions spring up. Businesses arrive to service the subdivisions; paved roads are built to tie the whole thing together. Eventually the island is a city, little different from the cities the new residents have left behind. The values the original settlers sought on these once lonely stretches of sand have long since fled.

That is approximately the state of most of the Atlantic barrier chain today. The problem is worst in South Florida. Subdivision after subdivision, mile after depressing mile, the string cities in the ocean extend along their little bits of sand. In defiance of — or, more likely, in denial of — the geologic forces that are literally moving this restless and temporary landscape, inch by inexorable inch, along the shoreline, the cities in the ocean sprout what their builders are pleased to think of as "permanent" structures: expensive houses, shopping malls, multistory luxury hotels. On Hutchinson Island near Fort Pierce, Florida, on the outside edge of a lagoon system called the Indian River, the catalog of "permanent" structures includes a large, two-reactor nuclear plant, erected most unbiblically on a foundation of sand and named (with an irony that probably escaped its designers) for Saint Lucie, the patron saint of the blind.

The barrier islands themselves have long since disappeared, at least in an ecological sense. The beaches remain for the most part unbuilt (there are exceptions), but everything behind them is reconfigured to human design, producing a landscape that is little different from suburban Miami — or, for that matter, suburban Kansas City. Crabs tracing their ancient paths from surf to lagoon are flattened by the hundreds on the highways. Herons patrol back yards and shipping channels, seeking remnants of salt marsh. Sea turtles heave themselves ashore by night and search ponderously and bewilderedly for traditional nesting sites now covered by pavement. Around the St. Lucie nuclear plant, Florida Power & Light has carefully preserved a substantial amount of turtle nesting habitat — an act that almost redeems the power plant. Elsewhere in South Florida, the habitat is nearly gone.

Note the three-way identity that exists among the incremental effect, the economist's fallacy of composition, and the ecologist's concept of synergy. In all three cases you are placing together a number of individual components and coming out with a whole that is very different from a mere summation. In this context it is useful to note that one of the most common popular definitions of synergy — "the whole is greater than the sum of its parts" — is seriously in error. The whole may just as easily be *less than* the sum of its parts: in fact, it may be less than any individual part taken by itself.

The fallacy of composition and its relatives show up in a bewilderingly broad variety of contexts: rural land development, taxation, wilderness preservation, and (in the variant known as free-riding) the use and misuse of those resources owned by all of us, such as clean air, clean water, and public timber and grasslands (more on this in a moment). They show up in southern California's Lake Arrowhead Basin, where new homes are now squeezed in several tiers back from the water and where public access to the lake has become limited to a tiny waterfront park and a few feet of sidewalk behind a very upscale McDonald's restaurant. It shows up at Niagara Falls, where dozens of tourist attractions, each situated to take maximum advantage of the view, have created a sea of distractions that nearly overwhelm the great waterfall itself. It shows up in Yellowstone, where bumper-to-bumper traffic forces drivers to concentrate so thoroughly on the road that they have no time to look at the scenery they may have driven several thousand miles to see.

A particularly striking example is provided by freeway traffic. If only one driver decides to use the freeway, he has vastly improved his ability to get from one end of town to the other. If everyone gets on the freeway at once, you get what we refer to, somewhat laughably, as "rush hour." Traffic slows dramatically; in those very common cases where gridlock develops, it stops altogether, and nobody gets from one end of town to the other at all. That is what happened in Seattle that memorable morning in 1967. Even with the express lanes closed, most people still thought of the freeway as the best way downtown. But this could be true only as long as most people didn't think so.

Before we go any further here, an important distinction needs to be made. Despite the close and obvious relationship of the fallacy of composition to Adam Smith's famous "invisible hand" — the force that, according to free-market economists, is supposed to make individuals' numerous self-interested decisions in the marketplace tend toward a balanced equilibrium that distributes society's resources in the most equitable and efficient way — the two phenomena are not the same. The fallacy of composition describes the *sum* of the results of a series of individual acts; the invisible hand describes the *average* of those results. Where the fallacy of composition simply adds to the mass, the invisible hand helps find the point of balance.

A look at Storm King Mountain may help demonstrate the difference between the invisible hand and the fallacy of composition. Storm King is a massive block of Precambrian granite that rises directly out of the Hudson River just north of the West Point military academy, about forty miles above New York City. Humping steeply more than 1,200 feet above the water, its precipitous, almost bald slopes emphasized rather than disfigured by the thin, ragged line of the Storm King Highway chiseled out of its face about a third of the way up, the mountain is one of the chief scenic features that make the Hudson Valley one of the great riverscapes of the world. It is also important in another way: at least 85 percent of the striped bass in the Hudson River system breed in the shallows about its base. Put those two facts together and you have, in the unspoiled mountain, a resource of immense value to the state of New York.

It is also, however, an almost perfect site for a pumped-storage power plant — one in which off-peak power is used to pump water into an elevated reservoir so that it can be drained out again to generate extra power during the peak periods (those of high electrical demand, such as summer afternoons when everyone's air conditioner is on). In 1962, recognizing this near perfection, New York's Con Edison utility announced plans to build not just any pumped-storage facility but the *world's largest* pumped-storage facility at Storm King. It had added up all the benefits of the site without considering the impact of the whole package — a clear case of the fallacy of composition.

New York environmental groups immediately went into action. For the next eighteen years, the Storm King controversy swirled in and out of the courts, the legislative chambers, and the newspapers. These tactics delayed the project, and they certainly made the power company begin to question the overall benefits of developing the site in terms of its cost in poor public relations, but they were not successful in killing it. What finally did the project in was an agreement between the principal environmental petitioners and Con Edison. Announced on December 19, 1980, the agreement boiled down to a simple exchange. Con Ed agreed to drop all plans for the Storm King power plant and to donate its lands on the mountain to the state of New York, to be made into a park. Environmentalists in turn agreed to drop their opposition to three other power plants Con Ed wanted to build in the Hudson Valley.

Remember the basic rule of exchanges: no voluntary exchange can take place unless both sides feel that they are better off after the exchange than they were before. Therefore, both the environmentalists and the power company must have felt that the agreement made them better off — and if such diametrically opposed forces both feel better off, chances are everyone in between is better off, too. In other words, this exchange, based ultimately, as with all exchanges, on the principals' self-interest, has moved society to a better place. The invisible hand has triumphed again.

Thy Neighbor's Sacrifice

T HE FRAGMENTATION that results from breaking the ownership of a resource into many discrete chunks — building lots, or automobiles, or factories, or livestock pastures — makes the incremental effect the principal means through which the fallacy of composition acts on private property. The incremental effect is notable in the public sector, too — it often makes sense to cut down one tree in a national forest, but it rarely makes sense to cut them all — but it is no longer quite so crucial. For public resources, a second pathway usually becomes more important. This is the self-interested but ultimately self-defeating phenomenon, mentioned briefly earlier, known as *free-riding*.

Free-riding is exactly what it sounds like: taking a ride on someone else's actions in regard to a common problem. If benefits are available no hesitation is displayed in grabbing them, but if the situation requires sacrifice the free-rider always lets the other person do the sacrificing.

Put that way, the act sounds aggressively antisocial. It *is* antisocial, but the element of aggressiveness is usually lacking. Free-riders don't normally see their actions as relating to sacrifice at all. They see them, instead, as a logical reaction to a lose-lose situation — one that develops out of the somewhat curious economic role played by publicly owned property.

In order to be made private, economists say, a resource must meet two tests. It must be *separable:* there must be some means of clearly delineating it from other things, some way of stating precisely where one person's property stops and another's starts. And it must be *excludable:* once the property has been separated, it must be possible to keep others in the community from using it.

Note that neither one of these conditions, by itself, is enough. A reach of river is excludable but not separable: you can build fences along its banks, but as long as water continues to flow in at the upstream end of the reach and out at the downstream end, separation of "your" water from other riverbank owners' water is not possible. The view of a mountain, on the other hand, is separable but not excludable: you can define the area viewed quite precisely, but you cannot keep anyone within sight of the mountain from looking at it. People can own access to a river or a view, but they cannot own the river or the view itself.

Anything that meets the two tests of separability and excludability is, or can be made, private. Anything that does not meet both of these tests is, by definition, a public good.

In addition to nonseparability and nonexcludability, most public goods have two other characteristics. They tend to be *nonrivalrous* — that is, use of them by one person does not keep others away. And they normally show what might be called *simultaneity*. The use of a public good usually takes place at the same time that the good is provided. You do not take a view home with you to look at later. You may take photographs of the view home; but these are not the view itself, and they are private goods, not public ones.

Public goods pose a significant problem for market systems. Because they cannot be bought and sold, the market does not deal with them. One can often charge for access — someone who owns land with a particularly good view can charge admission, or ask a premium price when selling the land for a homesite — but one cannot charge for the good itself.

So in a pure, laissez-faire market economy, public goods are underprovided. The demand may be high — everybody wants clean air and majestic scenery — but no one can make any money meeting that demand. You cannot sell what you do not own. I pay nobody for the air I breathe; I only pay, with my health and my view, when someone damages it.

All of which suggests two things. One is that, even in a world with a perfectly functioning market economy that was regulating itself, some government would be necessary. Governments are the only bodies in a position to take responsibility for public goods. Things that belong to no one belong, in a very real sense, to everyone. Everyone must therefore take responsibility for them. And that requires coordinated action by everyone for the good of all. Governments are the most effective way of providing this.

The other thing that an examination of public goods suggests is that, despite their underrepresentation in markets, *they remain economic goods.* There are costs associated with them, and someone must bear these costs. Air is free, but keeping it clean costs money. The view of a forest is a public good, but the lumber the forest represents is private, or at least privatizable; not cutting that lumber has a sizable opportunity cost associated with it. And since this is true — since public goods are nonmarketizable but still economic — market functions are going to have trouble dealing with them.

The principal problem arises when you try to make exchanges. Since no one owns a public good, any exchange relating to that good cannot be isolated to the people agreeing to the exchange. All costs and all benefits accruing to the public good are borne by everyone. And this means that people not even remotely involved in the exchange can reap a substantial part of its benefits. Free-riding follows almost as a matter of course.

Public goods cannot be owned by an individual. There is a related but not identical category: property that can be owned by an individual but isn't. Economists refer to this class of goods, or resources, or real estate, as *common property.*

Common property, in its broadest sense, is simply property that is owned by two or more people — property held "in common" by a group. All public goods are held in common, but not all common property is public goods. A national forest is separable and excludable and thus fully meets the economic definition of private property, but it is commonly held by the citizens of the United States. A farm owned by a commune or other type of intentional community is listed on the private tax rolls, but it is commonly held by the members of the commune or community. The house my wife and I own together is common property: neither of us holds title to it alone.

Common property poses an interesting problem for economics. Shared ownership means shared responsibility, and shared responsibility creates an opportunity for free-riding. With benefits and responsibilities both shared, there is a constant temptation to try to gain as much as possible of the former and carry as little as necessary of the latter. This is true even in a two-owner commons. My wife and I care deeply for each other, but that does not stop the division of household chores from being a difficult task. The temptation for me to ride on what she does, and for her to ride on my work, is always present. Sometimes the only thing that keeps the chores properly balanced is the fact that, as a married couple, we also enjoy doing things for each other.

If the free-rider problem is difficult in small, committed groups like families, it is almost impossible in large, loose ones like states or cities or nations. The impersonal nature of contacts within these groups lowers commitment to ethical behavior, and even if the commitment is there, the exercise may seem futile. When a resource is held in common by a large number of people, the impact of each individual's action on the resource is diminished. It is the old problem of margins, wrapped up in a new guise. You may fit your car with a pollution-control device, but the money spent on it is largely wasted if no one else does; the marginal contribution you have made to the solution is not significant enough to make a dent in the problem. And if everyone else installs the devices, your money is still wasted. Since your car only contributes marginally, the air would not be detectably dirtier if you didn't bother to clean up your exhaust. You can ride on everyone else's contribution and save the money you would put into pollution control for something else.

Even a cursory look at the free-rider problem shows its close similarity to the fallacy of composition. In fact, free-riding is really just a special case of the fallacy. The free-rider is taking an action that makes perfect sense on an individual level, but when it is added to the similar actions of others it creates a whole that nobody, including the free-rider, wants at all. The pollution-control devices on my car cost money, and reduce performance, and make no sense at all on an individual level (my one car is such a small contribution to air pollution!). It would be perfectly and indisputably logical to disconnect them. But if I did that, and my neighbor did that, and the woman down the block did that, pretty soon there would be no air pollution protection at all.

Other People's Garbage

EVERY ACTION has both intended and unintended consequences. We breathe in and out to exchange carbon
dioxide in our lungs for oxygen in the surrounding air, but
this action also moves microorganisms from our lungs into
the air and microorganisms from the air into our bodies,
increasing our chances of becoming ill and of passing on
diseases to others. We turn on the television to watch the
news, but the action also increases the amount of electricity
that flows into our homes, raising our electric bills. We walk
to the store to save gasoline money; we get the extra benefits
of exercise, including stronger legs, increased lung capacity,
and a healthier heart.

In medicine, the unintended consequences of taking a drug
are referred to as "side effects." A common side effect of anti-
histamines, for example, is to make you drowsy, which is why
the warning labels usually tell you not to drive or operate
machinery while you are taking the medicine. The term is
useful enough that it has found its way into many other
contexts, and it is now common to refer to the unintended
consequences of *any* action as side effects. Our increased electric
bill is a side effect of turning on the news. Our increased
vulnerability to disease is a side effect of breathing. Our improved health is a side effect of our desire to save money —
perhaps because of that increased electric bill from watching
the news. That would make it a side effect of a side effect, a
much more common phenomenon than you might think.

Side effects can be either good or bad. If you get a cat to

rid your house of mice, you will also get a pleasant companion in front of the fire on cold winter nights; if you get a cat for companionship, you will also get rid of your mice. In either case, the side effect is a benefit. If, however, you were to get a cat, for either purpose, and then discover that you were allergic to cat hair, you would have encountered a side effect that was a detriment. The lesson here is an important one: side effects of the same action can be both positive and negative. A rational person will obviously attempt to maximize the positive effects and minimize the negative ones, but it is rarely possible to eliminate the negative ones altogether. If you have both a mouse problem and a cat allergy, you are going to have to learn to live with one or the other.

Up to this point, we have been discussing side effects that happen to you as a result of your own actions. But there is an important class of side effects that result from the actions of one group of people but happen to another group. They are the consequences of economic actions — resource development, market transactions, manufacturing — but they lie outside the direct framework of the action, and those they affect have no direct economic interest in their creation. British welfare economist Arthur Cecil Pigou, who began studying the problem in the 1920s, referred to this class of side effects as *externalities,* the term commonly used for them today.

Pollution is the easiest externality to understand, and is the one most commonly found in economic textbooks. If an industrial plant dumps its wastes into a river, the river carries the wastes away from the plant. They are no longer part of the economic pathway represented by the manufacturing process, and the plant's owner can gain no economic benefits from cleaning them up. But they are very much a part of the economic life of everyone living downstream from the plant. It is the downstream dwellers who will have to pay the costs of dealing with the polluted river, including (but not limited to) the expenses of water treatment; higher health care costs; lost revenues from sport fishermen; and the unpriceable — but not unvaluable — loss of the opportunity to swim in, to boat on, or simply to sit and contemplate the unpolluted river.

How do we deal with such problems? The traditional command-and-control approach suggests the creation of regulations forbidding the plant to pollute the river. This gives those downstream the satisfaction of punishing the plant responsible for harming them, but it does not solve the externalities problem. The waste is still external to the plant's operation. The only thing that has changed is that it is harder, legally, to get rid of the stuff.

Economics suggests a better way. Instead of punishing externalities, *internalize them*. Make the plant that produces them responsible for their costs. That way the plant will have good, financial, bottom-line reasons for lowering those costs as much as it can.

Note that this cannot be done with fines. Fines are too uncertain, and have too remote a relationship to the action they are supposed to serve as punishment for, to be thought of as a regular cost of doing the action. And fines are rarely high enough to make firms cease doing something even when they know a fine is going to be imposed. When the full costs of pollution are internalized, it usually proves profitable to discontinue, or at least drastically modify, the polluting action. With fines, it usually makes most sense to pay the fine and keep on polluting.

Even a cursory examination of current fine structures makes this clear. Although the U.S. Environmental Protection Agency has policies in place, dating back to 1984, which require all field offices to make certain that the fines they impose match or exceed the benefits companies have received from breaking the law, few appear to do so. Of 685 EPA enforcement actions looked at by the General Accounting Office (GAO) for a 1991 study, data on the financial gain the offending firms reaped from their infractions were reported in only 243 cases — less than 35 percent. In fact, the GAO found, the penalty policy was so poorly enforced that the EPA's internal forms for reporting fines did not even carry the necessary fields to enter the data needed to determine offenders' illegal benefits.

Businesses that run afoul of state and local antipollution ordinances do even better than those that face the EPA. Many states have caps in place prohibiting the charging of fines over a certain amount (usually far below the amounts firms can make through violations), and even those that don't are often reluctant to assess meaningful damages, for fear the companies involved will pull up stakes and move to a state with laxer enforcement policies. The EPA has the power to levy compensating fines in those cases where state fine structures are found to be "grossly deficient," but this so-called overfine power is almost never used. Faced with an almost complete absence of definition as to what constitutes "grossly deficient," EPA overseers are forced to resort to what they call the "laugh test": if you mention the amount of the fine and everyone laughs, overfining is probably called for.

Fines are not a day-to-day, run-of-the-process economic cost; fines are something that happen only when you get caught. They become part of the game that industries play with their regulators to see how much they can get away with. That model does not allow for internalization. To be internalized, an external cost must become a regular part of the production calculations, on the same level as the price of energy and raw materials. It must be a cost the plant cannot avoid paying through adroit gamesmanship. One simple example of internalizing pollution costs: require the plant's waste outfall to be directly upstream of its water intake.

Not in My Back Yard

T HE ACRONYM NIMBY stands for "not in my back yard"; it describes the phenomenon of objecting to some activity only when it directly affects the objector. Though there are exceptions, NIMBY people usually do not object on principle to the activity they are complaining about, only to its proximity to them. Nuclear power is fine, as long as the nuclear plant is not next door to them. Plastic is a good and necessary part of modern society, but don't dump the manufacturing wastes in my river. Mayor Louis Welch of Houston, Texas, captured the NIMBY phenomenon perfectly back in the early 1970s when his city was going through a difficult siting process for a new solid-waste dump. "Everyone wants us to pick up his garbage," the mayor complained to the press, "but nobody wants us to put it down."

NIMBY results from a combination of externalities, the frontier myth, and the fallacy of composition. Externalities, because what NIMBY people are objecting to is the external costs of a siting decision; the frontier myth, because there is always an implicit assumption behind NIMBY complaints that some alternate site can be found that affects no one; and the fallacy of composition, because — though the objectors rarely, if ever, understand this — the problems being complained about almost always arise out of the cumulative effects of actions that the complainers find perfectly reasonable, and which they themselves indulge in. NIMBY people see no inherent conflict of interest when they go to a hearing to complain about the siting of a nuclear plant or a new power line and leave the lights and the electric heater on so the house will be warm and welcoming when they get back. They sit in their new suburban homes and complain vociferously about the even newer suburb going in on the other side of the valley. This is not hypocrisy; hypocrisy requires one to make the connection and do the deed anyway. You can't be hypocritical and guileless at the same time. NIMBY people leave the heat on because they like coming home to a warm house; they object to power lines because they don't like their views blocked. That there might be a direct connection between warm houses and blocked views never enters their heads.

The phenomenon is not limited to complaints about environmental disruption, by the way; what some of us view as environmental enhancement often gets the same treatment. In 1973, still a wet-behind-the-ears young activist, I became chair of a group called the Red Buttes Wilderness Council which was attempting to create a wilderness area on approximately 65,000 acres of national forest land in the Siskiyou Mountains of northern California and southern Oregon. (We ultimately succeeded in obtaining wilderness designation for just over a third of this acreage, leaving the rest — as fully deserving as the set-aside third — totally unprotected. This was one of the key events that ultimately led me to believe that preserves, in their traditional form, are not a viable solution to the problem of wildlands protection. But I digress.) One of my tasks as chair was to take a slide show and speech to as many community groups as possible in the area immediately surrounding the embattled landscape. I had memorized what I thought were all the relevant arguments: the amount of wilderness set-asides in the region, compared with the total amount of forest land; the tiny commercial value of the timber within our proposed boundaries, and the difficulty of getting good reproduction on the soils there once the standing timber was cut down; the amount of recreational use, both current and projected; the area's contribution to water quality; and various similar facts and figures. But I was totally unprepared for the question one woman hit me with at a coffee klatch in the tiny town of Klamath River, California. "Why," she asked grimly, "are you trying to surround me with wilderness?"

Note the content of that question. Not "why wilderness?"; not even "why wilderness here?"; but "why me?" This is NIMBY in as pure a form as it comes. And there is no real answer. "You drink water, don't you?" almost came to my lips, but I fought it back. Flippancy is wasted on the guileless. All I could really do was shrug and try to move the conversation to the community rather than the personal perspective.

NIMBY, perhaps surprisingly, often appears to be strongest among new residents of an area, who usually make up a disproportionate percentage of the membership of local environmental groups. Old-timers regularly complain of these people that they want to lock the door after they have come through it, which is a very succinct statement of the NIMBY problem. The standard follow-up complaint, however — that the problem is caused by an influx of liberal, anti–private-property types — has rather less merit. Politics, liberal or conservative, probably has very little effect on the NIMBY syndrome. I strongly suspect two other causes.

The first cause is fairly obvious. It has to do with the psychological investment we humans tend to make in major decisions. The new-resident populations of the areas most subject to NIMBY are overwhelmingly composed of people who, for one reason or another, have specifically chosen to move there. Some have been transferred in by their companies, or by the military; some are aging parents who have moved to be near their children; some are simply restless; but by far the greatest number have come because the areas' amenities attracted them. This is particularly true of three groups: retirees, the independently wealthy, and young singles or couples who have made an active choice to "get away from it all." It is precisely these three groups that usually form the activist core of NIMBY and other local-preservation organizations. When the amenities they have chosen to live near are threatened, they take action.

The established residents, by contrast, are there primarily due to inertia. They may have been through a similar decision-making process at some time in the past, but that was a long time ago and they no longer have much of an emotional investment in it. Some have actively decided to stay, but most have simply put off the decision to move. More passive than the movers, they are not nearly so likely to strike out at those who want to change the landscape around them. They simply do not care as deeply, or as much.

The second reason NIMBY is prominent among newcomers is related to the first, but it is somewhat more subtle. It has to do with the pace and scale of change — or, more accurately, with perceptions of that pace and that scale. People who have lived in an area for a while become attuned to its changes and no longer pay much attention to them. They have a sense — unspoken, subliminal, but nonetheless powerful — that they are living in a dynamic landscape. Neighbors come and go; houses change color and sprout additions; landscaping is pulled out and redone in people's yards and in the city parks. In this context, the prospect of further change — even the type of major change represented by the replacement of a woodlot with a subdivision — seems less threatening than it does to newcomers who still have a static, snapshot view of their surroundings. It is much easier to cling to the idea that things have always been this way, and should always stay this way, when "always" goes back only twenty-six months.

NIMBY is expensive. It is costly in time lost attempting to meet unmeetable complaints; in money for project redesign, unnecessary but politically palatable modifications, and repeated hearings; and in goodwill lost between the project and its neighbors. On this last issue there is a very thin tightrope to walk. If the neighbors believe the project was thrust upon them without a chance for adequate input into the decision-making process, they will, with justification, feel put-upon and resentful, and even a well-designed and well-carried-out project will be disliked and rejected. If design after design and site after site are rejected, and progress on the project is constantly blocked by neighborhood lawyers skilled in the delaying arts of technicalities and regulatory minutiae, the project backers will feel, with equal justification, that they are not being listened to, and that the project's neighbors are a bunch of selfish, spoiled brats who deserve whatever ill effects the project brings upon them.

The easy, wrong solution in such cases is to attempt to find the site where NIMBY objections are weakest and put the project there. This has two particularly pernicious results. It increases external costs; the weaker the opposition, the more costs the project can get away with dumping on others. And it concentrates those costs on the politically disenfranchised. Often these are the poor: NIMBY is one of the principal driving forces behind the common phenomenon of locating "dirty" industries in ghettos, or routing new freeways or rail lines through lower-class neighborhoods. But the disenfranchised on whom NIMBY shoves things off are not always the poor. Sometimes they are simply those in neighboring political jurisdictions who have no direct say in the siting decision.

There is, for example, an immense trash incinerator in Detroit, Michigan, built in the mid-1980s, whose operating permits contain waivers that specifically allow it to violate federal standards on a number of pollutants in its stack emissions. The city of Detroit was able to obtain those waivers because the prevailing winds will blow virtually all those excess emissions across the Detroit River into the city of Windsor — a Canadian city whose citizens had no say whatsoever in U.S. siting processes.

Incidents like this one argue strongly for a primarily economic, rather than a primarily political, siting process for controversial projects. Rather than honing further a procedure that attempts to mitigate the political impacts of siting externalities, we should concentrate on finding ways to internalize them as thoroughly as possible into the plant design. If the internalization is thorough enough, project backers will often find themselves looking at a negative bottom line and will decide not to build. And those projects that do go ahead will be as environmentally benign as possible. These are precisely the results that political regulation attempts to achieve but does not.

But the best way to get rid of the NIMBY problem, once and for all, is to get rid of the frontier paradigm. When looked at through the lens of the ecosystem paradigm, the problem alters dramatically. John Muir said it best: *When we try to pick out anything by itself, we find it hitched to everything else in the Universe.* Ecosystems are comprehensively interconnected; everything affects everything else. In such a context, NIMBY becomes irrelevant. Where does my back yard stop?

The Prisoners' Dilemma

To HELP UNDERSTAND the range of problems resulting from the fallacy of composition, the free-rider problem, NIMBY, and similar flaws in humans' abilities to see reality realistically, economists often borrow an analytic tool from game theory known as the *prisoner's dilemma*. One common form of it goes as follows.

Two prisoners (call them Al and Bob) are assigned to adjacent cells. They can hand things through the bars of the cells to each other, but Al cannot get into Bob's cell and Bob cannot get into Al's. In the evening a guard comes around with a meal cart. He gives Al a bowl of gruel and an empty plate. He gives Bob a small loaf of bread and an empty bowl. What are Al and Bob going to do?

We need to make one basic assumption. Bob and Al, we assume, both like gruel and bread equally well. If this is the case, then we can assign equal values to Al's gruel and Bob's bread. The actual values we choose do not matter: for our example, we will assume a value of 2 (we could choose 1, but 2 makes the math easier later). Thus we have:

$$\text{gruel alone (Al)} = 2$$
$$\text{bread alone (Bob)} = 2$$

Since they can reach through the bars, they can share; if they do this, it will give each of them both bread *and* gruel. The total amount of food each would get wouldn't change, but the variety would increase. Assume variety has a value of 1. Then Al and Bob each get:

$$
\begin{aligned}
& \text{1/2 gruel} \ = 1 \\
+\ & \text{1/2 bread} = 1 \\
+\ & \text{variety} \quad\ = 1 \\
\hline
& \qquad\text{Total} = 3
\end{aligned}
$$

Al and Bob are clearly both better off.

At this point we need to create a table and begin filling it in. We'll put Bob across the top and Al down the side, and we'll give each of them the option of either sharing or not sharing: this will result in a four-cell matrix. Each cell will have two numbers, one representing the value the cell has for Al, and the other the value it has for Bob. For legibility (and for other reasons that will become apparent soon) we will separate each cell's two numbers with a plus sign, thus:

Al's value + Bob's value

So far, the matrix looks like this:

BOB

		doesn't share	shares
	doesn't share	2 + 2	?
AL	shares	?	3 + 3

In the upper left corner, neither prisoner is sharing, so each one receives value equivalent to two points (all the bread, or all the gruel, but no variety). In the lower right corner, both share, so each receives value equivalent to three points (half the bread plus half the gruel plus variety). Clearly, when only these two corners are considered, both Al and Bob are better off in the lower right. But what happens in the other two corners, the ones marked in our table with question marks?

Look first at the upper right. Al is not sharing; Bob is. So Al gets all the gruel and half the bread, and his score is:

$$\begin{array}{rl} \text{gruel} & = 2 \\ + \ 1/2 \ \text{bread} & = 1 \\ + \ \text{variety} & = 1 \\ \hline \text{Total} & = 4 \end{array}$$

Bob is not nearly so well off: he has given up half his bread for no gruel, and so — with only half the bread, no gruel, and no variety — his score is:

$$\begin{array}{rl} 1/2 \ \text{bread} & = 1 \\ \hline \text{Total} & = 1 \end{array}$$

In the lower left-hand corner of the matrix, obviously, the situation is reversed. Al is sharing and Bob is not, so it is Bob who gets the full four points and Al who is left with only one.

Look now at the whole table:

BOB

		doesn't share	shares
AL	doesn't share	2 + 2	4 + 1
	shares	1 + 4	3 + 3

Do the addition in each cell, and the prisoner's dilemma paradox will begin to emerge. If neither Al nor Bob shares, each will receive two points and the total social value of this two-person society will be 4; if both share, each can raise his point total to 3, and the total social value will be 6 — the maximum possible. If only one shares, the total social value will drop to

5, *but the selfish prisoner gets 4 of those points, 1 more than he can get in any other way.* The individual's maximum and the society's maximum do not coincide. By maximizing his own benefit, each prisoner reduces the total benefits this two-person society can enjoy. There, in stark mathematical form, is the fallacy of composition.

There is more. Look again at the left-hand column — the one where Bob is selfish. That column includes Bob's maximum benefits, *but it also includes his second-lowest benefits.* Bob's maximization depends not only on his own selfishness, but on Al's goodwill. If Al is a good guy, Bob is going to, as the saying goes, max out. If Al is selfish, too, Bob will get less than if both of them shared.

Now look at the right-hand column, where Bob shares. If Al shares, too, Bob gets more than if they were both selfish. But he gets less than he would if Al shared and he didn't; and if Al is a stinker, Bob gets next to nothing.

What does Bob do, if he is the economists' "rational man"? The not-sharing column contains a maximum value (for Bob) of 4, and a minimum value of 2; the sharing column contains (again for Bob) a maximum value of 3 and a minimum of 1. Both maximum and minimum are higher in the not-sharing column. It looks as if Bob should choose not to share.

But if Al is rational, too (and there is no reason to assume he is not), he will not share either, and this "rational" act on the part of each is going to lead to the situation with the least total social value — one in which both Al and Bob are both worse off than if they decided to cooperate. If they both share, they can avoid this trap. Now it looks as though Bob should choose to share, and hope that Al, having done the same analysis, has reached the same conclusion.

But it is not rational to depend on hope, is it? Al may agree to share and then fink out at the last moment, after Bob has already passed the bread across. Maybe Bob shouldn't share after all.

There is no end to this circle; it is like the snake in Hindu mythology that eats its own tail. If you don't share, you could be better off sharing. If you *do* share, you could be better off not sharing. Whichever way you choose, the other way always has at least the potential of leading to a better outcome.

If you extend this analysis to cover a society of 250 million Als and Bobs (and Carols and Doreens), you will very soon be overwhelmed by analytical detail, but the principles, and the results, will remain the same. Each person maximizes his or her own welfare by being selfish, but only if others share. If everyone is selfish, everyone loses. If everyone takes care of the commons, everyone gains; but the gains to each individual will be higher if someone else does the work and takes the sacrifice. We have just mathematically demonstrated the free-rider problem.

NIMBY is in that diagram, too, right there in the upper right and lower left corners. Of course no one wants a sanitary landfill, or a high-voltage power line, or another new subdivision, in his or her back yard; that would be the equivalent of accepting the 1 in each of those corners while someone else got the 4. Given that choice, we will try for the 4 every time. But if we are all successful, we end up back in that upper left-hand corner, suffering together in a society that is, as a whole, worse off. If we can find some way of sharing the sacrifice, we can all move down and right, to maximum social welfare. If we cannot, then perhaps we can at least trade sacrifices.

It is perfectly rational for each one of us to act selfishly, but the sum of these perfectly rational deeds is an irrational conclusion — the worst possible outcome for society. The whole is not the sum; or, perhaps more accurately, the whole is only one of several possible sums, and the most likely of these to happen is the one with the least total benefits. Failing to grapple with the fallacy of composition pushes us toward the upper left-hand corner of the matrix as surely as gravity pulls us to earth. Everyone wants a beach house; but if everyone builds one, the beach will become too crowded to enjoy. Those who build on the beach can fully benefit from their action only if no one else copies them.

There is, by the way, an interesting side result of the composition/free-rider/NIMBY paradox which shows up when you look at the sum of each of the four cells in the prisoners' dilemma diagram — a side result that calls into serious question the exhortations of those who tell us that if each of us acts morally and selflessly the world will automatically be better off. That sum, which represents the total welfare of the society under each set of assumptions, is at its lowest when no one shares. Each individual act of sharing raises society's welfare, exactly as ethics teaches us. But until sharing becomes general, *the rewards go to the wrong place.* By sharing, one improves society but reduces one's own lot. Selflessness always creates social gains, but those gains tend to accumulate among the selfish.

The task of the reformer is thus clear. We must not simply promote selflessness; we must find some way to reward it. We must discover ways to move society to the lower right-hand corner of the prisoners' dilemma matrix and keep it there, holding it tightly against its strong tendency to split two ways (or 250 million ways) and drift back, by individual paths, toward the upper left, propelled initially by the self-interest of the selfish, and later by the frustration and simple outrage of the selfless.

What Does It Cost
to Run a Country?

IT IS FRUSTRATINGLY APPARENT to most of us that
our taxes don't buy the value they used to. Taxes go up and
up while the level of government services drops. When I was
a boy in the 1950s, taxes were much lower than today; at the
same time, parks and streets were kept up better, crime was
lower, and most of the services government provided were
delivered more effectively. Admittance to virtually all state
parks was free, as were overnight stays in most national forest
campgrounds. Government did less, but it did it better.

Note that this is not an argument for less government
today. Despite the widespread grumblings of the tax-revolt
activists, it is impossible to go back to the conditions of the
1950s. The problem, like the prisoner's dilemma, is one of
simple mathematics. Population increases are geometric, meaning that they increase by multiplication rather than simple
addition. The services a population requires from its government grow even faster — by multiples of the population increase. The more people, the more services are required, not
just on an absolute basis but on a per capita basis as well.

The need for government services is dependent not on the
absolute number of people in a population but on the number
of connections among people: the more connections, the more
services. This is because most government costs are at heart
infrastructure costs, and infrastructure is concerned almost
exclusively with connections. We are speaking here not only
of tangible infrastructure like roads, and telephone lines, and
electrical service, and garbage collection, but also of intangi-

bles: access to parks, and clean air and clean water, and safe, litter-free streets. All these things are dependent, in one way or another, on connections. A lake, for example, forms a series of connections both in space and in time among everyone who comes to its shores. Each person's effect on that lake is visited not just on the lake but on every other person who comes to use it, now and for some distance into the future.

And connections among people in an expanding population increase much more rapidly than the raw population figures do. To see this, consider two populations, one of fifty people, the other of fifty thousand. Add one person to each population. The new person in each population can theoretically interact with everyone else who is already there. So in the smaller population, the number of potential connections, and hence, of potential needs for government services, has gone up by fifty; in the larger one, it has gone up by fifty thousand. And that is the impact of just one person.

It is this unavoidable mathematical trap that drives taxes up, not the imposition of the welfare state or inefficient bureaucrats or the air force's famous $6,000 toilet seats. The costs of the same level of government services are simply much more today, on a per capita basis, than they were forty years ago. And they will continue to increase in the future, as long as the population does. Economists call these increases *density costs,* and that is exactly what they are — the cost of increased density, all other things being held equal. No amount of tax-control legislation can get around them. Population control is the only way.

Density costs can be quantified, and a number of studies have done just that. One of these studies, reported in my local paper under the headline WE KNEW IT ALL ALONG: OREGON'S A BETTER DEAL THAN CALIFORNIA, compared Orange County, California, in Greater Los Angeles, with Jackson County, Oregon, where I live. The results were not flattering to Orange County. Housing in Orange County, for instance, ran approximately two and a half times the cost of housing in Jackson County. Electricity was almost twice as expensive (9.3 cents per kilowatt-hour in California, compared with 4.9 cents per kilowatt-hour in Oregon). Water costs were similarly inflated: a typical Orange County household spent nearly as much for water in the month of August alone as a Jackson County household spent over the course of an entire year. Other costs were in line with these.

The methodology of the Jackson County/Orange County study was extremely informal: two residents, one in each county, had simply compared their own bills for a year, backing up their conclusions with nothing more than talking with neighbors and scanning the newspapers. A more formal study conducted by the American Farmland Trust during the mid-1980s in Loudon County, Virginia, however, led to strikingly similar results. After looking at numerous cost and revenue factors, including, among other things, public school capital and operating costs; property taxes; road maintenance costs; law enforcement costs; federal and state grants to the county; and the costs and revenues of water and sewerage systems, the study concluded with stunning clarity, "For every dollar in tax revenues received by the county, $1.28 in services are demanded by residential land uses. For every dollar in tax revenues received by the county, $0.11 in services are demanded by open farmland."

The more a community grows, the more expensive it becomes to live in that community, and therefore the more taxes we have to pay. The biggest creators of new taxes are not the tax-and-spend welfare Democrats in Congress, but the economic development committees of the Chamber of Commerce. The more they are successful in promoting growth — the more new businesses they attract, the more new subdivisions they plan, the more their communities develop — the more the taxes about which they are typically the first to complain are bound, with mathematically inexorable certitude, to proliferate.

Five ৰাৎ

National Wealth and
the Wealth of Nations

Growing Pains

ECONOMIC GROWTH is a strongly frontier-oriented value. When the country was young, with a continent in front of it full of raw materials that no one seemed to be converting into economic goods, growth was an obvious goal. It was also relatively easy to accomplish: one merely shifted the "frontier" westward, taking in more raw materials. The country and the economy grew together. And somehow growth became entrenched in American thinking as an automatic good.

Then the expanding boundaries of what Americans defined as their nation hit the West Coast, rebounded, and filled in the Great Plains. Alaska and Hawaii were annexed; Frederick Jackson Turner declared the frontier closed. Physically, the country could grow no farther. Economically, however, there was still room — still new resources to be discovered, still new technologies to be developed which would squeeze more growth out of fewer resources. Economic growth became detached, conceptually, from physical growth; it seemed a frontier that would never close. Generations of economists and businesspeople grew up believing that the natural state of economies was to continue to expand indefinitely, and that an economy that was not expanding was necessarily unhealthy. This idea continues to dominate economic thinking. We get reminders of it in the newspapers almost daily, with phalanxes of earnest cheerleaders in the guise of business reporters urging us to root for the home team, applauding loudly when the GNP rises and moaning when it falls.

There are detractors, of course. Among the loudest of these

is David Brower, the maverick environmentalist who was fired from his position as executive director of the Sierra Club in the spring of 1969 for being too radical. "When rampant growth happens in an individual," remarks Brower trenchantly, in the well-polished speech he refers to as The Sermon, "we call it cancer." If the 4 billion years of the Earth's history were to be compressed into the six days of Creation reported in Genesis, Brower points out, the Industrial Revolution would have begun only one-fortieth of a second ago. "We are surrounded by people who think that what we have been doing for that one-fortieth of a second can go on indefinitely," he states to his audiences. "They are considered normal, but they are stark, raving mad."

Brower has plenty of company. There is, for instance, *The Limits to Growth,* the outspoken 1972 book by Donella and Dennis Meadows mentioned earlier in these pages. The Meadows team, reporting on a Club of Rome study of world resource depletion, pointed out the similarity of recent world growth rates of resource use to the mathematical curve known as the asymptote, which climbs rapidly toward infinity as it approaches some limiting value. Since growth obviously cannot become infinite on a finite planet, *The Limits to Growth* predicted that, at some point in the near future, asymptotic growth rates would reach finite resource limits and crash. The economy would crash with them. The concept was roundly criticized by economists, who complained once more that it ignored the effects of the market: as resources become scarcer, the economists pointed out wearily, their prices will climb, which will encourage the development of cheaper substitutes. Through these changes the economy can continue to grow essentially unabated. Notwithstanding these criticisms, the Meadows book made "no-growth" both an environmental rallying cry and a developers' epithet. The division continues to this day. Thus we have Daniel D. Chiras, in *Lessons from Nature: Learning to Live Sustainably on the Earth,* lecturing us on "creating a healthy economy without growth," while economists continue to speak broadly of increased economic growth rates as "recovery" and George Bush, campaigning hard down the homestretch for a re-election that ultimately fails, points dramatically to the "very good news" represented by a reported doubling of the growth rate of GNP in the third quarter of 1992. "The Democrats," he adds pointedly, "keep telling us that everything is going to hell, and they're wrong."

Caught in this verbal crossfire, with the mythic baggage of the frontier hanging over our heads, it is difficult to think objectively about growth. Nevertheless, I offer a few thoughts of my own.

· Despite the opinion of Brower (and others), continuous growth in the natural world is not solely a pathogenic phenomenon. Lichens, redwood trees, chambered nautiluses, and lobsters are all examples of organisms whose growth continues throughout their lives. Their growth often slows as they age, but it never stops altogether, and there is no theoretical limit at which it must halt. On the other hand, these organisms all share another trait in common besides continuous growth: they all eventually die. So they are not necessarily models that we want our economy to emulate.

· By themselves, economic growth rates are meaningless. It is only when they are compared to population growth that they take on significance. Economic growth rates faster than population growth mean that a society is, on the average, becoming richer; economic growth rates slower than population growth mean that a society is becoming poorer. Economic growth rates that exactly match population growth mean only that the status quo is being maintained. And all of these statements may themselves be meaningless, because the fact that a society is becoming richer or poorer does not necessarily correlate with whether individuals within that society are better or worse off. Individual wealth is a distributional issue more than it is a macroeconomic issue. And since people define "wealth" in many different ways, even distributional analysis may not help us very much to determine how well a society is doing economically.

• Growth is not fueled solely by resource use. The speed at which money changes hands is another important factor; so is the economy's ratio of spending to saving. And the exchange of services among members of a society — in contrast with the exchange of goods — does not require large inputs of raw materials from the environment, and thus is not subject to the limiting factor of the earth's finite size. As the authors of *The Limits to Growth* pointed out twenty years ago,

> Any human activity that does not require a large flow of irreplaceable resources or produce severe environmental degradation might continue to grow indefinitely. In particular, those pursuits that many people would list as the most desirable and satisfying activities of man — education, art, music, religion, basic scientific research, athletics, and social interactions — could flourish.

• Though there are exceptions, most firms are not as concerned with the overall growth rate of their industry or the economy as they are in the growth of their market share. This type of growth is almost by definition a social bad, not because of environmental restrictions but because its ultimate goal is a monopoly, and monopolies seriously distort the "free-market" forces we as a society consider fundamental to social progress.

• Growth is strongly subject to the fallacy of composition. What is good for General Motors is not necessarily good for the country. In the same way that it is impossible for everyone to be above average, it is impossible for an entire society to be wealthy. It *is* possible for a society to be *wealthier* (than its neighbors, or than it was in the past), but the comparison does not necessarily mean anything. An individual who becomes wealthier will almost invariably also become better off. A society that becomes wealthier may actually make itself worse off, if the wealth comes, as it often does, at the expense of ecosystem health.

· Finally, whether or not an economy is growing may not ultimately matter very much. If this is true, we in the environmental community have been doing ourselves a disservice by relentlessly focusing on the bad aspects of growth, because that is still a focus on growth. It makes the same mistake that relying on preserves does: it sets boundaries. Boundaries are a frontier phenomenon, and to the extent that we buy into them, in any form, we are still trapped in the frontier paradigm. In the ecosystem paradigm, absolute growth is really a side issue to the growth of complexity and the establishment of long-term stability. That is what an ecosystem works toward. It may or may not also increase its biomass, cover more acreage, expand the number of species it houses, or otherwise "grow." These are all irrelevant except as they assist or hinder movement toward the goal of stability.

Donella Meadows states it well, in this passage written twenty years after the publication of *The Limits to Growth:*

> Growth is a means, not an end. When it gets you to where you want to go, the sensible thing is to stop.

And later in the same article:

> Growth is a stupid goal. So, by the way, is no-growth. Growth is beside the point. The point is caring for people and resources and meeting real needs with the highest possible quality. When that is done, the growth will fall where it may and where it should.

Flows and Funds

ANYONE WHO OPENS a textbook on macroeconomics and a textbook on ecology, in either order, is likely to notice the striking similarities between the diagrams of financial systems in the one book and the diagrams of ecosystems in the other. In both, the primary dynamic is depicted as a circular flow. In economies, money flows from households through markets to firms and back, via salaries, wages, and stock and bond payments, to households again. In ecology, elements (carbon, nitrogen, phosphorus) flow from the soil through producers (green plants and photosynthetic microorganisms, such as algae and blue-green bacteria) to consumers (herbivores, which eat the producers; carnivores, which eat the herbivores) and back once more, via excretion, respiration, and death and decay, to the soil. In both systems there are shortcuts and side loops. Some money flows directly from firms to other firms; some elements flow from producers directly back to the soil, without cycling through consumers at all. Savings siphons money out of financial systems; geologic storage (sediments and fossil fuels) siphons elements out of ecosystems. Foreign trade results in both a loss and a gain of money through exports and imports; migration results in both a loss and a gain of elements through emigration out of the ecosystem and immigration into it.

These macroeconomic diagrams have embedded the ecosystem paradigm firmly into economics, where it already drives much of the theory. The principal place it does not do so, ironically, is precisely at the place where ecosystems and financial systems most commonly meet: the infusion, from the ecosystems into the financial systems, of natural resources. That is still driven by the frontier paradigm. And that, therefore, is where we must primarily focus the energy for change.

Natural resources divide neatly into two categories: those that can renew themselves within the frame of historic time, and those that cannot. The difference between them lies primarily in the nature of their response to sunlight. Those that have a linear response, or no response at all, are nonrenewable; those that have a circular response can renew themselves. Thus, living things are renewable: they use the energy of the sun to drive a cycle that runs from birth through growth, death, and decay to the birth and growth of new organisms. By extension, soil is renewable; it is created by living things as a byproduct of their cyclical path through the environment. Water is renewable; it flows to the sea, evaporates from there to form clouds, drifts over the land, and falls as rain to flow to the sea once more. Evaporation and cloud movement are both driven by the sun. Hydropower is drawn from falling water, so it too is renewable.

Aluminum ore, on the other hand, is not influenced by sunlight at all; it is nonrenewable. Chlorine is influenced by sunlight, but the influence causes it to combine rapidly with anything else in its vicinity; this is a linear response that leads to the extinction of the resource. Chlorine is therefore nonrenewable. Fossil fuels are formed from the remains of living organisms and so are theoretically renewable, but the rate of renewal is so slow as to take them outside the boundaries of historic time; hence they must be treated as nonrenewables. Iron ore is in much the same category as fossil fuels; fair amounts of it appear to be the result of the metabolism of iron-fixing bacteria (living things), but the time scale is geologic, not historic. For policy purposes, iron ore must also be treated as a nonrenewable.

And for policy purposes, the difference between renewable

and nonrenewable resources is fundamental. Renewable resources, if used at rates less than their rate of renewal, will always be with us. Nonrenewables will not. To use a nonrenewable resource at all is to use part of it up.

To emphasize this fundamental difference, resource economists today do not generally speak of renewable and nonrenewable resources, but of *flow resources* and *fund resources*. Flow resources are those that move in cycles of renewal; if one harvests only the flow, the renewal will continue. These resources may safely be treated as infinite in time, although not in quantity. The flow is forever, but the quantity available at any one time is restricted to the amount flowing past at that time — the flow rate. Fund resources have no cyclical response, no flow, so whatever one uses represents an amount removed from the resource's total fund.

There is a useful analogy to financial capital here. Flow resources are interest-bearing accounts; if one takes care to live strictly off the interest, the account's principal will not shrink, and may even expand. Fund resources pay no interest. Any withdrawal from these funds is always withdrawal from the principal. The principal always shrinks: it cannot hold steady, and it cannot expand.

Flow resources are not necessarily environmentally benign; their development can, in fact, create large environmental costs. Dams, for example, harness the energy of falling water (as renewable as resources come), but few environmentalists would suggest that their effects on the environment are positive. Wood is renewable, but burning it in poorly operating woodstoves creates immense air-pollution problems. Harnessing the wind for energy production — a strategy pushed hard by environmentalists seeking a benign substitute for nuclear power — requires dedicating immense areas of land to forests of large metal machines with whirling blades. Driving through areas where this has been done — Tehachapi Pass, in the extreme southern sierra east of Bakersfield, California, for example — does not encourage an image of wind farms as environmental goods. Row upon row, ridge upon ridge, the phalanxes of great creaking metallic insects march off into the distance, peering down from every height, standing against every skyline, entirely dominating the scene. One wishes urgently for a successful Don Quixote.

As flow resources are not necessarily good, fund resources are not necessarily environmentally evil. Given a choice between burning the cottonwoods along a prairie stream and burning coal from a prairie hillside, one would probably do less damage to the environment by opting for the coal. A hardrock mine, even a fairly large one, often has less effect on its surroundings than a large clear-cut does, even though the clear-cut is (at least theoretically) harvesting a renewable resource. Fossil water — water trapped in ancient aquifers that have been cut off from their sources of recharge, either because the climate has changed or because impermeable rock or clay has covered them — can be tapped by wells in an environmentally benign manner, and in fact one might as well do so. As New Mexico state engineer Steve Reynolds put it a number of years ago, "The alternative is to leave it underground and simply enjoy knowing it's there."

From the standpoint, strictly, of the harm they do there is thus no significant difference between flow resources and fund resources. Nevertheless, flow resources are a much better choice for developers to use. Their advantage lies not in their effects, direct or indirect, but in their longevity. Fund resources are usable only until they run out. Flow resources are usable, for all practical purposes, forever. Fund resources are frontier resources; flow resources are ecosystem resources. To build an economy on fund resources is to plan to fail. Flow resources are our only hope for anything resembling permanence in the way we live our lives.

Vigilance is still required. We still need to be on guard for problems of scale, and external costs, and assurances that we are within the flow rate of the resource. We cannot assume that, simply because we are using renewables, we are automatically environmentally correct. A solar-powered chain saw can clear-cut the last habitat of an endangered species as well as a gasoline-powered one can.

But flow resources offer us a gateway out of the frontier paradigm. The use of flow resources forces us to concentrate our attention on rates of flow instead of rates of growth. We study cycles; we deal, of necessity, with limits. And eventually we may even come to understand, not just intellectually but intuitively, precisely what Donella Meadows meant when she said that growth was beside the point.

Future Imperfect

GOOD BUSINESSPEOPLE always try to protect their financial capital, investing it carefully and trying to make it grow. They should have exactly the same attitude toward natural resources, because exactly the same principles hold. Natural resources are functionally equivalent to natural capital. If you take care to focus on the interest-bearing accounts — the flow resources — and do your best never to touch the principal, your real wealth will grow. If you do not, it will shrink.

But conservation is not really quite so simple as that. There may be times when it is legitimate for some types of natural capital to shrink. The difficulty lies in knowing when, and by how much. Ideally, this should depend on how much the resource in question will be worth to the planet in the future. To determine this we need some means of looking at the future. A crystal ball would be nice. Discount rates are what is available.

Discount rates are the primary tool used by economists to attempt to compare the present with the future. They are often described as a means of putting a value on the future, but this is misleading; what they actually do is put a value on the present in terms of our *expectations* of the future.

Suppose you are given $100 in cash. Your bills are all covered: you don't need to spend any of that $100 on food, or rent or mortgage payments, or car payments, or paying off the charge card. You can use it any way you want. Do you spend it all now, or do you hold some or all of it to spend later?

Your answer is going to depend on a great many factors —

how long you expect to live, how steady you expect your income to be, whether you have a son or daughter about to enter college — but all those factors will have this in common: in one way or another, they will all look at the value of that $100 to you in the future. If you expect to die next week, money will be worthless to you in the future, and you might as well spend it all now. Your personal discount rate is 100 percent (value now, $100; value next week, $0, a loss of 100 percent of the current value). If, instead of expecting to die soon, you expect to be fired, money will be worth a great deal to you in the future — as a replacement for lost income — and you are likely to hang on to it. Your personal discount rate is zero (value now, $100; value next week, $100 — no loss of the current value).

In most cases, of course, your personal discount rate will be neither 100 percent nor zero, but somewhere between the two. Exactly where in that broad range it will fall will depend primarily on how settled your future seems. If your future looks solid and secure, your personal discount rate will normally be low; if your future is uncertain and unpredictable, your personal discount rate will normally be high. Higher discount rates translate into a higher propensity to spend. A homeless person may use that $100 immediately; a stockbroker is likely to invest it.

All of this works very well for money. What about the environment?

First we must note a business truism: in order for an investment in goods, services, or other nonmonetary commodities to be viable, the rate of return on that investment must equal or exceed the discount rate. If it does not, the *value* of the invested funds will be declining, even if their actual *amount* is increasing. If money grows at the rate of 5 percent annually, but the discount rate is 10 percent, $100 will grow to $105 in a year's time — but that future $105 is worth only $94.50 today ($105 − 10% of $105 = $105 − $10.50 = $94.50). Since $100 is greater than $94.50, maximizing the value of that money to you requires spending it now rather than investing it.

But when we say the rate of return must equal or exceed the discount rate, what discount rate do we mean? Businesspeople often assume that, because money is involved, the discount rate to be used is always the discount rate for money. But the discount rate for money applies to money *as a commodity,* not as a measuring tool. Different commodities have different discount rates, and they are not necessarily transferable. If the power to your refrigerator fails, you are going to eat the most perishable items (those with the highest discount rates) first. You are not going to use the spoilage rate of lettuce to determine how fast you should eat the ice cream.

Economists understand this, but they differ considerably on how to apply this understanding to environmental goods and services. It is relatively easy to determine the discount rate for a dam; since the dam's value is 100 percent when it is new and declines to zero when it reaches the end of its useful life, the discount rate is simply the inverse of the expected life span (if the dam will no longer hold water at the end of eighty years, the dam declines in value by one-eightieth each year, so the discount rate is 1/80, or 0.0125). It is far more difficult to determine the discount rate for the land the dam's reservoir will cover. What will real estate prices be in eighty years? How much would eighty years of crops bring in? How do you value whitewater rafting on the undammed river? Will the value society places on these things increase or decrease over the life span of the project? All these questions must be answered before an accurate discount rate can be determined.

Answers are not usually forthcoming, however, or even sought. What we use instead are assumptions. And these assumptions differ radically, depending upon which camp — that of the environmentalists or of the developers — we happen to be attached to. Environmentalists tend implicitly to assume that the discount rate for an untouched tract of land they wish to preserve is zero, or possibly even negative — that is, they assume that it will have at least as much value at any given time in the future as it does today. Developers tend implicitly to assume that the discount rate for the same tract of land is 100 percent.

If you are a developer, it is easy to calculate the rate of return on a logging operation: it is the amount of money you will earn for the logs minus the amount you will spend harvesting them and getting them to market. This monetary rate of return can be compared with the interest rate to determine whether you would make a higher return by investing the money elsewhere. In doing this, you have compared the discount rate for the money spent on the logging operation with the discount rate for money placed in other investments. But you have ignored the discount rates for the trees, the land, the displaced wildlife, and the disrupted scenery. And you can only ignore them if you assume these commodities have zero value — in other words, by discounting them 100 percent.

In a true frontier situation — a finite number of settlers facing an infinity of truly unsettled land — there would be some justification for setting the discount rate in this manner. If using up all the resources on a piece of land does not reduce the overall resource base, there is no reason not to use up all the resources. This works for intangible resources (scenery, spiritual values, and the like) as well as it does for tangible ones. If there are an infinite number of Grand Canyons, any single Grand Canyon is expendable.

In a pseudo-frontier situation such as the one that faced the first European settlers on this continent, it is still reasonable to set resource discount rates this way. The continent was pretty close to infinite compared with the tiny footholds the colonists were carving out. There was justification for paying little or no attention to the fact that they were reducing the value of the lands they were defacing. In that situation, the value of the developments themselves was paramount.

But if this frontier type of discounting was not wrong in Adam Smith's day, it is certainly wrong in ours — and it has set a pattern that has proved almost impossible to alter. The assumption of high discount rates for natural resources has been woven thoroughly into our national way of doing things, as unassailable as motherhood and baseball. It tends to be self-perpetuating: the higher the discount rate, the higher the implied interest rate, and the greater the return seems to be on your investment. Money wealth climbs. Real wealth may decline, but real wealth is not normally tradable in the marketplace.

The biosphere is like money placed in an interest-paying account: it grows. In a year's time, a forest or a grassland or a desert puts on a certain measurable percentage of extra biomass, and this percentage figure can be used in lieu of interest. Since in monetary systems the discount rate is the same as the interest rate, it is tempting to use the percentage growth of biomass for the discount rate of nature, as well.

But natural systems differ from interest-bearing accounts in one important way: they have limits. The amount of biomass in an ecosystem can never exceed the carrying capacity for the land base the ecosystem is built on. Interest keeps on accumulating forever. Organic growth, at least in an overall sense, stops.

This means that, in a mature ecosystem, growth in one part of the ecosystem always comes at the expense of another part. If the system is at carrying capacity, there can be no such thing as sustained overall growth. All there can be is a change in the part of the ecosystem that biomass is accumulating in. If the trees are gaining mass, the soil is losing it. At carrying capacity, the energy input from the sun merely drives transfers.

So the interest rates (the growth rates) of different segments of the ecosystem have to balance out. They will be positive in some places and negative in others. The overall growth rate will be zero.

If the interest rates do this, either discount rates will have to do it too or the equality between discount rates and interest rates will no longer hold. Therefore, assuming the equality remains valid, in an ecosystem, and in an economy based on an ecosystem paradigm, some discount rates are going to be negative. They have to be, to balance the positive ones.

One of the major tasks of the conversion to an ecosystem paradigm is to establish which parts of the economy have negative discount rates. I do not propose to tackle this task here, but I would like to cite an example: work experience. As a worker gains experience at his job, his value to the firm that employs him increases. We recognize this by offering higher wages to experienced employees. This is functionally equivalent to a negative discount rate; the employee is more valuable, rather than less, in the future. Is it too much to suggest that natural resources might function in much the same way?

Double, Double . . .

AN IMPORTANT FACTOR to keep in mind when discussing growth — organic growth, economic growth, or any other kind — is the concept of the *doubling rate*. The doubling rate is exactly what it sounds like: the length of time it takes for a growing substance to double in size, given a specific, steady rate of growth. It does not, however, behave the way we might intuitively expect it to. It is a geometric rather than an arithmetic rate, involving multiplication rather than simple accumulation, and the human mind is simply not set up to grasp geometric rates.

Consider a growth rate of 1 percent — a very small amount. Intuition might suggest that something growing at 1 percent per year will double in size in about 100 years. But this ignores the fact that each year's extra 1 percent is calculated, not just on the original amount, but on that amount *plus whatever growth has taken place since the calculations began.* If the original value is taken as 100, the first year's growth takes you to 101 (100 + [.01 × 100]). But the second year's growth takes you, not to 102, but to 102.01 (101 + [.01 × 101]). The effect is cumulative, and accelerating. By the fifth year, you are up to 105.1; by the tenth, to 110.4; by the twentieth, to 122. Doubling takes place in 70 years, 30 years earlier than you expect.

Nor is this all. Since the 1 percent growth rate is now working on twice its original amount, the growth rate has effectively doubled (1 percent of 200 is the same as 2 percent of 100). This dramatically speeds up the rate at which the growing substance accumulates. Starting with 100 (100 dollars; 100 cats; 100 suburban dwellings), the second 100 took 70 years to accumulate; *the third 100 will take only 41.* Seventy plus 41 equals 111. Instead of doubling the original amount in the 100 years your intuition expected, a 1 percent growth rate has nearly tripled it.

Any other growth rate will be similarly compressed. At 2 percent, it takes 36 years to double something, and only 56 (not 72) to triple it. At 3 percent (considered "healthy" for a national economy by most economists), doubling takes place in 24 years, tripling in 38, quadrupling in 48. Given that "healthy" growth rate, the nation's GNP should be four times today what it was during World War II. (It is actually sixteen times as much, indicating an even "healthier" rate of about 6 percent.)

The really alarming thing about all this is how the doubling rate allows things to sneak up on you. Ecologists are fond of giving an example that runs something like this: Suppose you have a species of duckweed that doubles in numbers every week. (This means that it covers twice as much of a body of water each week as it did the week before. For duckweed, this is not a totally unrealistic assumption.) You seed a patch one foot square into a 100-acre pond. How long will it take for the duckweed to cover the entire pond?

The answer is 26 weeks. But that is not the really alarming figure. The point the hairs begin to rise on the back of your neck is when you ask yourself a related question: how long does it take the duckweed to cover *half* the pond? It takes only a little reflection to realize that, if the duckweed patch is doubling in size every week, *half the pond will be covered exactly one week before the whole pond is.* For 25 weeks you have looked at the pond and thought to yourself, Hey, no problem; it's less than half covered. One week later, and the whole thing is gone.

And that is what scares environmentalists most about growth. Not that it exists; not that it is bad; but that it is, psychologically speaking, so very, very sneaky. It does not give the right signals to trip our internal alarms; because of the effect of the doubling rate, we tend to be complacent about environmental damage until it reaches a rate that is too high to be reversed in the amount of time we have left ourselves. If you start with a million acres of forest and clear-cut only 1,000 acres of it, the damage does not look great. If you increase the size of that clear-cut only 10 percent per year, the damage still does not look great — for a while. But half the forest will be gone in 42 years. And the whole thing will be gone in 49.

National Wealth and
the Wealth of Nations

THE SIZE of an organism can be determined by weighing and measuring; the size of a population can be determined by counting. The size of an economy, however, depends on processes as much as it does on numbers or physical dimensions, so it cannot be directly measured but must be calculated. The most common means of doing this is to calculate the economy's gross national product, or GNP — a "measurement" so widely reported, closely watched, and heavily relied upon that we sometimes forget that it was not handed down to us on stone tablets from Mount Sinai. It was born in the Depression, it is slightly under sixty years old, and it is very much a child of its times.

It was, interestingly enough, a Russian immigrant who first came up with the idea for GNP. Simon Smith Kuznets was born in Kharkov, near the base of the Ural Mountains, in 1901. (The city was then in Russia; boundary lines drawn during the Soviet era put it into the Ukrainian S.S.R., and since the demise of the Soviet Union it has been considered part of the Ukraine. Boundaries here have — as usual — not proved particularly useful for answering questions of ownership.) The young Kuznets left the region shortly after the Russian Revolution, ending up in 1922 at Columbia University in New York City, where he took a degree in economics in 1926. He joined the staff of the National Bureau of Economic Research a year later.

In 1929 the stock market crashed, the world economy

collapsed, and the Bureau of Economic Research suddenly found itself trying to explain what the hell had happened. Numerous theories were floated, but none were proved. In fact, Kuznets realized sometime around 1930, none were provable. Economists were pondering the question of why the economy was no longer growing, but they had not stopped to ask themselves the more basic question of what a "growing economy" was. Tools for measuring economic growth did not in fact exist.

Kuznets set himself the task of creating those tools. By the time the young economist left the Bureau of Economic Research in 1936 to take a teaching post at the University of Pennsylvania, he had formulated the concept of the gross national product. Acceptance by the professional community was slow; it was not until after World War II that federal statisticians began using the measurement on a regular basis. The real turning point came in the four years between 1946 and 1950. The economy had been expected to plunge following the war, as factories faced conversion to civilian production, world politics faced total reconfiguration, and the labor force faced the influx of hundreds of thousands of just mustered-out soldiers whose primary occupation for the last several years — killing other soldiers — involved skills not readily transferable to the marketplace. Instead, economic well-being soared. GNP turned out to be both the best handle on, and the best predictor of, this growth.

In 1971, Simon Kuznets was awarded the Nobel Prize for economics. The citation referred specifically to the "new insights" into global economic well-being provided by the concept of the GNP. Unnoted at the time of the ceremony was the fact that, out there in the real world, the notion of GNP as an indicator of national welfare was already beginning to come under serious question.

There are two theoretically equivalent methods used by economists today for measuring GNP. One measures income; the other measures expenditures. The expenditures method is the more reliable. To calculate GNP by this method, one begins by summing all consumer spending — all money spent by private individuals, in the regular marketplace, on goods and services — throughout the reporting period. One adds to that the sum of all spending by firms on capital investment, on the rental of manufacturing and office space, and on raw materials (*not* on salaries and wages: since salaries and wages are the source of consumer spending, to sum them into firms' spending as well would be to count them twice). A third category, government spending, is piled on top of those of the consumers and the firms. (Again, this is adjusted to make sure nothing is counted twice: transfer payments — social security, welfare, and the like — and the wages and salaries of government employees are deducted from the mix. This is why government spending as a factor of GNP always looks so much more reasonable than it does when it is spelled out in the federal budget.)

Finally, net exports are added. It has to be net (exports minus imports), not gross (exports alone): spending on imports is spending on the products of other countries, and it belongs in their GNPs, not ours.

The sum of these four categories — consumer spending, capital investment, government expenditures, and net exports — is, theoretically, the total flow of money that has moved through the country during the year and is therefore a good indicator of the overall state of the country's economy.

The second method for calculating GNP is known as national income accounting, or simply the "income approach." It relies, interestingly enough, on the circular-flow model of the economy — which is to say, it relies on an unrecognized but nonetheless real application of the ecosystem paradigm.

The circular-flow model, you will remember, states that money in an economy flows constantly around in a circle: wages are paid to workers, who pay merchants, who pay wholesalers, who pay manufacturers, who pay workers again. Goods flow the opposite direction, from manufacturers to wholesalers to merchants to workers. (The goods circle is not complete: workers do not sell the goods back to the manufacturers when they are done with them. This hemorrhage of one of the two economic circles, unmatched by a similar pattern in the other, is one of the major causes of environmental damage.) The two flows — goods one way, money the other — have to balance each other. Therefore, expenditures (a money measure of the flow of goods) must always equal income (the flow of money itself). So calculating total income will give you a figure that is equal to total expenditures — that is to say, it will give you the GNP.

Calculating GNP by the national income accounting method is somewhat simpler than using the expenditures method, because the figures are more readily available. One begins with "national income," defined as the sum of all salaries, wages, proprietors' earnings, corporate profits, net interest, and income from rent; statistics on all of these have already been assembled by the IRS in the process of collecting taxes, so they are easy to come by. Add depreciation on capital goods (the "capital consumption allowance"; figures for this are also collected by the IRS) and the so-called indirect business taxes (sales tax, excise tax, property tax, and any other tax — at any level of government — that is not levied directly on a factor of production). You now have a figure representing the total income received by all individuals, corporate bodies, and government units in the nation, plus a corrective figure for income lost to capital depreciation. In theory, this figure should equal the total expenditures by all individuals, corporate bodies, and government units.

In theory. In practice, it never does; so here economists do one of those things that drive noneconomists mad. They assume that the difference is due to measuring errors, not flaws in the theory, and they make it all better by adding an arbitrary amount — known blatantly as "statistical discrepancy" — to the national income accounts. Voilà! The two sides of the ledger magically balance.

They have a point. The figures are taken from different sets of data, collected in wholly different ways, so it is reasonable to assume measurement discrepancies. But the size of these "errors" — in the early 1990s statistical discrepancy was running at roughly minus 7 percent, which works out, in a $5 trillion GNP, to $350 billion — and the facile way in which the correction is incorporated into the data set are blunt reminders of the arbitrariness of the whole procedure. All by themselves, they make an excellent case for wondering if the slavish way in which we peg our opinions on whether the nation is doing well to whether the GNP is rising is not seriously misguided.

There are other reasons. The GNP, it turns out, has some serious built-in flaws as a measure of national wealth. It does not, for example, look at any exchanges or account for any work in which no money changes hands: barter and trade, housework and home maintenance done by the homeowner, and similar categories (which clearly make people better off) are not reflected in the GNP at all. Neither, cynics note, is the vast "underground economy": purchases that, for one reason or another, are never reported to the authorities, including informal contract arrangements between friends, most sales through the classified ads, and the purchase of illicit goods such as drugs or the services of prostitutes. (A few years ago, California's agriculture department put out a report listing the state's number one cash crop as marijuana. The report was immediately suppressed, as agriculture officials knew it would be; they had merely wanted to make a point. And the statement, as it happens, was quite literally true.) Sales of second-hand goods do not appear in GNP either, on the grounds that the items sold have already appeared once, when they were new, and to add them in again would be double counting. Thus perisheth the whole reusable/recyclable industry. Recy-

cling may make excellent economic sense, stop the hemorrhage in the goods cycle, and add immensely to our national
well-being, but it goes unreported in our standard measure of
national economic health.

There are worse flaws. GNP calculations take into account
capital depreciation, but they make no allowance at all for
natural-resource depletion; if a timber-dependent country were
to cut down every single stick of timber it owned in the course
of a single year, the GNP would look tremendously healthy
but the country would be facing bankruptcy. Even sillier:
GNP makes no attempt whatever to deal with externalities.
This is a flaw that turns out to be double edged. Not only are
the costs of environmental and social damage not subtracted
from GNP; the expenses of dealing with these problems are
actually added. Thus, as many critics have pointed out, when
the *Exxon Valdez* hung up on Bligh Reef in the middle of a
March night in 1989 and spewed 11 million gallons of Alaska
crude into the previously pristine waters of Prince William
Sound, the effect on GNP was to *raise* it by more than $2 billion.

These and other flaws render the whole process of GNP-
counting questionable, and a number of suggestions have
been made over the years to improve it or replace it.

The simplest of these suggestions merely calls for an adjusted gross national product (AGNP) that would incorporate
some of the big-ticket items the GNP leaves out, such as
external costs, natural resource depreciation, and the barter
economy (no one except the California Department of Agriculture has ever seriously suggested the inclusion of the illicit
economy). This is a Band-Aid-and-sling approach that would
patch up some of the more grievous wounds of the system but
would not deal with any of its systemic problems.

A slightly more radical transformation has been proposed
by William Nordhaus and James Tobin: the Measure of Economic Welfare, or MEW. Starting with the standard GNP,
Nordhaus and Tobin add estimates for the value of leisure
time, amenities, and homeowners' in-kind contributions to

their own welfare in the form of housework and home maintenance. They then subtract external costs; losses to crime and other social maladjustments; and the costs for maintaining what they refer to as "regrettable necessities": police forces, regulatory apparatus, and national defense. The MEW, they have shown, is growing at a significantly slower rate than the GNP. Tobin, for other reasons, won the Nobel Prize for economics in 1981.

Other critics call for the total abandonment of the GNP standard as beyond help. The United Nations Development Programme, for example, has replaced GNP in its own evaluations with a measure it calls the Human Development Index, or HDI. The HDI factors in, with equal weights, life expectancy at birth; literacy and length of schooling; and adjusted per capita gross domestic product, a highly modified form of GNP which subtracts all exports, divides by population, and multiplies by the purchasing power of money in the local economy. The Overseas Development Council uses a similar but simpler calculation: its Physical Quality of Life Index (PQLI) merely factors together life expectancy, infant mortality, and literacy rate. Mark Lutz of the University of Maine has taken the PQLI one step further, adding in a human rights index (he uses the one published annually by the British journal *The Economist*) to come up with something he calls, in tongue-numbing academese, the Authentic Socioeconomic Development Index (ASEDI for short).

Among the most widely admired of these "new" national-wealth indices is one put together by an unlikely alliance between a theologian and an economist, John Cobb and Herman Daly's Index of Sustainable Economic Welfare (ISEW). In their 1989 book *For the Common Good* (Beacon Press), theologian Cobb and economist Daly suggest starting with the personal consumption figures used in the calculation of GNP and skewing them around with multipliers based on natural-resource depletion, erosion, distributional inequities (that is, the gap between rich and poor), and long-term environmental damage (ozone depletion, global warming, and so forth). Graphing the ISEW, Daly and Cobb demonstrate a slow rise in the post–World War II wealth of the United States which peaks in the late 1970s and has been declining ever since — a pattern they and many others believe matches the way the nation has felt about itself.

But perhaps all this begs the real question: why are we attempting to measure such a subjective concept as total national welfare at all? Such measurements are inherently flawed; they all presume that society can agree on what constitutes total national welfare. Ask a billionaire and a monk what constitutes the "quality of life" and you are likely to get widely divergent answers. All of the measurements discussed above, from GNP through HDI and ISEW to ASEDI, assume that we can tell which of those answers is correct. We cannot. Both are correct, or neither is. Only the monk and the billionaire are qualified to judge, and then only for their own answers.

The insistence on comparing levels of national wealth both encourages the frontier paradigm and feeds off it. When we publish those figures, we are doing two things. First, we are encouraging countries to improve the figures; to increase their ratings, to raise their standings among the other nations; in a word, and against all long-term interests in this finite world of ours, to *grow*. And second, we are establishing a pecking order, a ranking among societies which enables us to draw a line and say, We are inside this line and you over there are outside it. We are civilization, you are beyond the frontier. It is the nature of frontiers to expand. We have not only a right but a duty — a Manifest Destiny — to shove the line forward and bring you inside.

As Mark Twain once put it, even a burglar couldn't have said it better.

Translated out of its high-sounding rhetoric, all that Manifest Destiny really amounted to was a rationalization for transferring resources belonging to one group of people, by brute force, to another group. The frontier paradigm hides this fact, but it doesn't make it go away. It dresses up its thievery in moral dress and calls it progress, but the thievery remains, at heart, thievery.

Under the frontier paradigm, wealth equates too easily with acquisitiveness. If there is a limitless amount of resources out there, the person who grabs the most wins. This makes wealth both comparative and strongly present oriented: I am wealthier than you because I control more possessions *at this moment.*

This implies, of course, that I may not continue to be wealthier than you if I don't watch myself. Since there is a limitless pool of things to draw on, if you continue to draw from it while I slow down or stop, you will eventually pass me. If I want to maintain my position, I must continue to acquire things, and even increase the rate of acquisition if possible. That way you cannot pass me, and I maintain my position as (comparatively) wealthy while you maintain yours as (comparatively) poor. The actual level of resources accumulated under your control, and mine, does not matter for this game. If resources are limitlessly available, it does not make any sense to compare the amount we own with the total pot; the total pot will always be infinitely greater. We can compare only with each other. If we want to be wealthy, the only way to do it is to be wealthier than someone else.

The moment you adopt an ecosystem paradigm, however, this concept of wealth becomes meaningless. In an ecosystem paradigm, there is no limitless pool of resources passing from "out there" through "in here" to "used up"; there are only the same resources, going round and round an endless circle of being and becoming. The circle branches, giving rise to other circles. Connections form and dissolve. It is a dynamic, shifting, kaleidoscope world, a world in which the frontier paradigm's three distinct pools — raw resources, resources-in-use, and waste — become largely meaningless. They are only stages on a journey. What matters, for wealth, is the state of the journey.

So wealth becomes not present oriented but time oriented. It is still comparative (I may be better equipped for the journey than you), but it no longer looks only at current accumulations. If current accumulations are only a stage in a circular process, the real question becomes how well the process is doing, and whether the current accumulations are assisting it or blocking it.

And thus one must look to the future, not to the present or the past. If what we view as "wealth" interferes too greatly with the flow of the resource cycle, it will eventually impoverish us. We must stop thinking of those among us with the most possessions as the wealthiest; wealth does not consist of how much we have grabbed, but of how well we have positioned ourselves in the flow. Wealth and sustainability are tightly connected; in fact, they are very close to being synonyms.

Buckminster Fuller was right. "Wealth," he said back in 1969, "has nothing to do with yesterday, but only with forward days. How many forward days, for how many lives are we now technically organized to cope? The numerical answer is the present state of our true wealth."

Must we measure something? Then let us at least measure something useful. Let us try to get a handle not on how riotously well we are currently living but on how long we will be able to keep it up.

We don't really need to know how many trees we are cutting down or how many we are preserving. The relevant question is, how are the replacements doing?

The size of that portion of our economy based on fossil fuels is not as relevant as how long those fuels will last and how smoothly we can make the transition to the next fuel source.

The amount we can afford to spend on housing in this country measures only how fast money is moving through our hands. It has nothing to do with how long we will be able to house our people comfortably. And what is "comfortably," anyway?

Ecosystems do not care much about quantity. They do not pay much attention to quality, either. What they depend on is *adaptability*. And that is determinable only by how long the ecosystem can survive, and how resilient it is in the face of environmental changes. A forest is "wealthier" than a desert. But a forest is "better" than a desert only at the art of being a forest.

Six ❧

Time for Good Behavior

Getting Our Money's Worth

THERE IS A DEEP-SEATED SUSPICION among both environmentalists and those in the business community that economics and ecology are natural and implacable enemies, and that any attempt to reconcile the two is therefore inevitably doomed. In this book I have argued precisely the opposite: that economics and ecology are both doomed unless we reconcile them. The theoretical basis for this stand has, I hope, been made abundantly clear. The practical questions remain. How do we effect this reconciliation? How do we bring these two hostile and suspicious armed camps together onto the same piece of ground and convince them to enter the same tent and sit down at the same table?

The key, I think, lies in the recognition, by both sides, of one basic, unavoidable truth. It is this: *the laws of ecology and the laws of economics are, at heart, the same set of laws.* For years, now, free-marketers and environmental regulators alike have been denying that identity. Both sides need to move past that denial. Environmentalists need to see that any regulations they promulgate that do not conform to economic laws, or that attempt to overrule those laws, are doomed to failure and will probably do more harm than good, both to society and to the environment. And free-marketers need to realize that much of what they have been defending as "the market" is actually a set of market distortions brought on by attempts to escape the laws of economics. These distortions harm the market as much as they do the environment. There is a deep-seated and unavoidable need for some forms of regulation: *those forms that move the market away from its distortions and toward the perfect market envisioned by classical economic theory;* the market that conforms, in all essential aspects, to the perfect ecosystem envisioned by classical ecologists.

We need to build a society that conforms as completely as possible to both ecological and economic principles. But that should not be difficult. The two sets of principles are the same.

Environmental protection costs money. We must begin by recognizing that. Pollution-control measures add to the cost of goods. The preservation of forest land takes away the incomes of those who would earn it by cutting down the forest. Banning the automobile might make sense ecologically, but there are people in whole classes of industries — auto workers, highway engineers, gasoline refiners and distributors, even fast-food operators — who would suffer financial ruin. We cannot deal with these problems by denying that they exist.

But environmental damage costs money, too. Every species lost to extinction, every river fouled by pollution, every hillside stripped of its trees represents an economic loss to someone. The bill may not come due immediately; those who feel the pinch may not be the same as those who rang up the tab; but sometime, somewhere, someone is eventually going to have to pay.

Consider, to begin with, the potential impact on the world economy of a 2°C rise in global temperatures — the bottom-end estimate for global warming. One result of such a temperature increase would be a rise in sea level of anywhere from twenty centimeters to two meters (eight inches to six and a half feet). If the upper end of the estimate proves valid, roughly 20 percent of the country of Bangladesh will be inundated, displacing between 10 and 15 million people and destroying much of the nation's agricultural capacity. Nor would Bangladesh be alone; significant portions of our own Atlantic and Gulf coasts would be affected as well. Much of this coastline is, like Bangladesh, barely above sea level, and a few feet of rise in that level will mean the inundation of hundreds of square miles of currently "dry" land. The broad, bird-filled Georgia sea marshes, the Florida Everglades, the immense and intricately interwoven bayou and estuary system of Louisiana — all of these, and the miles upon miles of flat, heavily developed lands adjacent to them, are deeply at risk. One study estimates that, in Florida alone, up to 1 million residents will have to be relocated.

Seawalls will have to be constructed at most of the world's port cities to protect them from flooding. Continental-shelf oil-drilling platforms will have to be raised. Even at the low-end estimate, large numbers of coastal fresh-water aquifers will be invaded by salt water and rendered undrinkable. Substitute water supplies will have to be developed for the many cities that depend on these aquifers. The cost could run well into the billions.

As temperature shifts, rainfall patterns will shift, too, becoming wetter in some places and dryer in others. Agriculture will have to reconform itself to the new shape of the climate. Leave aside the question of whether there will be more or less farmland available following the readjustment: the relevant point here is the cost of moving. Our entire agricultural infrastructure is aimed at Iowa corn and Kansas wheat and Idaho potatoes. It will have to be dismantled and rebuilt to serve North Dakota or Montana or Manitoba or wherever the vagrant rains decide to settle down. The value of lands in the old farm belts will plunge with their productivity; farmers attempting to relocate will find themselves stuck with essentially worthless real estate while the prices of the lands they are trying to buy go through the roof. Economists call these sorts of things "decision costs." No firm estimates exist for the size of the decision costs associated with global warming, but they are likely to be in the same neighborhood as the costs for controlling and abating damage on the seacoasts. The overall price tag varies according to which school of economists you happen to be talking to: it has been pegged at anywhere from $10 billion to $20 trillion.

But it is not necessary to look at a large, planetary-scale problem like global warming to see the economic costs associated with environmental degradation. In fact, *all* environmental damage costs money. A gaggle of recent examples:

• In November 1990 the U.S. Department of the Interior announced that it would be "aggressively pursuing" a lawsuit against the state of Florida to force it to pick up at least part of the costs of cleaning up environmental damage to Everglades National Park caused by reckless use of agricultural chemicals in the park's watershed. The total estimated bill: $200 million.

• In 1984 the Michigan legislature passed a law, the Michigan Environmental Response Act, aimed at cleaning up the state's more than two thousand known toxic waste sites. There is a large probability that the legislators did not know what they were getting into. Annual appropriations to enforce the act have run around $15 million. As of 1990, the state's Department of Natural Resources estimated that total cleanup costs would eventually reach a staggering $4 billion. At the current, seemingly high level of appropriations, raising that money will take 266 years.

• On November 5, 1992, papers were filed in the U.S. District Court for Los Angeles committing approximately 150 cities, public utility districts, and other public bodies in four southern California counties to cleaning up and restoring the waters of the Pacific Ocean adjacent to their coastlines. The formal commitment was part of the settlement of a two-year-old lawsuit filed by the National Oceanic and Atmospheric Administration, the U.S. Department of the Interior, and three California state agencies against a Torrance, California, pesticide-manufacturing firm called Montrose Chemical Corporation. The public bodies' share of the cleanup costs: at least $45.5 million.

· In March 1991 the New York Department of Environmental Conservation announced a set of recommended alternatives for cleaning up eight separate toxic waste disposal sites at a single ALCOA Aluminum manufacturing plant at Massena, New York, on the St. Lawrence River. Depending upon the combination of alternatives chosen, the costs could range from $46 million to $52 million. At least five other known sites at the ALCOA facility were not included in the recommendations: under the terms of a consent decree filed in 1985, ALCOA must clean up these sites, at an as yet unknown cost, as well.

· And on November 22, 1991 (the twenty-eighth anniversary of President Kennedy's assassination), the Small Business Administration released a report prepared by a firm called OMNI Environmental Services of Beaverton, Oregon, on cleanup costs for a twenty-acre plywood mill site on the Columbia River at the city of Astoria. There were no PCBs, pesticides, or other hazardous waste spills involved, just the accumulated effects of forty years of oil and grease dripping from the plant's machinery onto the soil. OMNI's estimate of cleanup and restoration expenses: $2.2 million.

It is important to recognize that all of the dollar estimates cited above are for cleanup costs alone; they do not address actual damage to the environment. This is not unusual. The actual costs of environmental damage can be surprisingly hard to estimate, due largely to the diffuse nature of these costs and the difficulty of proving connections. Fisheries have been declining on the Columbia River; is any of that decline the result of the oil and grease pollution at that Astoria plywood mill? If so, how much? What proportion of the health costs incurred by residents of the Akwesasna Mohawk Nation, an Indian reservation just downstream from ALCOA's Massena plant, are attributable to pollution from those eight expensive disposal sites? How many tourist dollars have been lost to communities surrounding Everglades National Park due to reductions in wildlife numbers caused by upstream agricultural chemical use? The fact that these questions are difficult or impossible to answer should not be taken to mean that the effects are small.

But there is something else wrong with the cost figures here, as well. As economists will be quick to note, they are only half the story. Are the costs of cleaning up pollution in the United States $86 billion each year, as the Environmental Protection Agency estimates? Are they twice that? Ten times that? Half of that? It doesn't really matter, because *costs are meaningless without benefits to measure them against.*

It is not the absolute size of our expenditures on environmental damage control that matters. It is whether we are getting our money's worth. If the benefits of what we are doing to the environment exceed, in absolute terms, the costs we are incurring, then we should keep doing it. If they do not, we should stop.

This test, by the way, applies equally as well to regulations as it does to the actions the regulations attempt to regulate. The point is not to get away from regulations, but to get away from inefficiency and cost ineffectiveness. It is not regulations per se that are the problem: it is regulatory minutiae, the attempt to compel socially responsible behavior by weaving a noose of footnotes around it. We need to get away from defining environmentally destructive activities as morally wrong and start defining them as fiscally irresponsible. Submitting things in triplicate satisfies our urge to tinker and micromanage, but it has a very poor track record when it comes to actually solving environmental problems. It is too tied up with the same flawed worldview that gave rise to the problems in the first place — the frontier paradigm.

Look, for example, at regulatory limits on pollutant discharge — as essentially and thoroughly a frontier-paradigm concept as any that ever came down the pike. It's the old line-in-the-sand approach; as long as the bad guys stay on their own side of the line they're all right, but as soon as they step across it the marshal and his posse will come down upon them like booted and spurred waves of an avenging sea and haul them off to jail. There is a certain amount of comfort in this. Civilization is on this side of the line; the Great Beyond is on the other. A boundary has been marked out — a line in the sand, a frontier of pollution — and we know where we stand in relation to it. The fact that this boundary cannot, by its nature, have anything to do with reality is conveniently ignored.

Let us stop ignoring it for a moment. A regulatory limit, like any other boundary, is meant to separate two unlike regions, in this case acceptably dirty and unacceptably dirty. (We could use the words *unhealthful* or *environmentally damaging* in place of *dirty;* the principle would be the same.) This presupposes a stairstep model of the regulated pollutant's effects. The pollutant is harmless in small amounts, harmful in large amounts; the point where it becomes harmful (the "threshold," in regulatory terminology) can be pinpointed precisely, and that point separates the acceptable from the unacceptable, for regulatory purposes, as the riser of a step separates the lower step from the upper, or the twelve gates to the city in Revelation separate the elect from the damned.

Ecosystems do not work that way. Ecosystems do not have thresholds, they have gradients. Communities, water chemistries, soil types, light conditions — everything that makes up the ecosystem — all grade gradually from one state to another, and there is rarely a point where you can say with certainty that one stops and the next starts. Even such a major difference as the soil-air interface is not precisely definable; air permeates the top layers of the soil, dust rises into the air, and though we think we know where the surface of the earth lies we cannot say exactly where the air stops affecting the soil or vice versa.

Go back to the regulations. Imagine one concerning a hypothetical substance — say, oobleck. Assume, for the sake of argument, that scientists from the Oobleck National Regulatory Council (ONRC) have determined that the regulatory threshold for oobleck in water should be one part per million (1 ppm). We have an industrial-plant effluent that is meeting regulatory goals — the concentration of oobleck in its effluent is less than 1 ppm — but a key element of the oobleck-control equipment has begun to malfunction, and the concentration of the dreaded substance in the effluent is slowly rising. It reaches 0.999999 ppm. Nothing happens. It then increases by 0.000001 ppm — one part per trillion. Bells ring, lights flash, sirens wail, and the embarrassed plant owners find themselves facing a $30,000 fine.

The question we have to ask ourselves is this: Is that extra one part per trillion worth $30,000? Does it change the effects of the oobleck on the environment by that significant an amount? To make sure we understand the problem, we can make it one part per quadrillion, or one part per septasextillion (that's a decimal point followed by 231 zeros): the principle involved will be exactly the same. The environment simply does not discriminate that finely. Large levels of any pollutant are harmful, but the definition of "large" varies from one pollutant to another. Progressively smaller levels are progressively less harmful. There is no bottom threshold. There *is* a level — the assimilative capacity of the environment — below which the ecosystem the pollutant is being discharged into is capable of smothering its effects, altering its chemistry, or otherwise rendering it harmless; but this level is not an absolute, varying from place to place, year to year, and even time of day to time of day, as the ecosystem itself changes. Regulatory thresholds cannot take such shifts into account, and thus rarely do anything better than approximate assimilative capacity.

All this is understood, implicitly if not explicitly, by both the regulated industries and their regulators. This converts regulatory enforcement into game playing, rather like a gigantic soccer match in which both sides attempt to score goals against each other — industry by coming as close to the line (the regulatory limit) as possible without stepping over, the agencies by catching the industries every time they *do* step over. The fancy two-step that results has little or nothing to do with environmental quality.

The first step toward solving a problem is to prove that it exists. The regulatory two-step does not and cannot do this. Putting accurate prices on environmental damage has a much better chance.

At this point a caveat should be inserted. The overwhelming majority of environmental activists (and I count myself in that majority) believe strongly that what the human race is doing to the earth is not just expensive but immoral. "Not for the first time," wrote the Welsh author and adventurer Colin Fletcher upon seeing a clear-cut in the California coast redwoods, "it occurred to me that one life-form had no damned right to do such things to another." In *A Sand County Almanac,* Aldo Leopold wrote of the need to develop in the human species what he referred to as a "land ethic" that would create within us a moral and ethical need to treat the entire living environment in the same tender way we treat our families and our friends. The phrase has reverberated endlessly through environmental literature ever since. There is a wholeness in the pure and undiluted world, a wholeness that can be distinctly felt but can only be properly described in theological terms. This is why environmental writing is so full of phrases like "the cathedral of the forest," "union with nature," and "the sanctity of life." It is also why environmental activists are so passionate and aggressive in their work. We feel the same moral outrage at a clear-cut that others feel when a rape is committed in a church.

I have no wish to deny the validity of any of this. But it is only fair to note that there is another school of morality, one that suggests it is immoral to let anything utilitarian go unused. This morality, too, is deeply felt. Many years ago I walked through a proposed wilderness area in northern California with a high-level Forest Service official named Zane Grey Smith. Zane is a land-ethic forester, but as we passed through this untouched landscape he was recalling a friend and colleague who felt quite differently. "Wonderful man, just wonderful," he said. "But he believed that there was something immoral about watching a tree grow up and die and fall down."

That is why we must turn to economics. Not because we are wrong; not because they are wrong; but because Adam Smith was right. Under the proper conditions, each of us acting from our own motives and our own morality will move society, as if by an invisible hand, to the best possible common solution for the society as a whole. And "society" can be taken here to mean the society of the redwood and the ant as well as of the human race.

Our job is not to deny that reality. Our job — that of environmentalists and developers alike — is to create those proper conditions.

Amid the low, oak-covered hills southeast of Sacramento, California, on the eastern fringes of the Sacramento Valley where the flat floor of the valley is about to stand on end to become the Sierra Nevada, there stands an abandoned nuclear power plant. Two immense cooling towers rise from the surrounding farmlands like the smokestacks of Mordor, but no steam rises from them. Acres of asphalt parking lot lie empty and deserted beneath the hot California sun. Only birdsong breaks the silence. The effect on the visitor is extraordinarily eerie, as if he or she has stumbled across a high-tech ghost town.

The plant is called Rancho Seco, and it belongs, lock, stock, and empty barrel, to the Sacramento Municipal Utility District, a publicly owned electric utility that is known popularly by the unlovely acronym of SMUD. As late as the mid-1980s, SMUD was what could only be described as a financial disaster area, its consumer confidence level sapped by rate increases and poor service performance, its bond rating, as established by independent financial rating services, an industry-trailing "C." Today there has been an almost complete turnaround. Customer confidence is at a near-record 97 percent approval level; the same financial rating services that classed SMUD bonds as "C" only a few years ago upgraded that rating to "A" during 1991. And in 1992 the American Public Power Association honored the company with its annual E. F. Scattergood Award, given to the utility that has done the most during the preceding year for "enhancing the prestige of public power and improving service to customers."

When did this remarkable turnaround begin? Ask Ed Smeloff, the utility's president during that crucial period, and you will get a straight answer. It happened, he says, "when we got rid of that albatross around our necks." The "albatross" in question was the Rancho Seco nuclear generating plant.

Abandoning Rancho Seco was not SMUD's idea. It was the voters'. The utility was proud of its nuclear facility, which had been providing Sacramento with electricity since 1974; its 913 megawatts of installed capacity represented approximately 55 percent of the district's power-generating ability. It had just been through a two-year, multimillion-dollar upgrade that had greatly improved the caliber of both the plant and its operating personnel. So when a small group of activists succeeded, in the spring of 1989, in qualifying a citywide ballot referendum to close the plant, it was not surprising that the utility fought it so hard. At that time, the plant's estimated book value was in the neighborhood of $945 million, not including the costs of decommissioning the closed facility or of replacing the lost power. One could not casually shove aside a resource of that size without risking total economic ruin.

Sacramento voters didn't buy that argument. On June 6, 1989, the utility's ratepayers voted themselves out of the nuclear power business. On June 7, the fuel rods were pulled from the core and laid aside. The process of shutting down Rancho Seco had begun.

Closing a nuclear plant is a long, difficult, expensive operation. It had rarely, or never, been done with a commercial facility the size of Rancho Seco, so the process was full of dangerous unknowns, like taking a blindfolded swim, wounded and trailing blood, through a tankful of barracudas. The hard value of the plant would have to be written off as a dead loss, along with all future earnings from the sale of its power. The reactor would have to be "cooled" to a safe level of radioactivity before it could be dismantled — a process, it was estimated, that would take at least sixteen years. During that time the facility would have to be guarded, kept clean, and maintained in what for all practical purposes amounted to running condition. As late as 1992, three years after closure, the company was still carrying 172 employees on its payroll who did nothing but work at Rancho Seco.

All these expenses were essentially deadwood that would have to be borne by SMUD ratepayers — in addition to the price the already financially staggering utility would have to pay for replacement power. Industry analysts gloomily predicted a company awash in red ink for the rest of its short, unnatural life.

It didn't happen that way. The vote to close the plant, Ed Smeloff says today, was a wake-up call: it forced the utility to tighten up what had been a very loose operation and demand that it run efficiently. With little choice, SMUD began aggressively pursuing conservation. Utility representatives fanned out to homes and businesses throughout the community, offering free energy audits and recommendations for saving electricity without diminishing consumers' lifestyles. A refrigerator recycling program replaced approximately eighteen thousand older, energy-wasting home refrigerators with more efficient new units in the course of a single year; a similar program aimed at electric space heating assisted in the installation of more than one thousand heat pumps. In what some observers saw as a bizarre move, the utility embarked on a massive tree-planting program, with the announced goal of placing half a million trees on Sacramento streets and lawns within ten years. The trees, utility officials pointed out, would cool the city significantly in the summer; they estimated a 30–40 percent savings in air conditioning costs. They told the public they were building a utility plant "a piece at a time." By early spring of 1992, the capacity of this conservation "plant" had reached 271 megawatts — nearly a third of Rancho Seco's lost generating ability. The average cost of providing power to the city had dropped to 3.9 cents per kilowatt-hour. Power from Rancho Seco had been costing over 25 percent more.

At SMUD headquarters in Sacramento later that spring, I asked the attendant at the lobby information booth how the utility company's employees had viewed the ballot measure that closed Rancho Seco. He hesitated for a moment before answering. "It's been mixed," he said finally. There was a "feeling of frustration" that they had just spent an enormous amount of money upgrading the facility and now it would all be wasted. There were mutterings about lost jobs at the plant, and lost power fed into the grid, and lost political face. A general feeling persisted that the environmental extremists had done it to them again.

But had the feared damage materialized? Had there been any adverse economic effects that he was aware of from suddenly taking on roughly a billion dollars in what should have been financial dead weight? This time the answer was immediate. "Oh, no," he said, shaking his head and smiling. "Virtually none."

Falsifying the Market

A S WE APPLY market solutions to environmental problems, we must not delude ourselves as to what "the market" entails. It is remarkably easy to be seduced, from either
side, by what can perhaps best be called "pseudo–market
solutions" — solutions that emulate market processes but do
not play by the same rules. These include, on the one hand,
demands for the sacrosanctity of private rights and for free,
unregulated access to public lands; and on the other, incen-
tive-based but nonmarket approaches such as tax rebates,
"green" taxes, and consumer boycotts.

Private-rights and free-resource fallacies are dealt with at
length elsewhere in this book. Here we will look at the opposite side of the coin — attempts to green up the tax code and
the marketplace through well-meaning but ultimately self-defeating means. We begin with taxes.

Americans have a long history of tinkering with the tax
code to try to achieve social goals. All such attempts can be
classified into either (or occasionally, both) of two broad categories: tax breaks and tax punishments.

Tax breaks take the carrot approach: they encourage what
society perceives as good behavior by rewarding it with lower
taxes. In this category fall tax deductions for home insulation;
property tax reductions for lands maintained as open space;
and tax rebates of various kinds, such as soil-bank programs.
These are promoted as means of creating incentives to do
environmentally beneficial things. It is true that they do this;
but, because the incentives are decided by politics rather than

by markets, there is no guarantee that they will have any bearing on reality. A society that simultaneously offers tax breaks for energy efficiency (insulation) and energy profligacy (oil depletion allowances) has not even begun to come to grips with its real problems.

Tax punishments — the stick approach — show problems similar to those of tax incentives. The intention is usually to correct for external costs by using taxes to raise an item's price. But with the amounts and the target goods both set politically rather than by markets, it is too easy to aim for popular approval rather than economic efficiency. And taxes have an additional problem: it is too easy to get sidetracked from the goal of creating behavioral incentives to the goal of raising revenue for the government. Some of the energy tax proposals bandied about, in all seriousness, in the early days of the Clinton administration demonstrate the difficulties that can arise. Among the worst of these was a proposal to tax all energy sources on "equivalent" carbon content. A tax on actual carbon content might have some validity as a means of encouraging energy production from noncombustion-based sources. A tax on equivalent carbon content carries no such incentive. It raises the price of energy, thereby encouraging conservation, but it does nothing to advance the equally important task of driving energy production toward those forms that produce the lowest externalities.

A good case history for examining what is wrong with green taxes is provided by the so-called feebate concept currently being pushed by some segments of the environmental community. A feebate would be a combined fee and rebate (both the carrot and the stick). Governments would levy a fee on gas-guzzling cars and those that failed to meet emission standards; at the same time, they would offer a rebate to owners of cars that exceeded fuel-efficiency and exhaust standards. The program could be at least partially self-supporting, with the rebate moneys coming from the guzzler fee; it would thus fall under the rubric of "transfer payments," with the government functioning primarily as a conduit for moving money from one segment of society to another. Transfer payments are generally easier to sell than flat-out taxes are. And the program would definitely act as a financial incentive for drivers of small, clean cars and as a financial disincentive for drivers of large, filthy ones. On the surface, the program looks like a good one.

Deeper down, though, there are some serious deficiencies — and some potentially embarrassing questions. Whom, for example, are we transferring funds to and from? It is the poor who tend to drive the older, dirtier, less fuel-efficient cars; it is the rich who can afford to purchase the new, clean, gas-sipping vehicles that would receive the rebate. The poor cannot afford the decision costs involved in the change, which in this case amount to the cost of a new car. If social equity is part of the goal, the feebate is built backwards.

If some cars receive rebates and others are assessed fees, this means that, at some level in between, both the fee and the rebate are zero. What, or who, should determine that level? Should we average EPA mileage figures for the current model year, or set an arbitrary target? How do we weigh fuel efficiency against emissions cleanliness? On the average the two rise and fall together, but there are always exceptions, and dealing with those could prove knotty.

And why are we rebating anyway? Why are we *paying* people to drive cars, even fuel-efficient ones? Most of the externalities associated with automobile use are not fuel related. Freeway and parking lot sizes are determined not by the efficiency or cleanliness of the cars using them but by their sheer, raw numbers. Rush-hour slowdowns are also number-rather than size-determined: the faster traffic flows, the more space is required for each vehicle (this is due to increased reaction times and braking distances, neither of which is notably changed by changing the size of the car). A freeway will physically hold only about half as many cars at 60 mph as it will at 30. As more cars squeeze on, speeds have to decrease in order to accommodate them. If feebates make cars easier to purchase, rush hour will become less rushed than ever. Is this what we think we are paying for?

Urban sprawl results from the mobility provided by the automobile, and as mobility becomes cheaper (as a result, say, of driving a car that gets higher mileage, and then getting money from the government for doing so to boot), sprawl is likely to increase — hardly a result the feebate designers could have had in mind. And it must never be forgotten that even a clean, fuel-efficient car is still pretty wasteful and dirty. No matter how thoroughly you gloss over the fact with gas-mileage charts and inspection-and-maintenance programs, in an ecological sense the internal combustion engine is still primarily a device to convert scarce fossil fuels into too much carbon dioxide and smog. The feebate idea tinkers with the figures in that equation, but it doesn't alter the basic equation at all.

When you come right down to it, a feebate is not a market solution at all. It is a means of enforcing a regulatory standard. The standard is that combination of emissions levels and fuel efficiency for which the fees and rebates average out to zero. Feebates may be a more efficient and effective way of enforcing standards than traditional command-and-control approaches are, but the standards are still standards. They are still arbitrary; they still divert society toward the goal of meeting the standard rather than toward that of eliminating the problem. And they are still the wrong way to go.

Feebates do not internalize the external costs of the automobile, they merely transfer them from one group of drivers to another. If we are serious about solutions, we need to do better than that. One possible approach would be a miles-traveled surcharge on annual auto license fees, computed at different rates for different classes of cars: subcompacts would be assessed a lower rate than midsized cars, which would be charged less than luxury sedans. This would encourage both the purchase of more fuel-efficient automobiles and a reduction in overall automobile use. And it would do it at a point where the government is already intruding in the car owner's life, so consumers would have fewer grounds for complaint. In fact, if the system were installed properly, some people — drivers of high-efficiency cars who used them sparingly — might actually see their annual license fees go down. The fee-bate goals would be realized without the feebate drawbacks.

Green consumerism is, on the whole, closer to a true market solution to environmental problems than green taxes are; but it, too, has some flaws. Green consumerism uses what is squarely a bottom-line supply-and-demand approach: if demand for an item drops, production will have to drop as well; if demand for an item rises, production will be likely to rise to meet it. By buying green products, we encourage their production; by boycotting dirty products, we discourage them.

The concept is sound enough (I am not about to discourage it, or to discontinue my own practice of it), but as a tool for large-scale social change, it is doomed. It comes up against the combined forces of externalities and the free-rider problem. Generally speaking, the greener the product the more externalities it has internalized, and therefore the higher the price. And that means that, though society will be better off if I buy green, I personally will be worse off. I have paid more for the green product than I would have for a precisely similar dirty one, and have therefore tied up more of my scarce resources than I absolutely needed to in order to do the job. Only ethics can make me do that, and even ethics are not always sufficient. I am in the process of converting the light fixtures in my house to compact fluorescent bulbs. There is no question that these are environmentally sounder; they even make more economic sense, in the long run, than incandescents do, because of their lower energy use and longer lives. But each one has an initial cost — a decision cost — of around eighteen dollars; whereas I just picked up two 60-watt incandescents for eighty-nine cents. Six months ago, I put a compact fluorescent bulb in the dining room; a month ago, I added two more in the living room. Despite the best of intentions, I have yet to convince myself to go beyond this token group of three.

Purchasing goods because they are environmentally friendly thus faces some daunting problems. Similar problems crop up when you look at the other side of green consumerism: *not* purchasing items because they are environmentally surly. This is particularly true of the standard form of organized nonpurchasing: the consumer boycott.

There are real questions as to how effective organized boycotts are as a means of influencing corporate environmental behavior. Firms look on boycotts as a political tool, and tend to fight them politically. They usually have more resources for this than environmental groups do. They can spread the word quite effectively about what they refer to as environmental blackmail (sometimes called "greenmail," although this term has other uses and may not, therefore, be reliably understood). The stubborn American spirit of fair play is easy to evoke on the issue of blackmail. Organized boycotts thus often fail exquisitely on a part of the moral turf that they have claimed but neglected to defend.

Disorganized boycotts, however, are another matter. If consumers stop purchasing a product because they are morally uncomfortable with the choice, the purposes of a boycott have been served even if no specific request has been made to avoid the product in question. At the same time, if no formal boycott has been declared, firms have no target to focus their own weapons upon. All they can do is respond to the specific allegations, something that is usually much harder to do. If an organized boycott is launched, tuna firms whose fishing methods kill porpoises can complain they have been singled out for special treatment over other porpoise-killing technologies (say, oil shipping). If environmental groups limit themselves to pointing to the numbers of porpoises lost to tuna nets, coupled with a request for consumers to consider whether they feel comfortable continuing to support this, the moral high ground of the antiblackmail crusade is lost by the firms.

They must respond directly to the complaints, either by disproving them or by changing their fishing processes. The alternative is a consuming public increasingly uncomfortable with tuna, and thus less and less likely to buy it. Market forces will work on moral problems if adequate information is supplied. The trick is supplying that information reliably, dispassionately, and in a form consumers can easily digest and firms cannot easily bluff their way around.

Green consumerism is not a market solution, but a moral approach to making market decisions. As long as we recognize it for what it is, it can remain a legitimate tool. The best means to do this is to put the moral choice squarely where it belongs — on the individual. When people no longer *want* to buy nongreen products, no one can make any money selling them. Then, and only then, they will disappear from the marketplace.

A story beloved by Quakers for over three hundred years is that of the courtier William Penn, newly converted to Quakerism, approaching the sect's founder, George Fox, and asking him, timidly, if it was permissible for him as a member of a pacifist group to continue to wear his sword to court. Fox's reply to the future founder of Pennsylvania was instructive. He demanded neither a boycott (no sword) nor accepting the status quo (wearing the sword). What he said was, "Wear thy sword *as long as thou canst.*"

Pay As You Go

MARKET FORCES offer an efficient and highly effective means of promoting environmental protection, but only so long as all costs and benefits, both internal and external, are included in the accounting spreadsheets. Thus, ways must be found to internalize the externalities — to include, within corporate and government financial planning, not only those costs and benefits of an action which accrue to the corporation or the government entity, but also those which are borne by the rest of society. Examples include the costs of pollution to people downstream or downwind; the costs of soil-productivity loss to future generations; the benefits of observing and recreating within unspoiled environments; and (we must not be anthropocentric about this) the reproductive health of other species of living things.

How do we assess those costs? Environmental economists have suggested three primary ways: effluent charges, user fees, and side payments.

EFFLUENT CHARGES

Effluent charges provide a market-based means to get around the limits the frontier paradigm imposes on regulations. Instead of standards and fines, regulatory agencies can levy a unit fee — an effluent charge — for the amount of pollution a firm discharges into the air or the water. If the fee is $100 a gram, a firm that discharges 10 grams a day will pay daily fees of $1,000; a firm that discharges 100 grams a day will pay daily fees of $10,000. No penalties, no levels to match, no recriminations, and no games. Just a simple fee schedule, like buying gasoline at the pump.

Environmentalists have traditionally shied away from such an approach. Putting an effluent-charge system in place, we have said, is equivalent to selling licenses to pollute. If a firm wants to dump a ton of dioxin in a river, all it has to do is pay a ton's worth of fees and dump. The firm will be legally entitled to do so; no one can stop it, or charge it afterward for the amount of damage the ton of dioxin causes.

All of which is correct but largely irrelevant. The point missed here (and it is a critical one) is the price, in dollars, of that ton's worth of fees. If the fee for dumping dioxin is low, of course the firm will dump. If it is high, the firm is going to look for cheaper alternatives. And for something like dioxin, the fee should be set very, very high.

An effluent-charge system does indeed sell something, but it is not a "license to pollute." It is the assimilative capacity of the environment. Assimilative capacity is measurable, and therefore priceable. It is a good that has value to firms, and which therefore they ought not to mind paying for. As with any other good used in production, they will shop around to try to keep the price down, and they will attempt to reduce the quantity they need to use. They will do both these things from purely practical motives, as means of lowering production costs. Under a regulatory system, firms have no incentives to lower their effluent discharges below arbitrary regulatory limits. Under an effluent-charge system, they have an incentive to drop their discharges as low as possible. The ideal goal of the firm's managers becomes the same as the ideal goal of environmentalists: zero discharge. Only at that point will the costs to the firm of buying assimilative capacity become irreducible.

Effluent charges are environmentally sound. They are based on the ecosystem, not the frontier, paradigm: they assume connections and gradients. They allow for local variation.

They are cyclical, not linear. That which comes out of the environment as raw materials is returned to it as wastes, which break down into raw materials again; the rate of this breakdown determines the assimilative capacity, and is thus figured, through the amount of the effluent charge, directly into the firm's costs.

You are already paying effluent charges, after a fashion: that is what you do every time you pay the sewer bill. But sewer rates are not currently set as a function of assimilative capacity. That is the next logical step. It will mean that, where assimilative capacity is high (on the Ohio River, say), rates will be considerably lower than where it is low (on the Gila River, or the Los Angeles, or the Passaic). We will have to get ready for a dramatic increase in the variability of sewage rates from one part of the country to another.

There will, of course, be complaints about this. Why, the complainers will want to know, are sewage rates so much higher in Tucson than in Louisville? There will be two possible answers to this question, depending upon the nature of the complaint.

Some of the complaints will revolve around fairness and distributional-equity issues. How, the questioners will want to know, can we charge poor people such exorbitant rates to pee? Which do we expect them to do — burst, or go out in the bushes where the effluent will *really* be untreated? These complaints can be answered satisfactorily through the use of lifeline rates, discussed later in this book.

The rest of the complaints will be based on what the complainers will think are economic grounds. If we charge these rates, they will say in Tucson or Los Angeles or Passaic, all our manufacturing industries will move to Louisville. We will lose jobs; we will lose industrial base. It will be an economic disaster, right?

Wrong.

It will be a political disaster; it will be a chamber of commerce disaster; but it will not be an economic disaster. It will be an economic gain.

Assimilative capacity is a good, and economics must treat it like any other good. The more efficiently it is used, the higher the productivity one can get out of it, *ceteris paribus.* On that point economic and environmental values correspond precisely. Yes, firms will move to Louisville seeking lower effluent-charge rates. But that is precisely the point. If assimilative capacity is higher in Louisville, *we want them to move to Louisville.*

USER FEES

As the size of a group increases, the number of connections per capita also increases; and since government services deal primarily with connections among people, government spending per capita must also increase. This is a mathematical fact of life; it is not something that can be wished or willed away. As populations climb, governments simply get more expensive, and there is nothing the most fervent antitax activist can do about it.

As governments become more expensive, ways must be found to meet their costs. The means chosen in the United States for the past several decades has been deficit spending, but this is obviously a short-term solution that cannot continue indefinitely without severe harm to the environment. The focus, in the 1992 presidential election, on the size of the total federal deficit indicates that most voters and most politicians understand this. What neither voters nor politicians appear to have grasped yet, however, is the fact that, if deficits are not used to meet costs, revenues must be. The mathematics are inexorable: as long as the population keeps expanding, spending cannot be cut by any more than token amounts without gutting basic government services.

So revenues must be raised. What means should be used to do this? The immediate assumption is that taxes will have to be raised. But the immediate assumption is not necessarily correct.

Before 1913, when the Sixteenth Amendment to the U.S. Constitution was ratified and income taxes became constitutionally allowed, the federal government received almost all its operating income from tariffs on foreign goods. In an increasingly interconnected world economy, this practice is no longer viable, but it does remind us that means other than taxes for raising revenue are not only possible but can be made practical. Alternative funding sources could replace a substantial part of today's tax load, too. Of the various possible alternative sources available to us today, the most attractive are user fees.

Under the frontier paradigm, resources are free. One merely goes out beyond the frontier; picks something up from the limitless pool out there; adds the value created by the labor of finding the resource, extracting it from the environment, modifying it, and transporting it to market; and passes the whole thing on to the consumer, charging a price based on the added value. The system makes perfect sense, but only if you assume the existence of a frontier with free resources beyond it.

If there is no frontier, and no limitless pool of resources, then the picture changes. In a limitless world, taking a resource from the public lands affects no one; if others need the use of some of that resource, they can go out beyond the frontier and get it from the still-limitless pool that remains. In a world with limits — the real world — taking a resource from the public lands reduces or eliminates someone else's opportunity to use that resource, either for the same purpose or another. There are, in other words, opportunity costs associated with the use of resources from the public lands. Mining reduces the ability to use a piece of land for grazing; the value of the lost grazing (measurable through reduced beef and wool production) is a cost of doing the mining. Cattle compete with antelope for food, so putting cattle on a piece of rangeland reduces the number of antelope the rangeland can support; this reduction (measurable through reduced spending in local stores by hunters and wildlife viewers) is a cost of grazing. Mining and grazing on the public lands do have value, but to compute only the values while ignoring the costs is to view only half the picture. What goes around, comes around; ecosystems are loops, and affecting any part of a loop eventually affects the rest of it. The costs are real. Someone must bear them. Who should it be?

Economics provides a straightforward, logical answer. Obtaining resources from public lands is a transaction; and, as in any transaction, those who receive the benefits should also pay the costs.

Hence user fees, which may be defined as *fees collected from the users of public goods and services in order to recover the costs to the public of providing those goods and services.* To be fair, and consistent with good market practices, "costs" in this definition should include opportunity costs. The government, in other words, should be allowed to make a normal profit.

There are numerous (almost numberless) places where user fees can be employed. Water activists have long argued in favor of waterway user fees: requiring boat and barge owners to pay transit fees through locks and canals and dredged channels which are high enough to recover all the costs of building the locks and canals and dredging the channels. The fees for patenting mineral lands need to be dramatically raised in order to cover both the environmental costs of mining and the lost value to the government of passing publicly owned raw resources worth billions of dollars into private hands at what is, now, essentially a zero price. Grazing fees for public rangeland, currently running from one-half to one-fifth the fees the private neighbors of the public lands charge for the same service, need to be raised to reflect market realities. Sales of timber from the public lands, too often a money-losing situation today ("welfare for timber companies"), should be required to at least meet costs, not only on a programwide basis but on a sale-by-sale basis as well.

Environmentalists will applaud all these changes. They will

be less happy with others. Consistent application of the user-fee concept will require the collection of realistic recreation fees for the use of wilderness areas, parks, campgrounds, wildlife refuges, and public lands in general. Hikers should pay the costs of trail building, fishermen of spawning bed restoration projects, hunters and birdwatchers of habitat preservation. We may not like these fees, but if we are not going to be hypocritical we had better support them. It is no less reasonable, logical, and right to pay for the privilege of hiking to and camping in a mountain meadow than it is to pay for the privilege of running cattle in it. Hikers and campers generally do less damage than cattle, and the fee structure should reflect this. But hikers and campers should no longer expect to get along without fees altogether. That is the same free ride we have been accusing the resource-exploiters of taking.

Most states already charge for use of their state parks; most national parks also have entrance fees. These approaches are on the right track, but they suffer from two significant problems of fairness. They are haphazard: what is essentially the same experience can cost wildly different amounts depending upon where in the country you happen to be. And they are restrictive: they tend to shut out the poor. Access to nature is a basic human right, one that should not be shut off due to poverty. Some means must be found to allow everyone access to parks, *and* allow the parks to collect realistic user fees.

This seems, on its face, impossibly contradictory, but it can be done. One possible tool is the multiagency park permit.

A multiagency park permit would work like a driver's license. It would be good for a specific length of time, probably four years (the driver's license standard). The user would carry it in his pocket. A separate license, similar in function to an automotive license plate, would be attached to the car window. Food stamp recipients could receive "park stamps." Or they could be allowed to pay for park permits with food stamps. Either method would guarantee access to nature for the poor.

An approximation of this system already exists. Most states sell annual park permits; you can also buy a Golden Eagle passport from the national park service which will, for a limited time, get you into any unit of the national park system. What is missing from the scenario is the key element of *exchangeability*. Like car licenses and driver's licenses, park user's licenses should be universally accepted — an Oregon license should get a person into an Arizona or a Texas park, and vice versa. They should also be accepted by all levels of government, from city and county parks up through the great federal reserves. The access paid for should be access to *all* nature, not just to specific little bits. The fees could be pooled by the agencies involved, but this would not be necessary; the law of averages would spread purchase of the permits out far enough that every level of government would have no trouble getting its share.

A refinement of the parks license, which could both raise additional revenue and help manage park use, is the special-use surcharge. As driver's licenses now have extra-cost endorsements for such things as commercial vehicles and motorcycles, so parks could have them for a variety of uses. The license could be validated for boat use, or camping, or fishing, or hiking, with the validations costing extra fees but good for the life of the license. In this way, marinas, campgrounds, lake-stocking programs, and trail building could all receive funds from users in proportion to their actual use. The concept is already partially implemented at most state parks, which charge more for camping than for day use and usually tack on an extra fee for boat launching. There is no reason this concept could not be extended and formalized.

Consider, for example, the possibilities inherent in a radio surcharge. Some places (Fire Island, New York, is one of them) have designated "radio free" and "radio allowed" zones. Why not go further and charge a small extra fee to carry the radio in? Handled properly, that could reduce or eliminate one of the biggest irritants of public campgrounds: the jerk who plays his radio until two in the morning.

User fees are efficient and fair. They place the burden for paying for new connections among people squarely on those who are using the connections, meeting the pay-as-you-go principle. They also allow those who disapprove of a particular government activity — waterway dredging, for instance — to avoid subsidizing it. With user fees, you pay primarily for the government services you actually receive. (There are some exceptions to this: public-good resources, such as clean air, cannot by their nature be kept from non-fee-payers, so user fees will always underfund them.) And the presence of user fees, if set by the market instead of by fiat, allows market forces a voice in what government services will be offered. If government activities such as timber management are going to be marketized — and the resulting environmental gains are going to be realized — the institution of user fees is a necessary first step.

How soon is it going to happen? Don't hold your breath.

I have at hand a letter from my congressman, Bob Smith (R-Oregon) — one of those self-congratulating puff pieces that members of Congress regularly send out over their frank to the voters of their districts. This one concerns Smith's opposition to efforts to control the federal budget deficit through tax and fee increases. In our context, it is interesting primarily because of the way it lumps taxes and user fees together.

The two are alike only in that both accrue to the government. With taxes, the revenue-raising and service-dispersing functions of the government are severed from each other. Taxes may be levied on specific items, but the rates charged are unrelated to services provided. Usually the moneys raised either go directly into the general fund, or are earmarked for reducing damages caused directly or indirectly by the item taxed — health care funds from cigarette taxes, for example. There is no exchange, no money traded for goods or services

received. A tax is not a transaction, but a transaction cost —
a market friction, a reducer of efficiency. It makes other transactions more expensive. It raises the effective price of a good
or service, and thus skews market curves, but it is not itself
affected by market forces.

User fees, on the other hand, *are* market transactions. They
are payment for services or goods. A rancher paying grazing
fees on public lands is buying the right to graze; a miner
paying royalties for coal under national forest lands is paying
to buy something the government owns. If market forces are
allowed to set these fees, they *reduce,* not increase, market
distortions, and thus promote rather than hinder efficiency.
Fees that are too low have the same type of effect on the
market as do taxes that are too high: they skew it out of
shape. Politicians who support the free-market system can
logically oppose taxes. If they oppose user fees, they are shooting themselves in the foot.

So here is Bob Smith, the owner of a large cattle ranch in
eastern Oregon, lumping user fees and taxes into the same
category: "higher taxes." The Clinton administration's budget
plan includes "a variety of tax and fee increases" that add up
to "the largest tax increase in American history . . . tax and
fee proposals which would harm Oregon's economy." I do
not propose at this point to argue the tax increases with Bob,
although, as I have noted elsewhere, per capita increases in
government spending brought on by simple population growth
require per capita increases in government income to match
them, and that money is going to have to come from somewhere. I do, however, take issue with the inclusion of user fees
in the same category as taxes. Smith should know they are
different. I suspect that he does. But he also grazes cattle on
public land, and the charging of market-based user fees for
this service would cost him a fair amount of money. User fees
will not hurt Oregon's economy, but they *will* hurt Bob Smith's.
And as long as we have congressmen in that position, free
resources are going to win out over the free market every time.

SIDE PAYMENTS

As economists define them, *side payments* are payments made to balance the costs of externalities. They pass between the person (or firm) creating the external costs and the person (or firm) on whom those external costs fall. They do not directly affect the environmental impact of externalities, which under a side-payments arrangement may or may not be cleaned up. All they do is mitigate the financial costs, which are a side issue; hence the name.

Side payments can take either of two forms. Look, for example, at a hypothetical case in which a firm is dumping wood wastes into a river. The wastes are clogging the intakes of a municipal water-supply system downstream. How, using side payments, can we address this problem?

There are two possible answers. The firm can pay for the installation of screens over the water system's intakes, and send someone regularly to clean them. Or the municipality can pay the costs of treatment machinery at the plant which will keep the wood wastes out of the river to begin with. The first is a side payment from the firm to the city. The second is a side payment from the city to the firm.

Which method do we choose? From the standpoint of economics it does not matter; as economists have long suspected, and Ronald Coase and others have recently confirmed, the two alternate forms of side payments are functionally equivalent. This is because every external cost is also an external benefit. The firm that is dumping the wastes is foisting an external cost off on the water-supply system; but it is also receiving an external benefit — a cheap means of waste disposal — *from* the water-supply system. Internalizing either the benefit or the cost into the firm's books will balance the economic equations. Economics alone cannot tell us which to do. So which form of side payments do we choose?

Simple fairness would suggest that the firm should bite the bullet and pay the municipal water system's costs. But simple fairness would be wrong. In this case, the most effective use of side payments is to have the municipality pay the firm to stop polluting.

Environmentalists in general do not like this approach. It violates what economists refer to as "PPP" — the Polluter Pays Principle. Those who pollute, the argument goes, are morally bound to pay for the damage they cause. The water-supply system has not imposed the pollution on itself; it should not have to bear the costs of cleaning it up. Paying a company not to pollute is a form of bribery and is therefore immoral.

I am not going to argue this point. It strikes me as immoral, too. But we must come back again and again to the basic question: are we trying to punish the perpetrators, or are we trying to clean up the river? If we can do both, fine. If we cannot, we had better choose the cleanup. Otherwise, we are in serious danger of being a highly moral species in the middle of an absolute disaster area of an environment.

And in this case we cannot have it both ways. If the water system pays the plant to do a better job of waste disposal, the river will be cleaned up. If the plant pays the water system to install and maintain screens on its intakes, only the water in the system's pipes will be cleaned up. Bribery or not, if a clean river is our objective it is fairly obvious which direction the side payments ought to go.

One form of side payments that was in broad use in the United States until very recently was federal grants to cities for the construction of sewage plants. Begun by the passage of the Federal Water Pollution Control Act of 1948 (the direct forerunner of the Clean Water Act), the municipal sewage grant program trickled to a halt in 1990, on the grounds that cities should be paying for their own sewage treatment. But if the cities are discharging their sewage into the nation's waters, there is no reason why those who benefit from keeping the waters clean — downstream dwellers, consumers of down-stream-produced products, and recreationists from other parts of the country — should not pay at least a share of the cleanup costs. The same principle that underlies user fees holds here: those who get the goods should pay the price. Municipalities have every right to demand that taxpayers foot a fair part of the bill for keeping the taxpayers' rivers and lakes clean. In fact, the concept can be logically extended to industry. If taxpayers are receiving the benefits from the installation of treatment equipment that keeps dioxin out of a paper mill's effluent — benefits in the form of dioxin-free rivers — why shouldn't they help pay for the equipment? That is not a subsidy to the paper mill operator. That is an at-cost purchase of clean water. We would be getting exactly what we paid for.

Ecosystems are amoral. The wolf is not being "bad" when it eats a fawn, any more than the fawn is bad when it eats a blade of grass. Trees are not sinning when their shade keeps sunflowers from growing at their feet. Ecosystems are not made of chains of right and wrong, but of chains of cause and effect. If it makes the ecosystem work better, an action is "right," no matter what it may look like in our eyes.

Such must be our approach to aligning economics with the ecosystem paradigm. The obviously immoral — thievery, murder, political corruption — must be guarded against. Otherwise we must look primarily at connections, and how they will function toward the paired, indissoluble goals of a healthy economy and an intact ecosystem. PPP is morally sound, but it is ecologically corrupt. It comes from the frontier paradigm, from the world of boundaries, the model where actions can be isolated from one another and where simple acts have simple consequences. When I cut the first tree out of a forest of 10 million, I can afford to choose which tree it is on moral grounds. When I cut the last, I had damn well better have a good functional reason.

The Public Lands

ONE OF THE PRINCIPAL PROBLEMS with the labor theory of value is that it assumes a resource has no value until it is modified by human endeavor. If all of the value of an object is attributable to the labor that went into it — locating the raw resources, mining them, transporting them to the factory, modifying them into the finished object, transporting the object to market, and selling it — then no value can be attributed to the resource itself. The resource must be free.

This is an attitude that can develop only under the frontier paradigm, with its essential separation of the world into "in here" (civilization) and "out there" (wilderness). Things "in here" are owned; things "out there" belong to no one. There is an infinite supply of "out there" (the frontier is the limit of civilization; therefore, things beyond it are by definition limitless); price falls as availability increases (the rule of availability), so a good in infinite supply has a zero price, which translates into zero value in exchange. Resources beyond the frontier are free.

In Adam Smith's day, with a whole new world waiting to be exploited, this concept made a certain amount of sense — at least from a Eurocentric standpoint. Looking out from their tiny, hemmed-in portion of the Eurasian continent, Europeans saw a world thinly peopled by "natives" who were not using the resources the same way Europeans would. They translated this into a belief that the natives were not using the resources at all. Out there beyond Europe's boundary — beyond the frontier — the amount of resources available dwarfed by an immense magnitude the quantities of the same resources that could still be found in the Europeans' own little used-up part of the world. Smith can be forgiven for seeing those resources as limitless, and hence free.

We have no such excuse today. We know resources are limited; we know they have value where they are, as well as wherever we might take them. So unmodified resources are not only a potential source of value once the labor is put into them but are valuable in their own right. The market recognizes this, and bids their price up — on private lands.

But on public lands, a curious thing happens. Public lands are still viewed as remnants of the lands beyond the frontier, so the resources on them are still viewed as free. It does not matter that their real size is limited, and that we can see those limits. Attitudes developed in the entrepreneurial mind when limits were much less apparent than they are today, and filtered through the paradigm of the frontier, still hold sway.

The western boundaries of the original thirteen colonies were only vaguely defined. The borders between the colonies generally began at the sea, followed natural dividing lines (usually rivers) across the Piedmont, then shot straight westward into the unknown. Georgia included what is now Alabama and Mississippi; North Carolina claimed Tennessee; Virginia's original charter gave it Kentucky, most of what are now Ohio, Illinois, and Indiana, and all points west to the Western Ocean. Connecticut was interrupted by Pennsylvania and New York, but beyond the western edge of William Penn's grant the colony claimed a vast Western Reserve that included northern Ohio and much of Michigan and Wisconsin. No one — no colonial governor, at any rate — knew what was really out there.

After the Revolutionary War, the colonies, now states, attempted to govern those western lands. But there were difficulties. Maryland and Pennsylvania each claimed lands that Virginia thought were hers; Connecticut's Western Reserve conflicted with all three, and with New York, which also thought it owned Michigan. North Carolina and Georgia fought their own battles over the location of what is now the Tennessee-Alabama border. These territorial conflicts threatened to tear the infant Republic apart. In order to preserve the peace with one another, and the federation they had entered into, the states began, one by one, relinquishing control over their western domains to the federal government.

The process began in 1781; it was essentially complete by 1800. State lands now stopped at the crest of the Appalachians, and federal land — the public domain — began there and ran westward. And a convenient fiction had been created. The western boundaries of the states, the Appalachian Divide, formed the edge of civilization, the frontier. The public domain was beyond the frontier. It did not take long, under these circumstances, for the public domain lands to be *defined* as the lands beyond the frontier. The political accident that created a fleeting identity between these two distinctly different geographic concepts was swept into history and forgotten.

The public domain lands have shrunk dramatically over the years. Homesteads, ranches, cities, and whole states have been carved out of them. The government's attitude toward them has long since passed from getting rid of them as fast as possible to husbanding them. In 1976, with the passage of the Federal Lands Policy and Management Act (FLPMA, known fondly to public-lands activists as "flipma"), the last of these lands passed expressly from public domain into public ownership. But their boundaries have remained associated with the frontier, and the resources beyond those boundaries are still viewed too often as limitless and are still treated too often as free.

Usually the people who hold these opinions are avowed defenders of property rights and the free market. But it is not really the free market they are interested in; it is free resources. Their definition of property rights stops at the border of the public lands. They cannot, or will not, see that the holders of those lands — all of us — should enjoy rights equivalent to those of any other landholder. By demanding that resources from the public lands be free, these people are demanding that they be allowed to take these resources from their owners without paying for them. And taking things without paying for them is the definition, in most dictionaries, of theft.

For the market to operate properly, prices must be allowed to seek their own level through the forces of supply and demand. By setting the value of resources on the public lands as zero, the free-resource thieves artificially depress prices, and thus interfere seriously with the workings of the market they so passionately defend.

There is a school of thought, promoted primarily by the New Chicago School and its associates among the so-called new resource economists, which suggests that the solution to the public-lands problem is to get rid of the public lands. Sell the national forests to the timber companies; sell the Bureau of Land Management grazing lands to the ranchers, and the national parks and wilderness areas to the Sierra Club and the Wilderness Society. Once this modern version of the enclosure movement was complete, every acre of land in the country would have a private owner directly responsible for it, and this clarification of lines of responsibility would allow us to deal forthrightly with externalities through nuisance and tres- pass laws (pollution is a nuisance when it's on your own property; it is a form of trespass when it crosses the line onto someone else's land). Free-riding would no longer be possible, because there would be no shared lands; if you shirk your responsibility toward your own land, you are the one who must bear the full costs of that shirking.

The privatization idea has a certain theoretical neatness about it, a sense of tying up loose ends, which makes it highly attractive. It appeals strongly to those who believe in the sacrosanctity of private property and those (often the same "those") who would shrink government. All the great creak- ing overhead of the federal land-management agencies could be pruned away. Private-property rights would be reduced in some areas (nuisance law) but strengthened greatly in others (law of trespass). And the technique might even work. Think of the motivation that would result if you knew that, every time your factory chimney belched fumes, one of your neighbors was likely to sue you for trespass. Compare that with the motivation that results from the knowledge that you may be fined if you happen to be caught in gross violation by the EPA. Only the most obedient, government-loving soul is likely to see the second possibility leading to as clean an environment as the first.

Nevertheless, I have my doubts. There are, in fact, deep flaws in the privatization idea beneath its attractive ideological veneer. As an environmental tool, privatization will work only if private property works — that is, if ownership of property automatically leads to improved stewardship. It does not.

We can begin with the free-rider problem. How can privatization solve that? The technique might be fairly effective at dealing with common-property problems, but what about the problems of genuine public goods? When the ozone layer is damaged, who sues for trespass? You may be able to deal with rivers by privatizing access to them — riparian property owners could, by stretching the trespass idea a bit, sue the owner of a factory whose dioxin-laden effluent was destroying riverine life — but how do you deal with the open ocean? Salmon breed in the shallow waters over gravel bars near the sources of freshwater streams, but they are caught for commercial purposes in the sea. Must the fishermen, to protect their stocks, buy up the headwaters of every salmon stream in the United States and Canada?

There is also the corporate-ownership problem. Corporations exist as legal fictions for two purposes: to provide legal continuity for a firm's responsibilities when its ownership changes hands, and to limit the individual liability of the corporate owners. The first might help the environment; the second certainly does not. It is far too easy, under limited-liability law, for greedy entrepreneurs to rake in profits off the damage their corporation does to the environment and salt them away where they cannot be touched when the owners of the damaged property come looking for the responsible party. There are good, solid legal reasons — social justice reasons — for keeping the limited-liability laws in place, but they do not bode well at all for the privatization idea.

Then there are the distributional issues. Do we limit the size of private landholdings, or do we allow the wealthy to accumulate as much as they can? Both approaches create environmental difficulties. If you limit the size of landholdings, you actually create externalities. If the site upstream where pollution is dumped in a creek is owned by someone who does not also own the site downstream where the damage is caused, the damage is an external cost; if the upstream owner's holdings are large enough to include the downstream site as well, the same damage becomes an internal cost. On the other hand, if you do not limit the size of landholdings, you create the possibility, almost the certainty, of a landless class, a group of people who own no real estate but merely rent from others. As any landlord knows, renters take far poorer care of the environment than owners do; indeed, the whole purpose of privatization as an environmental tool is to give those people who might damage property a vested interest in keeping it clean. If all you have done is switch property ownership from big government to big landlords you have not really touched this problem. All you have done is shift it to parties who are less well equipped, politically and financially, to deal with it.

A more fundamental difficulty with privatization is that it ignores the effects of the fallacy of composition. It assumes that what is good for the individual is automatically good for the community. The Smithian invisible hand, in this view, always pushes the individual and the community in the same direction. Economists, of all people, should see the fallaciousness of this: it was their science that developed the idea of the fallacy of composition in the first place.

To pick just one example out of the many possible, consider a four-acre pond in a forest. If one family purchases land on the shore of that pond and builds a home there, that family is better off. If a second family builds a home on the opposite shore, the action improves the lot of the second family, but it decreases the well-being of the first, whose members no longer have the solitude they once enjoyed and can no longer look at the unbroken forest on the far shore of "their" pond. Is the community of two families better off? Probably; but it is less than twice as well off as the first family was alone. The fallacy has begun to show itself.

By the time you get to the twentieth family, or the two hundredth, the situation has become ludicrous. The new family has made itself marginally better off (it now has waterfront access, where before it had none), but the community as a whole is worse off — more crowded, less attractive, and with most of the amenities that brought the first family to the pond having long since disappeared. The only way, under privatization, to avoid this result is to limit the number of people who can purchase property at the pond. Besides being totally anathema to most privatization theorists (these are the people who fight land-use controls, not those who put them in place), such limitations take away the public's right of access to the pond. If these limitations are universally in place, they take away the public's right of access to all ponds. This makes the pond owners better off, but it makes the community worse off. The fallacy of composition cannot be avoided. If you still think it can, drive through Incline Village sometime, on the Nevada side of Lake Tahoe, and try to get down to the lake.

But the greatest problem with privatization is more fundamental, even, than ignoring the fallacy of composition. The greatest problem has to do with a very deep misunderstanding on the part of privatization theorists of just exactly what *private property* really means.

Economists recognize two different types of property. (Lawyers recognize the same two types.) One type, *personal property*, consists of items that the owner can carry around, such as books, stereo equipment, food, appliances, a boat, the family car. (If it takes a stretch to imagine toting a boat or a car on your back, remember that the term *carry* originally meant simply "to transport.") The second type, *real property*, is that which is fixed in place, such as a lot, a home or commercial building, or a concrete driveway. The term *real* suggests opposition to "fake," as if land and buildings were somehow more *actual* than, say, clothing or diamonds, but this is probably an accident of homonyms; though most dictionaries bring the etymology of *real estate* down from the Late Latin *realis*, meaning actual, it is more likely that it derives from the Old French *reial*, meaning royal. In the European tradition, all private land — all real estate — was once royal estate, held by others only through the pleasure of the king.

The difference in portability between real property and personal property makes a profound difference in their economic functions. Personal property can literally change hands: you can hand the keys of your car to its new owner in Newark, and he can take it to San Francisco, removing it entirely from its former economic milieu. Real property cannot do that. If you hand the keys of a house to a new owner in Newark, the house is going to stay in Newark. No matter who owns it, its economic impacts will always remain attached to the same place. The owner may be in San Francisco, but it is Newark that will have to deal with the fire hazards from uncut, dried-out grass, and the costs of protecting the home from break-ins, and the pollution that results when the sewer line cracks open and overflows into the street.

A couple of things should be apparent from this discussion. One is that *absentee ownership creates externalities*; if the owner of a piece of property lives far enough away from it, none of the "bads" created by that property will affect him or her. Absentee owners do not judge value the same way those do who live on or near a piece of property. Their opportunity cost curves are skewed by their absence. The opportunity to enjoy the unspoiled property is suppressed; the opportunity to use the money it could provide is enhanced. Why should they preserve their ability to walk through the woods when the woods are three states away and they never get to walk in them anyway? When the opportunity is not there, no opportunity cost can be attached to it.

The property's neighbors, on the other hand, even though they do not own the property, do have opportunity costs connected with it. They are the ones who have the opportunities to walk through the woods, and to enjoy the wildlife and clean water they provide, and to benefit from the stability the tree roots bring to the soils. It is they who will suffer most of the lost opportunities from property damage, while the absentee owner gains most of the opportunities obtainable from the development that causes the damage. Looked at this way, it is easy to see that absentee ownership of property is a major source of externalities. In fact, it is almost the only source.

The second, and closely related, thing is this: despite its name, *real property is actually less real than personal property.* It cannot be owned as completely; there is always an element of the commons connected with it. Economists deal with this by stating that people do not own a piece of land: what they own is a bundle of rights attached to that land. This bundle is not absolute, but is defined by society. The definition may change at any time.

In Issaquah, Washington, there is at least one developer who now knows about this. Once a separate community, Issaquah is now a rapidly growing suburb on the eastern fringe of the Seattle-Tacoma megalopolis. The north end of town is flat and open, spread out on the plains east and south of Lake Sammamish. The south end, the original town, is confined by geography into a narrow valley between Tiger Mountain on the east and Squak Mountain on the west.

It was in this southern portion of town that the developer owned property, or at least held title to it. The land in question consisted of eighty-one acres of steep hillside and climbing wetlands sprawling up Squak Mountain from the banks of Issaquah Creek, the valley's cold, clear, still trout-filled stream. On that land the developer proposed to place 163 dwellings. The local planning commission turned him down. He appealed to the city council. The council, facing a solid phalanx of neighbors dead-set against development, turned him down as well.

"He kept saying he had a *right* to develop that land," says Larry James, my brother-in-law and one of the leaders of the neighborhood opposition, "and we kept saying, 'What about our rights?'" — such as the right to enjoy the neighborhood as they had built it, with its quiet streets (the development would have added approximately a thousand trips a day) and its access to woods and wetlands (the development would have removed those entirely). "The planning staff kept saying those wetlands had no social value," Larry says, grinning. "I had to tell them I thought my kids had turned out pretty well. They were raised playing out there, learning the names of the plants and animals. It was a lot better for them than doing drugs."

Privatization is a frontier idea: it can work properly only under the assumption that there is a limitless amount of land to be privatized. As soon as you recognize the existence of limits the idea begins to lose its viability, and it disappears completely when you recognize the existence of both limits (the absolute amount of woods and wetlands; the absolute number of homesites that can exist around that four-acre pond) and connections (the effects each developer, or each homeowner around a pond, has on the rest of us). If we are going to be true to the ecosystem paradigm, we are going to have to do much better than that.

One possible alternative to privatizing our public lands which has been suggested by a few maverick resource economists — most notably Randal O'Toole of Cascade Holistic Economic

Consultants (CHEC) in Eugene, Oregon — is what O'Toole
refers to as *marketizing*. The idea is strikingly simple. Instead
of taking away the federal agencies' land base, O'Toole says,
we should just take away their budgets. Zero them out of the
federal appropriations process; make them compete for funds
in the marketplace with the rest of us slobs.

At first glance, the idea looks preposterous. If the Forest
Service has to sell timber to make money, won't it sell all the
timber? No, says O'Toole, it won't; it will, in fact, sell considerably less than it does now. Many, perhaps most, Forest
Service timber sales currently lose money. If the Forest Service
had to fund itself out of its own receipts, it couldn't afford to
do that. It would sell only that timber on which it could make
a profit. Everything else, including most of the highly scenic
but largely unproductive low site-class lands conservationists
wish to protect, would remain uncut.

In O'Toole's view (and in the view of many others who have
studied the problem) the federal agencies are driven economically by a desire not to maximize profits, but to maximize
their budgets. They are in what amounts to competition for
market share; but their market is the federal budget, their
competitors are the other agencies, and their consumers (the
purchasers of their services) are the congressional appropriations committees. Whatever they can persuade Congress to
fund increases their market share. Whether or not a budget
item is cost-effective (and therefore profitable) doesn't affect
this scenario in the least; it is driven not by the net size of the
transaction but by its gross size. The larger the better, ipso
facto and the devil take the hindmost.

Zeroing out the agencies' appropriations would eliminate
this. To meet their payrolls and stay in business the agencies
would have to look at the net, just like any other firm. Under
those circumstances, a lot of hallowed but fiscally questionable practices — building roads with public funds for private
timber haulers, for example, or selling timber below cost in

order to keep open a tottering mill that competition should have closed long ago — would quietly fade away.

A number of ramifications twine out from this idea, not all of them things environmentalists would like to see. Regions where timber could be sold at a profit would bear the brunt of all future harvest efforts, concentrating the effects in smaller areas (an overall gain) but impacting those areas more heavily than before (a local loss). Management areas under an agency's control which could not be marketized would receive less funding than they do today; and we could expect, as a corollary to this, that as many areas of the agency's operations as possible would be marketized. That means seeing fees imposed for hiking, fishing, hunting, horseback riding, and even scenic viewing. It means entry into parks, wilderness areas, and other reserves restricted to paying ticketholders. It means selling firewood off the public lands at market value, not issuing inexpensive permits that essentially sell one hundred dollars' worth or more of the public's resources to private individuals for five dollars or less. All these approaches raise important issues of distribution and access. Some are dealt with elsewhere in this book; others probably cannot be dealt with at all, through any means, and we would simply have to live with them.

Overall, however, I believe that marketization is about as sound an idea for resource-agency reform as we are likely to get. The strong marketplace connection between underpricing and overuse has been too firmly established by economists to ignore. If we are serious about curbing abuses, that is the place we need to start. And if this means an alteration in our current free recreational access pattern to public lands, then this is a change we are going to have to live with. Free access, after all, is a frontier idea. If we are going to evoke the ecosystem paradigm, we cannot stop with the other fellow's frontier delusions; we will have to rid ourselves of our own as well.

How Much Is a River Worth?

THERE IS AN UNSPOKEN DIFFICULTY with all the pay-as-you-go schemes discussed in the preceding chapter. They fail to quantify anything: they suggest means of collecting money for environmental damage, but they offer no means of determining how much to charge. It is easy to demand payment for the damage done to a river. It is far more difficult to determine with any precision how much the river is worth.

In order to internalize costs, we must first have some idea what they are. Hence the supreme importance that has come to be attached, by economists and environmental reformers alike, to the practice known to its adherents as "full-cost accounting": a change in the accounting practices used by firms in order to cause the full costs of each product or service they sell — environmental and social costs, as well as those of labor, transportation, and raw materials — to be reflected in the price charged to the consumer.

There are a number of obvious advantages to such a reform. It uses a familiar tool, price, to inform consumers of the consequences of their actions, and allows them to make choices based on that information. It encourages the purchase of environmentally friendly products, because firms that are able to lower their environmental costs will be lowering their overhead as well, and will be able to sell their goods for lower prices. It makes certain that funds are available to cover environmental damages caused by the production of consumer goods, and it collects those funds from the consumers themselves, thus following the Polluter Pays Principle to its logical conclusion. And it avoids most of the pitfalls inherent in green taxes; the increased cost to the consumer is highly product-specific rather than blanketed over broad product categories, the costs are set by market processes rather than by fiat, there is little regulatory overhead, and there is no government revenue-raising function. This last item is more important than it may sound. No revenue-raising function means no revenue, hence no incentive for regulating agencies to use the increased costs to consumers as a budget-padding tool rather than as a means of correcting flaws in the pricing system.

On the other hand, there are also some significant difficulties with full-cost accounting — beginning with the accounting problem itself. How do you figure the costs incurred in reducing spotted owl habitat to produce lumber, or destroying wetlands to build shopping centers, or releasing small amounts of dioxins and furans from an incinerator stack? It is relatively easy to price the depletion of fund resources such as ores or fossil fuels, but how do you price the depletion of flow resources? How far into the future do you look, and what assumptions do you make concerning the influence of natural factors and of other industrial uses, not under your control, on the resource's rate of flow? How, in short, do you put a price on change? The scope of the problem begins to become apparent when you realize that virtually all environmental damage is, in one way or another, actually damage to a flow resource. It is not usually the present we are concerned about, but the indeterminate future — the future that will be affected by the reduction or elimination of the flow of some good (wilderness, clean water, wildlife) whose continuity we have come both to value and to take for granted.

There are also human barriers, perhaps insurmountable, to implementation. Two of these are particularly important. First, prices on most consumer goods would rise dramatically, bringing screams of anguish from consumer-advocate groups who might not like to be reminded that industry was merely ending the consumer's free ride on the backs of future generations. And second, companies less socially responsible than others would face an almost irresistible temptation to leave some of the costs out of their "full-cost" accounting, thereby lowering their prices and obtaining a competitive edge over their more responsible brethren. A little bit of that and we could be right back where we started. For the process to stand any chance of success, everyone — every industry, every industrial supplier, and every consumer — would have to be completely on board. If you think that is going to be easy, look again at the chapters of this book on the free-rider problem and the prisoner's dilemma. We are facing here some very fundamental paradoxes in the way the world works.

And suppose the accounting difficulties can be overcome and the implementation barriers removed, and we proceed. How do we actually pay the external costs? I am not talking about the difficulties in raising funds, but the direct mechanical and logistic problems of the transfer. Suppose the price of lumber were raised to reflect the true cost of all its externalities. The consumer pays that increased price — all of it — at his local lumberyard. How do the funds get from there to the places where the costs are incurred? The lumberyard owner pays the mill, which pays the millworkers, and the loggers, and the owners of the timber it cuts. Who pays the fisherman whose catch is reduced, or the rural homeowner whose spring stops flowing, or the hikers or mountain bikers or skiers or horse riders or motorcyclists who used to use the trails through what is now a clear-cut? Who pays the spotted owl? How do we guarantee that the price, once paid, does not simply pad some middleman's coffers, somewhere along the way?

Nevertheless, and despite all the difficulties, the process deserves a try. Two tools that may help are life-cycle analysis and Leontief analysis.

Life-cycle analysis (also known as cradle-to-grave accounting) is an attempt to trace all costs associated with a product through its entire existence, from the costs of prospecting for the minerals and other materials incorporated in it, right down through the costs of manufacture, sales, and use, to the product's eventual disposal as waste. Internal and external costs are treated alike in this process; any cost that cannot be measured is estimated as closely as possible. The result is a column of labeled costs that can be grouped and summed, allowing both proper pricing of the good at each stage of its life cycle and proper distribution of the funds that accrue from sales at that price. It also has the advantage of pinpointing for us what we do not know — that is, of highlighting the exact locations and limitations of those areas for which adequate cost-accounting methods do not yet exist — and thus pointing precisely to areas in need of further research. Its principal disadvantage is its vertical nature. Focused tightly on a single product and its external ramifications, this approach does not deal well with the effects of products on one another. There are hooks in the process for estimating outside influences on the product, and product influences on the outside, but nothing for the symbiotic effects the two may have on each other. The fallacy of composition is thus rarely addressed, or even recognized.

Which is where Leontief analysis comes in. Developed in the mid-1960s by Harvard economist and Nobel laureate Wassily Leontief (who called it, much more modestly, input-output analysis), Leontief analysis consists essentially of a horizontal broadening of life-cycle analysis to include the effects of all parts of the system on one another. The means of doing this are simple and elegant. The analyst prepares a table much like a highway-mileage chart, giving each factor associated with the production of a good (internal, external — it doesn't matter) both a column (labeled across the top) and a row (labeled down the side). The columns are inputs; the rows, outputs. The number at the intersection of each column and row represents the total amount of the input factor listed at the top of the column which is needed by the factor listed at the left end of the row to achieve the output summed at the right end of the row.

Creating an input-output table is a two-stage process. First, one must determine what Leontief refers to as the *technical input coefficients* of the various inputs: these are defined as the costs, in units of input, of each unit of output in an output row. These coefficients are then multiplied by the total amount of output to get the total input in each column.

An example may help clarify things. Here is one with figures taken from Leontief's own work.

Assume an economy composed entirely of wheat farmers and weavers. In order to produce a bushel of wheat, each farmer requires .25 bushels of wheat (for his own food) and .14 yards of cloth (for clothing, wheat-carrying bags, and so forth). Weavers also have needs; to produce a yard of cloth, they need .12 yards of cloth (for their own clothing) and .4 bushels of wheat (breakfast, lunch, and dinner — boring, nutritionally unsound, but hey, it's only an example). From these figures, the technical input coefficients, we can fill in a preliminary matrix. It looks like this:

Technical Input Coefficients

From	Into	
	Wheat	Cloth
Wheat	0.25	0.40
Cloth	0.14	0.12

Assume an annual production of 100 bushels of wheat and 50 yards of cloth. From this you can figure the inputs needed. They are:

Production

From	Into			Outputs
	Wheat	Cloth		
Wheat (bu)	25	20	(55)	100 bu
Cloth (yd)	14	6	(30)	50 yd

Note the discrepancies (third column). The output of wheat is 55 bushels more than is needed; the output of cloth is 30 yards more than is required. Those extra amounts represent production surpluses, which may be either sold or used directly as a means to make the producers' lives more luxurious.

Surpluses aren't automatic in any economy, of course. Look what happens if the technical input coefficient for cloth into wheat goes up from 0.14 to 0.5 (farmers suddenly require half a yard of cloth per bushel of wheat, instead of roughly one-seventh):

Production

	Into			
From	Wheat	Cloth		Outputs
Wheat (bu)	25	20	(55)	100 bu
Cloth (yd)	50	6	(−6)	50 yd

This economy is producing a deficit of 6 yards of cloth. One of the beauties of Leontief analysis is that it makes the causes of such deficits easy to pinpoint; in this case, it is obviously the increase in the cloth demands of farmers.

Real economies are, of course, much more complex than this, with hundreds of columns and rows. Here we will add just one more:

Technical Input Coefficients

	Into		
From	Wheat	Cloth	Pollution
Wheat (bu)	0.25	0.40	0
Cloth (yd)	0.14	0.12	0
Pollution (gm)	0.50	0.20	0

The production of each bushel of wheat results in the unavoidable production of half a gram of pollution; this is equivalent to saying that wheat "requires" half a gram of pollution per unit as a production input, giving it a technical input coefficient, for pollution, of 0.5. The same reasoning holds for cloth, which produces 1/5 gram of unavoidable pollution per yard of output. Pollution itself is a good (actually, a "bad") whose production we are trying to hold to zero, so its technical input coefficients are all zeros as well (zero unit production divided by any amount of input per unit results in a zero coefficient).

The technical input coefficient table allows us to calculate a production table:

Production

From	Into				Outputs
	Wheat	Cloth	Pollution		
Wheat (bu)	25	20	0	(55)	100 bu
Cloth (yd)	14	6	0	(30)	50 yd
Pollution (gm)	50	10	0	(60)	60 gm

The figure at the right end of the pollution row tells us how much pollution (which it doesn't want) the economy is producing at these particular commodity production levels (which, we assume, it *does* want): it is 60 grams, 50 from wheat farms and 10 from cloth mills. If the economy is seriously interested in reducing pollution, the table tells us that it should be concentrating its efforts on the agricultural sector.

You can do a lot with Leontief analysis. You can, for instance, replace all those unit-production figures with dollar costs; it is merely a matter of knowing the cost per unit of the various inputs. You can solve for any cell in the matrix in terms of the others; you can change a single cell or group of cells and watch what happens to the rest of them. The process is ideally suited to spreadsheet analysis on a computer. It takes a while to set up the matrix for a complex economy on a spreadsheet, but once you have done that initial work you can easily enter any assumed changes and watch their effects ripple through the economy like the waves of the sea.

The best thing about this form of analysis, though, is the overall picture it gives of the internal workings of an economy — an overall picture in which the differences between external and internal costs fade rapidly away. Every row and every column in the matrix is treated in precisely the same manner. The cost of blowing sulfur dioxide into the air from the stack of a coal-burning power plant looks exactly the same, in the Leontief matrix, as the cost of purchasing the coal in the first place. There is no factor that cannot be entered, and no factor that, once entered, cannot be looked at objectively. And although units must be consistent along each row, there is no requirement that all the rows use the same units (look again at those production matrices); hence, there can be no excuse for leaving out externalities on the grounds that their dollar costs cannot be estimated.

Leontief analysis is currently a drastically underused tool. If we are serious about getting externalities under control, every corporate accountant in the country should be doing the company's books following this system, and all the members of every board of directors should be fluent enough in it to understand them.

Will this happen? It is already beginning to. Consider this quote from a recent magazine article:

> Air, water, and land are not the "free goods" our society once believed. They must be redefined as assets, so that they can be efficiently and appropriately allocated — ideally, we should be living off their interest, rather than depleting the assets themselves. . . . Although it is fairly simple to place a dollar value on mineral and petroleum resources, it is significantly more difficult to place a value on a wetland, a forest, or a species. Nevertheless, a true picture of a nation's wealth should ultimately include an accounting of all its resources. Similarly,

industry must take into account both the resources it uses in production and the environmental impact of its products and services.

Relatively calm and straightforward stuff for an environmental magazine. But this was not an environmental magazine: it was *Chemical and Engineering News.* And the writer was not an environmental reformer. He was Frank P. Popoff, chairman of the Chemical Manufacturers' Association, and president, chairman, and CEO of one of the world's erstwhile largest polluters — the Dow Chemical Corporation.

Time for Good Behavior

TRAVELING THROUGH VERMONT in the summer of 1992, my wife and I came up against what we have since referred to as the Potty Problem. Along Vermont freeways that summer, what are delicately called "sanitary facilities" in all the rest areas were closed and locked from five o'clock in the afternoon until ten o'clock the next morning. Vermont officials told the press they were saving money this way. What they were actually doing was creating a massive, expensive, and totally unnecessary environmental problem. One does not stop needing to pee when the hands of the clock roll around to 5:00 P.M. If one is not provided with the proper facilities, one will make do, or in this case doo-doo, with what is at hand.

Hence the execrable condition of Vermont's rest areas. They were messy, unsanitary, and unsightly, and they produced environmental pollution of a particularly virulent variety (human wastes are far more likely to be biologically harmful to humans than are most other forms of pollution: they are primarily made up of bacteria, many of which are still living and most of which are especially adapted to reside in human hosts). And the whole thing could easily have been taken care of simply by leaving the bathrooms open, logic that evidently escaped the Vermont Highway Department. According to the Burlington *Free Press*, when the policy first went into effect porta-potties were placed on the sites for off-hours use, only to be removed almost immediately on the grounds that they were "unwelcoming." Used toilet paper blowing across the parking lots was apparently preferable.

Vermont's potty problem — and similar potty problems I have noticed over the years in many other states, including (but not limited to) Massachusetts, Texas, North Dakota, and New Jersey — stems partially from an incorrect assumption about what we can "afford" to do. The proverb says "A stitch in time saves nine," but most of us would still prefer to take our chances with the nine. Buckminster Fuller pointed out the absurdity of this position a number of years ago:

> [Humankind] says time and again, "We can't afford it." For instance, we are saying now that we can't afford to do anything about pollution, but after the costs of not doing something about pollution have multiplied manifold beyond what it would cost us to correct it now, we will spend manifold what it would cost us now to correct it. . . . We have no difficulty discovering troubles but we fail to demonstrate intelligent search for the means of coping with the troubles. This is primarily due to our misconditioned reflex which says that "we can't" afford to do the intelligent things.

Fuller is correct, but the problem actually goes beyond this. The truth is that we fundamentally distrust other people's motives, a failing that we are going to have to conquer to make any progress in solving the social and environmental ills that afflict us. We think it is necessary to order people to do right. Worse: we think it is sufficient. Actually, it is neither. The best way to get people to do right is to make it easier and more comfortable to do right than to do wrong. Given the chance, most people will gladly opt for behavior that does no harm to others. The key is to give them that chance. In many cases, what look like serious, intractable environmental or other social problems can easily be solved by simply setting out the tools and getting out of the way.

One well-tended litter barrel will do a far better job of keeping trash off the roadsides than any number of DO NOT LITTER signs can. The harder you make it for people to pay to use parks, the more people you will get who use parks without paying. When water pollution rules become so arcane and complex that few people can understand them, we should stop being surprised that few firms can meet them.

Not all our problems are that tractable, but even many of the seemingly insoluble ones will profit from the enabling-right-behavior approach. Traffic control in our historic cities is a case in point.

The day I visited New Orleans in September 1992, the Saints were playing the Browns in the Superdome, and when the game let up, midway through the afternoon, the ancient, narrow thoroughfare of Decatur Street was crammed with the cars of football fans going home. Bumper to bumper, the miasma of their exhausts floating around the old buildings with their delicate wrought-iron traceries, the cars fought for supremacy with the tourists and the street mimes and the roaring current of raw jazz pouring from the bars and cafés of the French Quarter. Most of the time, the cars seemed to be winning.

A few weeks before I had been in Provincetown, Massachusetts, out on the tip of Cape Cod. There was no professional football game there, but there might as well have been. Bumper to bumper, cars oozed through narrow, curving streets designed for carriages and pedestrians, lined with two-story frame buildings whose old, simple style contrasted jarringly with the traffic flowing past them. Both historically and environmentally speaking, automobiles in downtown Provincetown, as in the French Quarter, are an abomination.

And practically speaking, as well. One does not tour Provincetown or the French Quarter by car; one tours such areas on foot, or by bicycle, or in a horse-drawn carriage. The cars are a distraction from the current business of the towns, which is history. Why are they there?

The answer is inertia, and politics. Inertia, because it is easier to continue with the status quo than it is to change; politics, because the car has become associated with individual freedoms, and to banish it from a city seems somehow un-American. What about handicapped access? scream the automobile defenders. What about those who can't walk? What about those who don't want to? You can't cater just to the healthy, wealthy few.

Well, what about them? Actually, everybody walks a lot in these towns anyway, or gets around in a wheelchair. You can't expect to get a parking place in front of the store you are going to. People know that. They drive through the town to reach a parking lot, from which they walk back past everyone else doing precisely the same thing. Why not simply move the parking lots to the edge of town?

No new law should be necessary, only behavior enablement. Raise the parking fees downtown: triple them, quadruple them. Provide much cheaper (perhaps even free) parking on the outskirts of town. Put inexpensive (or free) shuttle buses to work between the lots and the town center, or provide cheap bicycle rentals. Make sure incoming tourists know of these conditions. If traffic downtown doesn't drop off dramatically, generations of economists from Adam Smith on down have been wasting their time.

Shopping malls provide us with a similar set of opportunities for using enablement in place of command-and-control to solve environmental problems. Shopping malls are looked upon by most environmentalists as an unmitigated disaster, and in many cases they are; yet with only a few changes in emphasis their potential for environmental good could be profound.

Consider the good points they already possess. They get people out of their cars and walking — one does not drive from shop to shop in a mall. They allow numerous businesses to share a common, integrated climate-control system, providing energy savings both through coordination of operation and through the fact that since the stores share a common space each one has fewer external walls than it would standing alone, and there is thus less chance to lose or gain heat in relation to the environment. The presence of so many stores of so many different varieties improves consumer choice, which dilutes and reduces monopoly power — and, as Gifford Pinchot pointed out long ago, monopolies are the natural enemies of conservation.

Malls are people-friendly. The stores and concourses are attractively designed and kept clean. They are often provided with greenery and falling water. They almost always contain numerous benches, places to stop and get out of the flow for a while. In this regard they are far better than our highway systems. They provide not only for the starting point and the destination, but also for the journey. Our freeway engineers could learn much from them.

And malls reduce stop-and-go driving. Those massive parking lots, with all their environmental drawbacks, have this advantage: once placed in the lot, a car is likely to stay there until its driver is ready to go home. Starting is the dirtiest part of a car's operation (every time an automobile engine is started, it produces as many pollutants as roughly six minutes of idling, and idling is the second-dirtiest part); consequently, the reduction in air pollutants can be immense, even when you take into account the extra distance most people have driven to get there.

Now take this scenario one step further. The same centralization that allows the mall to reduce stop-and-go driving should allow it to get rid of driving altogether. Clustering many different stores at one point of access creates ideal conditions for mass transit. All that is needed is a terminal, an efficient transit route from the neighborhoods that shop the mall most frequently, and a little incentive for people to leave their cars at home. Simply reducing the size of the parking lot could do that. If mass transit is a preferable way to get there (less costly in emotional terms), it will be used.

Developers have a number of rules of thumb they use in determining whether to proceed with a development plan. There is, for example, the "point four FAR rule": the observation that the ratio of floor area to lot size (the floor-to-area ratio, or FAR) should be in the neighborhood of 0.4 in order for a retail or office development to make money (this assumes that the remainder of the lot can be covered by parking). There is the "four per thousand rule": 1,000 square feet of office space can comfortably support four workers. There is the "600 foot rule": it is only with great difficulty that one can persuade a modern, car-owning American to leave his or her car behind for a travel distance of more than 600 feet. These rules (and others like them) determine a development's potential profitability. All other conditions, including the regulatory complex, are strictly secondary.

It is easy enough to denigrate this process, but we are going to have to face the fact that denigrating it has really done us very little good. We have postponed developments; we have reshaped them; we have moved them; but our track record at preventing them is very poor. Development will happen, and it will happen primarily at the pace of and on the terms of the developer.

But this does not mean that environmentalists must despair. It means, rather, that we have been fighting the battles with the wrong weapons. We have used laws, regulations, moral suasion. The developers have used rules of thumb for profitability. That is why we may yet get an office complex with a 518-car parking lot on the shore of Thoreau's Walden Pond. If we really want to succeed in controlling development, what we need to do is inject a few of our own rules of thumb into the developers' set.

These will, of necessity, be economic rules. We are talking here about influencing profitability decisions. Forget living lightly on the earth, or establishing the rights of trees, or creating sustainable development. These are all extraordinarily worthwhile goals, which is why nothing will ever come of them. The people we need to reach to be effective are not particularly interested in worthwhile goals. For them, costs and benefits will always ultimately be the deciding factors.

And they have to be rules of thumb. At the corporate process level — the controlling-the-pollutants level — you can get somewhere with Leontief analysis and similar tools. Developers are not influenced by anything that cannot be reduced to a mantra. They are practical, even flexible people, but they are not into deep analysis. They want results.

A profession that refers to pieces of natural, undeveloped land as "blanks" is not ever going to be strongly influenced by the niceties of ecology. We are going to have to learn to speak to them in terms they can understand.

I offer the following as a starting set of rules. In most cases I have made no attempt to quantify them; experience will have to do that. They offer not specific measures but directions in which to take the measurements. The actual measuring task is probably best done by the developers themselves.

Rule Number 1: The value of a development is inversely proportional to the amount of land in the vicinity that has been paved over. Pavement is ugly; pavement also increases the runoff rate of precipitation, and thereby reduces land capability. And pavement encourages automobile traffic, which detracts from housing value. Everyone wants to live on a quiet street; it is a fundamental part of the American dream. If we are going to achieve this goal, we must plan our developments for people, not automobiles. Pavement should be reduced to as close to zero as possible. If this can be done without reducing access to the community, value (and selling price) will go up.

Rule Number 2: Good walkways make good neighbors. Another major aspect of the American dream is the ability to take an after-dinner stroll through your neighborhood in comfort and safety, watching the kids playing on the lawns in the evening light, maybe stopping in for an ice cream cone at the neighborhood store. To do this, people need places to walk. Developments need to be planned with walkers in mind. Sidewalks need to thread between houses, converging on nodes, such as parks and stores, where people want to go. People want to get out of their cars, but our current neighborhoods won't let them. Planning properly can overcome this.

Rule Number 3: Thirty families equal one node. This is the only rule in this set that is easily quantifiable. The quantification comes from one of the developers' own current rules: the maximum distance that people want to walk is 600 feet. This means that no house should be more than 600 feet from a node of some kind — a park, a shopping center, a transit stop. A circle with a 600-foot radius has an area of a bit over 1.3 million square feet. Divided into 27,000-square-foot lots, that is forty-one lots. Allow a fourth of those for streets, walkways, and open space. Thirty homes — thirty families — can be comfortably provided for in that 600-foot circle.

Rule Number 4: The value of land for development is directly related to the ease of development of the land. The reverse also holds: the value of land in its undeveloped state is inversely proportional to the ease of development. It is a fortunate coincidence (well, probably not a coincidence, but fortunate nonetheless) that the land that is most difficult and expensive to develop — wetlands, steep hillsides, barrier islands, shorelines and so forth — is also the most valuable from an environmental standpoint. Developers fail to see this because they don't credit undeveloped land with any value-in-use at all; but once we get over that hurdle, the rule should be quantifiable. It is difficult and expensive to drain a wetland in order to build a mall or a housing development. If we set the wetland's value properly, the opportunity costs involved in its loss, added to the actual costs of draining and building, should drive cost-benefit ratios deep into a negative hole and send the developer elsewhere.

Rule Number 5: Plan the garden first. This rule actually subsumes, and therefore supersedes, all others. First suggested by the iconoclastic California architect Christopher Alexander, whose 1977 book *A Pattern Language* (Oxford University Press) should be required reading for all developers, rule number 5 has the practical function of making the site more important than the building. This is the order things should always take but seldom do. It does not preclude buildings; it merely requires them to be fitted to the land. It cares about connections; it is the ecosystem paradigm triumphant.

If we site structures to fit the environment, there are far fewer reasons not to build them. When human living patterns disrupt the forest no more than deer or trees do, keeping them out of the forest stops being necessary. The problem with development is not the buildings. It is the frontier paradigm they are built under.

Not Regulation-Free, but Barrier-Free

Economic Justice,
Environmental Justice

SOONER OR LATER in most discussions about environmental problems someone is likely to bring up the vast imbalance in resource use between the United States and the rest of the planet. With less than one-twentieth of the world's population, we manage to use more than one-third of its annual energy production, roughly one-sixth of its steel, 30 percent of its aluminum, 20 percent of its copper, and more than half of its molybdenum. Agricultural consumption is similarly biased: we use more than one-sixth of the world's meat supply and nearly one-tenth of its grain. Our per capita consumption of water is at least eight times that of the less fortunate half of the human race. Such profligacy, most environmentalists will tell you, is both wasteful and unfair. Wasteful because, if most of the world is doing without much of this, we clearly could do without a lot of it ourselves; unfair because, in a world full of grinding poverty, we should share our wealth more equitably with those in need.

I don't wish to disagree with either of these points. That we should waste less and share more is, I think, beyond argument. But I do wish at least to suggest the presence of a vast minefield of potential hazards awaiting those who attempt to do both these things together. Few issues show this more clearly than the demands, by large numbers of environmentalists and social activists, for "fair prices": ceilings above which prices may not rise (to keep goods affordable) and floors through which they may not drop (to keep income adequate).

Fair prices and fair distribution are often viewed as identical issues, but they are actually radically different. To speak of "fair prices" is to throw away centuries of economic theory and practical experience, to ignore the natural laws of supply and demand, and to abandon cost and benefit analysis altogether. Fair price *(justum pretium)* is a medieval idea, born of a cozy world of theological determinism, where earthquakes were punishments for disobedience to God and the lilies of the field were placed there primarily to be used for moral lessons. In such a world, God could assign a fair price to a good, and humans could think they had found it. That God might set a dynamic rather than a fixed price — a price dependent upon the smooth functioning of the rest of His creation — was both heretical and distinctly unnerving.

Fair distribution may indeed be a moral imperative, but fair prices will not help achieve it. When the price of a good is kept "fair" by fiat, it is kept either above or below market value, meaning that the good is either oversupplied or undersupplied. If it is oversupplied, who gets the surplus? Those who can afford it. If it is undersupplied, who gets what little is available? Those who can afford it. And the rich can always afford more than the poor. "Fair" prices thus turn out to be fair primarily to the rich. The welfare is being directed to the wrong recipients. To achieve fair distribution — "right sharing of the world's resources," to use the current liberal catchphrase — we are going to have to use a different set of tools.

An honest examination of the question of distributional equity challenges us, liberals and conservatives alike, to face some of the comfortable biases we use to shape our thinking about the world. Begin with the word *equity.* What does that mean? Does it mean equality? It does not; dividing the world up into precisely equal shares makes no allowances for differing circumstances. Kidney patients need dialysis machines; this does not mean that every home must be equipped with one. Sybarites wallow in big-screen TVs, leather upholstery, and 200-watt stereo amplifiers; ascetics are embarrassed by them.

Fairness — equitability — requires us to allow for these differences. Procrustes was not fair to the travelers he forced to fit his bed.

A more formal analysis of this problem can be made using the theory of diminishing marginal returns. The theory states that each additional unit of a good is worth less to the recipient than the preceding units were, and that therefore, since value is set at the margin, adding a unit reduces the value of all units. It does not say how steep that value reduction is, nor insist that the slope of the marginal return line be the same for all recipients. In fact, the steepness of the value-diminishment function varies strikingly from individual to individual; one can add the individual functions (to get a function for the society as a whole), but one cannot really compare them. The value of an additional dollar to a stack of dollars may mean the world to a miser and absolutely nothing to a monk. Neither is necessarily wrong. Can they be compared to each other? William Stanley Jevons, the father of marginal returns theory, didn't think so. "I see no means," he wrote in 1871, "by which such comparisons can be made."

We are thus led, by way of Procrustean analogies and nineteenth-century economic philosophy, to an inescapable conclusion. Equitable sharing of resources does not mean equal shares; equitable sharing means meeting legitimate needs. Surplus does not need to be shared equally, and probably cannot be (that would require either a uniform set of wants — a chimerical construct — or some sort of probably equally chimerical means of allocating resources so that the same percentage of everyone's radically different wants could be met). And nonsurplus doesn't need to be shared equally either, since different people have different needs (remember the dialysis machine). Equitable sharing requires finding some means of determining legitimate needs, filling those needs, and letting people compete for the rest.

But what is a "legitimate need"? That may be as difficult to determine as equality. Is a television set a legitimate need?

If so, how big a television set? How about a telephone? An automobile? Are two bathrooms a necessity, or just a convenience, for a family that includes three teenage daughters?

There are no right answers to any of these questions; all must be handled on an individual basis. One particularly promising tool for doing this is the concept of lifeline rates.

The term *lifeline rates* refers to a form of unit pricing in which the first few units are priced low, with additional units priced higher. The name comes from the fair access this kind of pricing provides to the item being priced. Low-income people are not shut away from it entirely; they are able to buy a minimum ("lifeline") amount. Those who can afford to buy more than they need pay extra for the privilege.

Those who press us to adopt lifeline rates are usually moved primarily by simple fairness. They argue that the poor should not be priced out of the market for basic necessities just because the rich use too much of them. Articles and speeches promoting the concept thus tend to focus on those situations where the lifeline appellation is literally true, picturing old people on fixed incomes freezing to death in their cold homes because they cannot afford the cost of gas, or young mothers unable to keep their children's food safely refrigerated because the electricity has been turned off.

But lifeline rates are more than a matter of simple fairness. They make sense from a conservation standpoint as well. If your task is to control demand, lifeline rates are much more effective than flat rates are, no matter how high you may set the flat rates. You can see why this is true if you remember to look at the margin. The primary constraint on demand is not the average price, but the *marginal price* — the price of each *additional* unit. Declining marginal prices encourage increased purchases; increasing marginal prices discourage them. Under standard marketing techniques, where bulk purchases earn a discount, the marginal rate obviously declines, encouraging greater consumption. Under lifeline rates, the marginal rate increases, encouraging conservation. What happens under flat rates?

It may not be obvious, but under flat rates the marginal price also declines, at least from a psychological standpoint. This happens because each additional unit is not looked at independently but as a part of a whole; and as the whole increases, *the percentage added by each unit becomes smaller.* Look at the following table and watch the marginal *percentage* price shrink:

No. Units	Unit Price ($)	Total Price ($)	Margin (%)
1	1	1	100
2	1	2	50
3	1	3	33
4	1	4	25
5	1	5	20
50	1	50	2
100	1	100	1
200	1	200	0.5

Thus flat-rate pricing, like bulk-rate discounts, encourages extra consumption — and the higher the absolute rate of consumption, the stronger that encouragement is. In our table, the purchaser of 50 units adds only 2 percent to his total outlay for each additional unit; the purchaser of 5 units adds 20 percent. Though the absolute marginal price is the same, the psychological margin is ten times as much. Clearly, the small purchaser is going to think a lot harder about that extra unit than the large purchaser is. If you are already using 100 gallons of water a day, the 4 or 5 extra gallons that a leak in the sink costs you are not going to seem very significant. If your daily use is only 20 gallons, you are probably going to get the leak fixed.

From the standpoint of full-cost pricing, too, lifeline rates make considerably more pure economic sense than flat or declining rate structures do. Externalities increase as production increases. When you add them into the accounting mix, per-unit production costs stop showing the steady decline beloved by efficiency-of-scale theorists: they decline less and less as quantities rise, and after a certain point they actually begin to go up. If a lumber manufacturer uses only 100 trees a year out of a million-tree stand, the external costs he imposes on the public are negligible. If he uses 100,000 trees a year, they are pretty significant. At a million trees a year, the external costs become most of the actual costs of the product.

Lifeline rates are relatively easy to apply for utilities with fixed points of delivery. All you need is a metering system and a reverse rate table. Reading the meter each month gives you the total amount used during that month; the table gives you the amount to charge. This system works very well for electricity, natural gas, and water. It can be used on sewage, though this is not normally necessary, as the quantity of sewage leaving a house is directly proportional to the amount of water flowing in. (In fact, if you disregard lawn and garden watering, the two figures are almost identical.) So if water use is cut by lifeline rating, sewage production will decline by very close to the same amount. It might help to install separate meters for indoor and outdoor faucets.

A type of utility where lifeline rating has recently been used with a great deal of success is garbage pickup. A low rate is charged for the first can of garbage picked up each week; rates climb, often very rapidly, for succeeding cans. A number of cities have experimented with this concept over the last few years, with uniformly good results. In Victoria, British Columbia, for example, $120 out of each residence's annual property tax bill goes to the municipally operated garbage collection agency; in return, the residence is allowed one free can of garbage pickup each week. Additional cans cost anywhere from $1.50 to $2.25 each. The program has cut household solid-waste production by approximately 15 percent.

The Minneapolis suburb of Farmington is trying a slightly different tack. There, garbage charges are assessed by weight. Garbage trucks carry scales; garbage cans are bar coded and entered in a central computerized database. As collectors make their rounds, they place the cans on the scales and scan the bar codes with supermarket-type laser scanners. The weight and code number are automatically entered in the database for billing purposes. "It puts the ball in the consumer's court," says Farmington solid-waste coordinator Bob Williamson. "Here's your garbage bill: you can reduce, reuse and recycle, and it will directly affect your garbage bill."

Lifeline rates are relatively easy to apply to services such as garbage collection, or to continuously vended, meterable substances like water, electricity, and natural gas. They are harder to apply to discrete items, especially those purchasable from many vendors. A tank of gasoline can be purchased at so many places that there seems no way for society to keep track of how much gas a consumer purchases each month without descending further into Big Brotherism than any of us care to. Food, too, is purchasable in many places, as are most other discrete consumer goods, such as books, computers, telephones, compact discs, videocassette recorders, cigarettes, and clothing. It is difficult, if not impossible, to apply lifeline rates to such items.

Big-ticket items like cars, homes, and yachts would seem at first glance to be even harder to "lifeline" than ordinary consumer goods. Paradoxically, however, it is actually much easier to create a lifeline system for these items than it is for food, clothing, and entertainment items. The key here is that society is already keeping track of these things. The monitoring network is already in place and is not particularly intrusive (dyed-in-the-wool libertarians might disagree with that last statement). We pay license fees on our cars; we pay property taxes on our homes, and we are allowed deductions on our income taxes for home payments. Boats are also licensed, and in some states they may, if large enough, qualify as second homes for tax purposes. Cars, homes, and boats all regularly carry large insurance loads. All of these — licenses, taxes, and insurance fees — are by nature single-vendor items with a measurable flow rate. And that means they can easily be lifelined.

Take cars, for example. A case can be made for car ownership as a necessity in American society. The design of our cities concentrates jobs, housing, and shopping in three separate areas. Mass transit is largely a joke. Without a car an individual quickly becomes marginalized, unable to hold a mainstream job, unable to shop easily even for basic necessities. Individuals do live under these circumstances (my brother Robert, approaching middle age, has never held a driver's license, choosing to travel everywhere by bicycle instead), but while their lives may be full (Robert has crossed the country twice on his bicycle, and regularly travels throughout his own corner of the state of Washington), they may not connect well to the lives of the rest of us (Robert lives in a one-room apartment and, though he holds a degree in city planning, makes his living as a part-time janitor). Until the advent of truly adequate mass transit, most of us are going to continue to need cars.

But if there is little question about the need for one car, there are good reasons to doubt the need for a second or a third. Many two-income families do require two cars, but most probably do not; one working spouse can often drop the other off at work, or at a convenient mass transit or car-pool depot. And it is a very rare family that actually needs a third car, which is almost always strictly a luxury item even in families with three or more drivers. Most high school seniors would like to own a car, and many do. Almost none of them actually need one.

So it would be fairly easy to apply the lifeline concept to automobile license and insurance fees. The fee structure for the first car could remain as each state currently handles it. But license and insurance fees for the second car should double. And for the third, they should triple. A household able to demonstrate that a significant portion of its income depended upon the ownership of a second or third vehicle could be exempted from the rate increase.

The case for a lifeline-type rate on second or third homes is even stronger than it is for second or third cars. Vacation homes are by no stretch of the imagination a necessity. In our peripatetic society, a husband and wife may hold jobs in different communities, and sometimes this requires one or the other to stay overnight regularly in his or her jobtown (if a hometown is where your home is, a jobtown must be where your job is); but in most cases this does not require home *ownership*. Rental will do the job nicely.

Second homes are luxury items and should be treated as such. The owners should pay the full social costs of owning them. This means an elimination of all tax breaks connected with second-home ownership. Mortgage payments on second homes should not be tax deductible. Building permits, property tax assessments, and homeowners' insurance rates for second homes should all double over those for first homes. For third homes, they should triple.

Luxuries are not bad per se, they are only bad when they infringe upon others' needs. Society cannot allow me to fill my swimming pool with water diverted from critical tasks such as filling lakes or keeping living things — forests, people, cactuses, crops — alive. Other than that, whether or not I fill my swimming pool is none of society's damn business.

Is This Job Necessary?

IN THE SPRING OF 1992, David Chism of the Northern California Association of Western Pulp and Paper Workers got up in front of an auditorium full of environmentalists and labor leaders and stated bluntly that labor unions, his own among them, were busily buying the wrong arguments about jobs and the environment. "Labor has been following industry's agenda and has failed to prepare its own," he said. By letting the timber industry scare them with threats of job losses, loggers and millworkers had been maneuvered into helping maintain corporate profits at the expense of their own future job security, because the forests could not sustain the current harvest level. "I tell my people repeatedly," Chism said, "that they've got to stop letting industry set their bottom line."

A few moments earlier, Tony Mazzochi had said much the same thing, only Mazzochi — the former secretary-treasurer of the Oil, Chemical and Atomic Workers International Union, now working for the OCAWIU as a presidential assistant — was even more blunt. "Workers who are threatened demand immediate remedies," he pointed out,

> and most of those remedies are provided by the employer. We need to frame the debate differently. We have to talk about walking away from facilities that employ tens of thousands of people. We have to think the unthinkable in the way of remedies. Old assumptions about work and who provides the work and the nature of work are going to have to be thrown away.

Elsewhere, Mazzochi has argued for what he calls a "Super-fund for workers" — a national, federally funded program for supporting and retraining workers whose jobs, for environmental or other reasons, have become obsolete. "Our vision entails a substantial pool of capital to fund this transition," he has written.

> Clearly, we are talking about tens of billions of dollars. But we know that the money is there. It is amazing how easily $500 billion is found to pay for the profligate practices of the savings and loan pirates. It is amazing how hundreds of billions of dollars are being set aside to clean up the waste at our military facilities. We certainly should be able to treat our working people as well as we treat dirt.

The preservation of jobs is not an economic issue; it is a political one. The often-heard complaint that economics has not been taken into account when jobs are lost to environmental protection is false. Economics itself often calls for the elimination of jobs. Usually they are the same jobs that environmental protection measures end up "costing."

It may be helpful here to frame the argument in a slightly different context. Traveling the back roads of America, one often comes upon tiny, boarded-up communities, their stores closed and deserted. It is almost universally the automobile that is responsible for these — the automobile, and the development of today's high-speed highway network. It has become so easy to go into the larger towns for shopping — the larger towns with their larger stores, whose prices and stocks of goods the little country stores cannot begin to meet — that no one in the rural areas shops these little community stores anymore. Without shoppers, of course, the stores die. You can almost see the tombstones in front of them, with the epitaph carved in block letters in the polished marble: KILLED BY GOOD HIGHWAYS.

When country stores die, they take jobs with them. Thus,

inevitably, good highways destroy jobs. Do we hear the chambers of commerce in these rural communities decrying this? Of course not. We hear chambers of commerce demanding new roads for "economic growth" at the same time they decry environmental protection proposals as "taking away jobs." This is the frontier fallacy at its most blatant. Roads represent a conquest of the frontier, and thus "progress"; nature preserves represent a continuation of the frontier, and thus the defeat of civilization. The fact that the real economic roles of the two are very similar is fudged over or, if brought to people's attention, not believed.

Things change, jobs among them. The world does not stand still. Old ways of making a living fade away, new ones arise. To attempt to hold on to the old ones after they have outlived their usefulness is wasteful, inefficient, and stupid. And to demand this economically destructive process in the name of "economics" (as the save-our-jobs people usually do) is either ignorant or amazingly cynical and arrogant.

None of this means that we should not be sensitive to the hardships caused to individuals by the loss of their jobs. In fact, we need to be very sensitive to this. No society that considers itself moral can afford to make some of its citizens go hungry or lose their homes merely to enable the rest of society to live up to some philosophical economic or ecological ideal. And even if we could set the moral issue aside (which we cannot) there is the purely practical matter that people with no incomes are a source of both economic and ecological harm: economic because they cannot participate in the money economy and thus keep it operating below its production possibilities frontier; ecological, because the immediacy of their needs robs the future of all value. One does not care about future generations when the present generation is starving. One may not even care very much about next week. If the aching in the empty belly is strong enough, one will cheerfully eat the last spotted owl on earth. Anyone who does not understand this cannot ever have been very hungry.

But this does not really have anything to do with jobs. It has to do with income, which is a separate issue. We need to preserve an adequate income for everyone, but we do not need to do it by preserving jobs that have outlived their social and economic usefulness. A guaranteed minimum income is one possibility; this idea is stridently opposed by the political right on the grounds that gaining income without working for it is morally decadent and somehow connected with communism, but these arguments ring a little hollow coming from people whose income derives from inherited wealth. It is difficult to see how getting welfare without working for it is morally superior to getting interest without working for it. The only difference between the two positions is which end of the horse you happen to be standing at.

And there are other possibilities besides a guaranteed income. One viable option is to shorten the work week. Dropping the standard work week from five days to four would mean that only 80 percent of the current workload would get done ($4/5 \times 100 = 80\%$), which would create an immediate 20 percent labor shortage — plenty of room to absorb today's unemployed. This approach would have the advantage of hitting the unemployment problem at its real source, which is the increased productivity of the American worker. Increased productivity means we are getting more production out of less labor. More production with less labor means that more leisure time is available. By holding tenaciously to a five-day work week, we prevent workers from getting the leisure time they have earned. But the leisure time does not evaporate. Instead of disappearing, it gets bundled into forty-hours-per-week segments and apportioned out to workers in the form of pink slips. No leisure for some and 100 percent enforced leisure for others is not an efficient way to deal with the problem. We can do better.

A four-day work week would require some adjustments, but none of the problems it raises is insurmountable. In fact, probably the best thing about this solution to the jobs problem is that we've met all of its challenges before — in the early years of this century, when the standard work week dropped from six days to five. By studying that transition, we should be able to help this one run smoothly. Certainly the time has come to try.

Management leaders will often privately agree with most of this. I remember particularly a conversation I had a few years ago with Ed Kupillas, an executive at a large Oregon timber company, outside one of the first major public meetings on the Northwest's spotted owl crisis. Ed and I have been attending these events for many years, usually as speakers on opposite sides of the agenda, and we can afford to be honest with each other. We spoke of jobs. "I have argued very forcefully in the councils of the industry," Ed told me, "that we are making a mistake by leaning so hard on the jobs issue. I think it's going to come back to haunt us. Everybody knows that employment in this industry goes up and down in cycles that depend on housing starts. We can't guarantee a job to anyone, and we're creating false expectations that we can. The next time we have to lay off people because of the economy, labor is going to come down all over us. We need to get off jobs and start talking about access to the resource."

Precisely.

We seem to have come a long way from environmental issues. But as long as job preservation is being used as an argument against environmental protection, job and income reform are environmental goals. When we get the employment picture right, job blackmail can no longer be used to hold up environmentally sound changes in our ways of doing things. Remember the ecologists' mantra: *all things are connected*. If we are going to establish an ecosystem paradigm for economic activity, we cannot be afraid to follow those connections wherever they might lead. Here is a somewhat unexpected one in an environmental context: the minimum wage.

The minimum wage issue is related to the jobs-preservation

issue. Both presume, falsely, that income and work must always necessarily be related. This has never been true, and with increased automation in the workplace it is less true today than it ever was. Work should be rewarded; one should have some hope of bettering oneself, and bettering society at the same time, through one's own efforts. For many of us, work is a genuine necessity, without which we feel degraded and useless. But work and the meeting of genuine needs should be divorced from one another, for the simple reason that the work and the needs are almost never in the same place.

Minimum wages are essentially price supports. The good being priced is labor. Like all price supports, minimum wages induce an increased supply of the priced good (supply is directly related to price) at the same time that they induce a reduced demand for it (demand is inversely related to price). With supply artificially raised and demand artificially depressed, a surplus develops. In the labor market, such a surplus is called unemployment. Minimum wage laws thus lead inexorably to unemployment. There is no way, given the laws of supply and demand, that they cannot. And as long as income is tied to employment, this means that minimum wage laws are increasing, not decreasing, income equitability.

But minimum wage laws do more than that. By adding the friction of a labor surplus to the market, they reduce the efficiency of production. They move the society off its production possibilities frontier. That means there is less for everybody — and, given the structure of political power in this or any other country, that decrease in production is going to be felt disproportionately by the poor.

Is this an issue for environmentalists? It is, for three reasons. First, thinking like an ecosystem requires connecting everything to everything else; there are no nonenvironmental issues. Second, and more directly, the fact that minimum wage laws have moved society off its production possibilities frontier means that the same goods we now enjoy could be produced more efficiently (with less resource cost and thus less damage to the environment) if we moved back onto it. Efficiency, wherever it is found, is always an environmental issue. Finally, and even more directly, the fact that the foes of environmental protection have chosen to fight much of their battle on the ground of jobs requires us to argue on the same ground. Jobs are not an economic issue, they are a political issue. Income, however, is an economic issue. The minimum wage laws, by tying income to jobs, aid and abet the free-resource thieves in their task of convincing the public that, by encouraging shifts in the structure of the traditional job market, we are somehow subverting the nation's economic well-being.

"I was a panelist at a conference on converting a military plant in Colorado to civilian production," Tony Mazzochi told his Portland audience.

> Everyone was talking about how conversion would save jobs. When my turn came, I had to point out that if we built subway cars instead of airplanes in the same plant, it would still be producing toxic waste. I said that instead of spending however many billions they were planning to on converting the plant, they should just give it to the workers in lump-sum payments and let them go sit in the Denver cafés and write poetry. Everybody laughed, but I was serious. I think you'd get more social good out of the money that way.

Here is one final comment on the issue, this time by an economist: Harry L. Cook, professor emeritus of economics at Southern Oregon State College in Ashland. "There are not many propositions that all economists, conservative and liberal, can agree upon," wrote Dr. Cook in the summer of 1989, as the spotted owl issue heated up in the Oregon woods,

> but one of them is that the appeal to use resources to "save jobs" is a false argument. It puts the cart before the horse. It says that the purpose of resources is to provide jobs rather than to provide goods and services to satisfy wants. Unfortu-

nately, the "save the jobs" argument has had a long and inglorious history, often temporarily successful, with weak and declining industries trying to postpone the inevitable as they are replaced by new and growing ones. . . .

Old jobs lost and new ones gained is a painful process for the displaced workers . . . but it is simply a necessary price that must be paid to have a dynamic and progressive economy.

Access to Nature

I T IS WIDELY RECOGNIZED that dwellers in the inner city have little or no access to nature. It is not so clearly apparent that travelers through the countryside do not. But that is what our modern transportation system has produced: a people with no roots in the natural world. We live in our neat suburbs, surrounded by tame things that have left their naturalness behind: mowed grass, weeded peonies, clipped roses. Traveling, we climb in our cars, insulated against outside temperature and atmospheric pollutants by their air conditioning systems, and point them down the freeway. There is no place to stop along the freeway, no pulling off to step for a moment into the deep cool smells of the woods or the bracing winds of the mountain passes. There are, at intervals, fraudulent connections to nature, the so-called rest stops; but these are almost universally full of lawns and flowerbeds and picnic tables, the stuff of back yards and city parks. The real world, the bugs and the cactuses and the forests and the swamps, lies beyond the fence where we cannot touch it.

Off the freeways, things are little better. Our roads are meant to get us from point A to point B, and they do that admirably. They do not help us to discover what is between the points. Even on America's back roads, one usually goes miles without a turnout — no chance to get off the road, to leave the snug cocoon of the car, to wander among natural things. The scenery scrolls endlessly by like a tape in a smoothly running VCR: you want to savor the landscape frame by frame, but no one has thought to provide you with a pause button.

The standard environmentalist approach to this problem is to press for the creation of more nature preserves. But preserves are not a solution; preserves are part of the problem. Preserves are creatures of the frontier paradigm, a separation of nature from human affairs rather than an integration of the two. A preserve boundary is a frontier that has been pinned down by legislation so that it can no longer advance. One side of it is wilderness, the other civilization, and never the twain shall meet. Outright laissez-faire, free-market developers wish to preserve the free access to untouched physical resources that characterizes frontier paradigm development, and in an age of coast-to-coast suburbia this is clearly no longer a viable option. Is preserving free access to the untouched spiritual resources of the frontier any more viable?

The answer is no. We on the preservation side cannot freeze time any better than the developers can. Change occurs, and we must adapt to it rather than try to halt it in its tracks. Drawing lines around preserves does not preserve them from anything except direct physical development. We need access to the pure and undiluted world, the world where only natural change takes place; we need this for spiritual as much as practical reasons; but we cannot get it by decreeing preserves. All we get that way is unconnected islands of nature in a sea of pavement. We need nature in all its sprawl and diversity, not bound up in neat borders but everywhere. Tear up the fences and let the wilderness out: let it come into the suburbs and the cities, twine itself in among the neat square fields of Iowa, insinuate itself into the megalopolis of the Middle Atlantic. Let life live.

Practically speaking, of course, we shall need the preserves until we get it through our thick skulls that wilderness is a legitimate economic use of the land. I am not advocating the immediate dismantling of the national park system or the national wilderness system. It is still necessary, for practical reasons, to support additions to those systems in those places where damage is occurring because the economics of natural systems have not been adequately integrated into the economics of development. But our first priority should be to perform that integration, and our long-term goal should be the same as that of the developers: dismantling the preserves.

What should we put in their place? Art Carhart had the right idea.

Arthur H. Carhart is a distinctly underappreciated figure in the history of the American conservation movement. A landscape architect by training, he spent most of his long life working for the Forest Service, beginning as a surveyor on the White River National Forest in Colorado and eventually rising to chief of recreation planning for the entire agency. Early in his career, in 1919, he became the first Forest Service employee actually to succeed in setting aside a chunk of Forest Service land (Trapper Lake, in the Colorado Rockies) to be kept free of all development, preceding his friend Aldo Leopold's Gila Wilderness in New Mexico by a good five years. In retirement he wrote a book, *Planning for America's Wildlands,* which was published in 1961 under the imprimatur of four conservation groups: the National Audubon Society, the Wilderness Society, the National Parks Association, and the Wildlife Management Institute. In it he argued strongly for a wildlands zoning system — a system similar to city zoning, flexible and modifiable rather than frozen into law, designed around the land rather than around political posturing, and set primarily through economic considerations, with *economic* here being taken in its largest sense (as we have tried to do throughout this book) to mean the choices based on the values, not necessarily the prices, inherent in the land and perceived by the land's users.

Carhart suggested seven zones: A, B, and C wilderness, Dude Ranch, Youth Camp–Private Cabin, Resort, and Semi-suburban. Only the class A wilderness corresponds completely, in its use patterns, to what we think of today as wilderness; the class B wilderness allows logging, and the class C wilderness allows motorized recreation. As with city zoning systems, use variations might be allowed, under special permit, in any zone. The planner, wrote Carhart, should always be thinking ahead: some areas zoned as wilderness today might be rezoned to something else tomorrow; some lands now zoned for other uses might eventually (or soon) revert completely to class A wilderness. Size and remoteness should be factors in designating class A, but they should not be absolute; small bits of class A wilderness zones could exist even within urban areas. The key was flexibility, and connections:

> To run a line around a portion of land, assign [*sic*] to it any singular high-priority type of use or uses without reference to other lands having physical and use relationships to the selected portion of land *is not zoning* as the land-use planner uses the term.

Nothing was permanent; nothing was frozen in stone. The key was always the highest and best use, which Carhart recognized could change with time. "All wildlands," he wrote, "are in *constant* change." Thus, we cannot tell today what the highest and best use might be tomorrow. Choices cannot be made for all time. Choices must be continuous. When you determine that the marbled murrelet is endangered, you need to stop logging its habitat — but maybe not completely. When you find bug-infested timber, you need to log it — but maybe not in all cases. Always the context must be considered. Always the connections must be looked at. Always the ecosystem paradigm must be honored. Life is in a continuous state of becoming. Our treatment of the biosphere must always reflect this basic, inescapable fact. Wrote Carhart:

> May I interpolate this thought: Altogether too much of land use programs has been the result of who arrived first on the scene, what might have been his over-riding interests, and the force he put into establishing that interest as the dominant

one. This applies to lumbering, reservoir building, stock-growing, *and* wilderness as well. What we are driving at right here is to try to set up a systematic, studied approach to land use planning of wildlands, based on intelligently determined, best suited use and uses for a piece of land, that will avoid impulsive, emotional, dollar-chasing or one-use land management.

Not Regulation-Free,
but Barrier-Free

D O M A R K E T S really work better than regulations do to achieve socially desirable goals? Do unregulated markets work better than regulated ones? The answer to both these questions is: maybe. It depends on the market, and on the regulation.

If a market meets the four criteria for efficiency — homogeneity, complete information, lack of friction, and adequate size for transaction independence — and if, in addition, accounting practices are used that allow externalities to be fully included in the cost and benefit figures, then the market is going to do a better job of husbanding scarce resources, protecting the environment, and meeting general social goals than any amount of regulation can. But the farther away the market drifts from these conditions, the poorer a job it will do, and eventually a point will be reached where regulation would be more efficient. At that point, it makes sense to switch to regulatory tools.

Virtually all regulations affect the workings of the market, but they do not all affect the machinery negatively. If a regulation helps counter market failures, it will actually improve the market's ability to function, not hinder it. Regulations can do this by taking away barriers to market entry; by improving informational structures (for example, requiring price posting); by breaking up monopolies and trusts; and by increasing product homogeneity.

Unfortunately, that is not what regulations, by and large, do. We have conceived our regulations through the distorting mirror of the frontier paradigm, and they have become as distorted as the mirror. Our regulations do not aid the natural laws of ecosystems and of markets, but hinder them. We use regulatory tools to try to get markets further out of the pollution-control loop; but our principal problem is that they are too far out of the loop already. Our entire regulatory apparatus is aimed at the wrong target.

Under the current regulatory approach, our attention has been too easily diverted to the question of how much it will cost to stop logging or clean up pollution. That is the wrong thing to ask. The real problem to be concerned with is not how much it will cost to stop doing these things, but how much it will cost to let them continue.

If we are going to apply the free market, reason suggests, we should follow that application to its logical conclusion.

We need to rid the market of all frictions and distortions. If we do not, we are defeating our own purpose. It is as if we attempted to use a jack to lift a building after purposefully bending it out of shape and rusting it shut. Markets, like jacks, will only work properly when we do not interfere with the laws of nature under which they operate.

We need to make sure the market provides full information. This means adequate price posting: if the market is going to adjust to Pareto optimum through the choice by consumers of the best good for the lowest price, the consumers need to know what that lowest price is. If one wishes to choose a motel on the basis of price, the prices of all motels must be visible from the street; if one wishes to choose between logging and wildlands on economic grounds, one must be certain that the opportunity costs of both (not just the logging) are fully understood. If free-market advocates expect us to make the rational choices their own theory requires, they must not hide the facts upon which rational choices are built. Bringing this about will almost certainly require strict controls over advertising. That is not what the free-marketers think they are asking for, but it is the best way to make it work.

We need to make sure that the number of firms and the number of consumers both remain high enough that no one firm or consumer can influence price. This will require strict controls on monopolies. Trustbusting is not an anticapitalist strategy: if one accepts market theory, it is a free-market necessity and thus a strong support for the values capitalists say they are for. Carried to its logical extreme, this proposition on firm and consumer numbers also requires us to institute a fair distribution of resources. If wealth is concentrated in the hands of the few, the many without funds will not be able to buy consumer products, and the requirement that the number of consumers be high enough to prevent any one consumer from influencing price will fail. Among the best things one could do for the market system — really — is to achieve an equitable income distribution in this country. Free-marketers call this communism. It is actually a prerequisite for the proper functioning of capitalism.

The free market is not regulation-free, it is barrier-free. We must not make the mistake of confusing the two.

Eight ✤

The World Is Not
a Wax Museum

Browse Lines

THE CULTURE OF AMERICA has always been strongly rooted in its geography. Tall, rugged mountains, rocky coastlines, conifer forests, and rushing rivers have bred the same types of communities in Maine and New Hampshire as they have in Washington and Idaho. Southern Louisiana feels much like southern Florida, West Virginia like southwest Oregon, eastern Montana like western Nebraska. Where the land is the same, the fit of the land and its people will usually be the same as well.

On top of these geographically determined cultural patterns, however, there is rapidly being superimposed another. It is a pattern created by the great restlessness of the American people, coupled with our intense longing for roots; our ability to manipulate building materials and heating, ventilating, and air conditioning systems (HVACs, in building trade lingo); and a certain amount of manufactured nostalgia for things that never were. The *Washington Post*'s Joel Garreau, who has devoted a book to the subject, refers to this new cultural landscape as "Edge City," a name that calls attention to the massive buildups where beltways around old-style cities intersect intercity freeways. I prefer a more general term, a term as applicable to small towns and clusters of buildings out in the middle of nowhere as it is to the margins of cities: *freeway culture.*

Freeway culture is the same wherever you are in America: the same interchanges, the same fast-food joints, the same motels, the same walled-off subdivisions with their huge California houses on postage-stamp Rhode Island lots. The same fancifully designed concrete-and-glass office complexes topped by immense corporate logos ("billboard buildings") rising above the trees of suburbia like Mayan pyramids rising from the jungle. The same stores, in the same malls. Well, perhaps not quite the same malls: an effort is usually made by mall designers to inject "local flavor" into their creations. The brick flooring, low ceilings, and wrought-iron signery of the Arcadian Village Mall in Lafayette, Louisiana, are a far cry from the Douglas fir trunks under soaring roofs at the Clackamas Town Center in Portland, Oregon. But the stores are the same. Always a Waldenbooks, always a Sam Goody's. Always at least two "anchor" stores, large multistory structures selling primarily clothing and dry goods and usually belonging to a chain. J. C. Penney. Mervyns. Nordstrom's. Sears. Plants, green all year, rising at the junctions of corridors, usually toward skylights. Fountains ("active water features"). Ramps. Benches.

A number of good things can be said about freeway culture. For coast-to-coast travelers, there is a soothing hominess about being able to find the same businesses wherever you pull off the freeway. The buildings are usually spotless, comfortable, and attractive. Mall food courts are fine places to eat while traveling; so, for that matter, are most of the national and regional fast-food chains, and if you want to step up to sit-down fare a Denny's or a Bob's Big Boy or a Ruby Tuesday will usually do the job quite nicely. Freeway culture motels are almost always cleaner, more comfortable, and cheaper than the locally owned variety. I take shameless, grateful advantage of these things myself.

At the same time, though, we need to be aware of some pretty serious problems. The same feature of the freeway culture that produces its advantages — the consistent, coast-to-coast uniformity — is also the principal source of its drawbacks. The most obvious of these is the disappearance of identifiable regional cultures. Sitting in a Burger King in Savannah, Georgia, is a virtually identical experience to that of sitting in a Burger King in Olympia, Washington — or, for that matter, to that of sitting in a McDonald's or a Roy Rogers or a Jack-in-the-Box, in either of those places or any-where else in the country. Remaining within the confines of the freeway culture allows you to drive across the continent without going anywhere. Only the pictures on the walls change. When you can go into a McDonald's in a small town in eastern Canada, as I did about ten years ago, and encounter a kiwi fruit milkshake as part of a Hawaii Days special, you know that the whole concept of regional culture is, if not dead, at least treading across extremely shaky ground.

Ecologists and economists alike know that monocultures are dangerous, always on the edge of maladaptiveness, always ready to fall prey to a simple calamity that in a healthy, diver-sified system would be quickly damped out but which here, in these artificially uniform conditions, spreads like the pro-verbial wildfire. Freeway culture is not immune to these dan-gers. Some hint of the problems they can cause surfaced in the winter of 1992–93 when an epidemic of bloody diarrhea caused by tainted meat at a small number of Jack-in-the-Box restaurants in the state of Washington came close to wiping out the entire chain — and depressed business in every other fast-food chain across the country as well. Local restaurants, sharing neither a uniform national image nor a centralized supply network, continued to thrive.

But it is not really the monoculture aspect of the sameness that is the main problem we need to deal with in the freeway culture. It is the sameness itself.

To come across identical-looking freeway interchanges in Boston and Tucson is to create, mentally, a geographic iden-tity that does not exist. There is an overpowering urge to believe, in the face of the freeway culture, that land every-where can be treated the same way. It cannot.

Land differs dramatically. It differs in stability, in rock chemistry, in angle of repose. It differs in ambient temperature, in annual rainfall, in wind exposure. Soil depth and fertility, vegetal cover, and proximity to water vary greatly from one part of the country to another — even from one part of the same county to another. The biosphere knows this; that is why we would think it absurd to find cactus forests on the summits of New Hampshire's mountains or alligators nesting in the sloughs of Puget Sound. It should be equally absurd to think of New York–style skyscrapers in Phoenix, or California-style adobe cottages in Iowa, or any permanent structures at all on Cape Hatteras. In the wake of Hurricane Andrew, complaints surfaced from the owners of what the papers called "Cape Cod–style" homes in Florida destroyed by the storm. The level of damage, they said, indicated that they had been the victims of shoddy building practices. No one stopped to consider whether the real problem might not be Cape Cod–style homes in Florida. The neat frame structures that serve so well anchored in the cool woods and stern morainal soils of New England are woefully out of place in the palmetto scrub and shifting sands of Florida. Storms strike these lands differently. If they are going to survive the storms, houses must be built differently, too.

Of primary concern are land capability and carrying capacity. Generally speaking, it is not the absolute size of a city that determines how well it functions; it is the size of the city in relation to the carrying capacity of its immediate environment. Seattle "works" better than Los Angeles does, not simply because it is smaller but because the carrying capacity of the Puget Sound region is much greater than that of the Los Angeles Basin. The scale of the city in relation to its environment is far better for Seattle than it is for Los Angeles. The verdict in the Rodney King case was the match that set off the Los Angeles riots in the spring of 1992, but the kindling was provided by the city's extreme overshooting of its carrying capacity. You cannot be a resident of a city that is taking water away from farms and forests and towns located as much as a thousand miles away without at some subliminal level beginning to feel like a thief.

When a species exceeds the carrying capacity of its habitat, the result is inevitably habitat degradation. Ecologists learn to look for signs of this: browse lines on trees, lichen lines on rocks, soils moved downslope. A reduction in the number of other species present, leading to a general simplification and destabilization of the ecosystem. Loss of ground cover. Invasion by exotic species.

We should pay attention to the same type of phenomena in human affairs. Widespread pollution, forest destruction, and ozone depletion are the equivalent, for the planetary environment, of browse lines and lichen lines. We are operating beyond carrying capacity — beyond the ultimate production possibilities frontier — and the results are to make the world less and less habitable for humans.

As I traveled across the length and breadth of the United States during the summer of 1992, preparing for this book, one of the things that struck me most strongly was the ubiquitousness of oaks. Not the same oaks, of course; the species I was seeing differed radically from place to place. But the genus was everywhere. Red oaks high up in the mountains of New Hampshire, white oaks in Ohio, black oaks in the Central Valley of California, and blue oaks in the nearby Sierra foothills. Live oaks on the Georgia Sea Islands; post oaks in the Carolinas; Gambel's oaks on Mesa Verde and in the dry, rocky Wichita Mountains of Oklahoma. Water oaks living in southeastern swamps. There were oak species with leaves like laurels, others with leaves like willows, others with leaves like poplars, and still others with leaves like holly. Here in my Oregon valley the white oaks and black oaks achieve massive dimensions, sixty feet tall and sixty inches through at the base; near the summits of the nearby Siskiyou Mountains there are Sadler's oaks (*Quercus sadleriana*), a species endemic to this area, low-growing and spindly like rhododendrons, rarely exceeding six feet in height or three inches through no matter how long they may live.

Oaks are almost literally everywhere. It is a good thing we appreciate them; we cannot escape them. Wherever humans have settled, oaks have almost always preceded them.

The oak genus accomplishes this feat by adapting, radiating through evolution into separate species. Whatever is needed, the genus's basic DNA seems to be able to come up with. Different oaks have learned to stand with their feet in the water next to cypresses, to compete with maples and beeches on the uplands, and to live among junipers on high, dry ridges. The tree's characteristics change as its needs change. The tiny, dry leaves of the blue oak (*Quercus douglasii*) help it survive on the hot windy ridges of the Sierra foothills; they would be of no help in the nearby Central Valley, where the winds are quieter and water is more available, so the oaks there are California blacks and whites (*kelloggii* and *lobata*), big trees with fair-sized leaves, trees adapted to growing on the flat alluvium. The hill and lowland species do not try to compete with each other, rarely if ever grow side by side, and are so different that, although they are both oaks, only a person reasonably familiar with trees will be able to recognize the characteristics that place them in the same genus.

Humans are all one species; though we have radiated into a number of races, each with characteristics that help adapt it to the environment in which it originated (dark skins near the equator, light ones farther north, for example), our principal means of adaptation is through culture. Over the thousands of generations since we first left Africa, the species has slowly, through trial and error, learned what it takes to survive in each new habitat it comes to, and has adapted its behavior and its lifestyle to match. Plains peoples have learned to hunt herd animals; river peoples have learned to fish; forest peoples have learned to gather the products of trees. Eskimos have learned how to dress for the cold, Arabs for the heat. People have taken native plants and animals and tamed them for agriculture; they have taken native materials (whalebone and ice, copper and stone, lumber, coal) and developed technologies through which these materials enrich their lives. This process has been going on for at least 3 million years. Like the oak, our cultures have radiated, adapting us to different climates, different conditions, and different places.

But in the last several hundred years a change has occurred. Technology has reached the point where it can adapt the place to us, instead of the other way around. And dependence on this technology has spread all over the world, replacing the variety of cultural adaptation with the single-mindedness of environmental manipulation. Instead of developing new cultures in new places, we are now wiping them out.

I am not going to argue the morality of this process, nor argue that modern technology is bad, nor demand that we go back to a simpler lifestyle. None of these stands is really defensible. It is nonsensical to argue that ethics require us to live in grass huts like the Yap when today's Yap huts have television sets inside them and motorbikes parked in front of them. We have no right to tell the Yap that wanting these things is wrong, nor do we have the right to demand that our own people begin living in the way the Yap are busily abandoning.

But we do need to be aware of what we are doing. In destroying indigenous cultures, we are cutting ourselves off from a vast body of knowledge of potentially great value. We are losing the human equivalent of the oak's storehouse of genetic adaptability: our storehouse of cultural adaptability. As a result, there are more and more places where we no longer know how to live appropriately. And as the materials that drive our technological culture become dearer, that loss of knowledge is going to seem more and more stupid.

Frontier paradigm economics can exist only by valuing indigenous cultures at zero. Frontier economics requires the illusion of untouched resources. Resources are not untouched if native peoples are already obtaining value from them.

But the romantic notion of preserving native cultures is really no better. It is the old problem: to preserve something, you must be able to draw a line around it and command it not to change. You do not abandon the frontier; you merely demand that certain areas, or peoples, stay forever on the other side of it.

We need to listen to George Tinker. A Native American theologian who teaches at the Iliff School of Theology in Denver, Tinker decries both those who would demand that native cultures remain unchanged and those who would try to drag them to full "equality" in the dominant European-based culture of the planet. To do either, he points out, is to take the choice away from the native peoples. And in the freedom to make that choice lies the only hope for a synthesis, a melding of the truths that have been learned by both technological and indigenous cultures. Given the chance, a new cultural species may yet emerge — an oak that remains an oak but has fitted itself to the local soils and rains and sunlight.

Exactly the same point can be made about ecologists and economists. To insist that either profession must be dragged kicking and screaming into the other's camp is wrong; to say that either must be shut completely away from the other is equally wrong. The only viable solution is a synthesis, an eco/nomics that conforms human economies to the economy of the planet as a whole. The conditions here in the hills of the waning millennium do not allow either lowland economics or lowland ecology to survive. What we need is not to level the hills; what we need is a new species.

Tinker compares the world to a lot with a house on it, with Europeans in the house and native peoples out in the yard. Come in the house, say some Europeans; stay in the yard and make room for us, say others. Neither course is right, for either culture. If everyone is forced to stay in the yard, no one is allowed the benefits of being in the house; if the natives are invited into the house, it is still a European house, and they are only guests. The problem here is neither the Europeans nor the natives; the problem is the house. And the solution is neither to drag the natives (or the environmentalists) inside or the Europeans (or the business community) out. The solution is to tear down the house and build a new one. Together.

The World Is Not
a Wax Museum

THE WORLD is not a wax museum.
It's not a set of Tinkertoys, either.

The world can be neither frozen permanently in a single flowerlike instant of perfect time, nor manipulated at will by blinder-wearing builders and their accomplices in other professions. The world does not conform to the desires, needs, or political agendas of either environmentalists or engineers. It has its own ideas, and it is going to bloody well follow them. The human race and all its works are at best a minor irrelevancy that can, if necessary, be easily brushed aside.

Oh, we can affect things. We can affect lots of things, and we can affect them drastically. We can affect ourselves right off the planet, along with many if not most other life forms, if we are not careful, and we may be on the verge of doing just that. But in the larger, geological, earth-centered picture, this doesn't really matter very much. Natural law carries on, and will continue to do so whether or not we remain a part of the picture. "Nature is trying very hard to make us succeed," Buckminster Fuller once remarked pointedly to an interviewer, "but nature does not depend on us. We are not the only experiment."

We humans seem to have a great deal of trouble understanding this.

One hot August night when I had just turned seventeen, as I lay soaking luxuriously in a tepid bath in my parents' home a few miles west of the Washington/north Idaho border, I saw the water suddenly begin to move. The tub had clearly been jarred, though I had not jarred it and no one in my family, all either sleeping or quietly reading, had done anything that could possibly have affected it, either. The next morning's papers resolved the mystery. An earthquake with a Richter magnitude of 7.2 had struck just west of Yellowstone National Park, changing the elevation of parts of the Montana Rockies by as much as 22 feet. One peak near the junction of Rock Creek and the Madison River had split wide open under the strain; 80 million tons of its face had peeled off into the canyon of the Madison, burying the Rock Creek Campground and the campers in it beneath 400 feet of raw wet earth and damming the Madison to create a brand-new, four-mile-long lake. Seldom has what we humans inappropriately refer to as terra firma been altered more completely and precipitously by a single act of nature; the only comparable events in U.S. history have been the volcanic explosions that tore the tops off of Katmai Volcano in 1912 and Mount Saint Helens in 1980.

In July 1991, nearly thirty-two years after the fact, I visited what used to be the Madison River Canyon and is now called Earthquake Lake, and came face to face with a large-scale personal dilemma. All my life I have been a fighter against man-built dams. What is it in me that causes me to cheer when nature builds one? For I was cheering very much, prowling that slide and its backed-up water, and had in fact cheered when it had been created, notwithstanding the loss of human life that had been involved. Suppose government engineers had built it, instead of God? Would I have cheered then? Would I have had reason to cheer? What difference is there between a Glen Canyon Dam and a Madison River Slide, other than how they happened to arrive?

It is a troubling question, made even more troubling by the knowledge that my opposing reactions to these two types of dams, natural and human-made, are far from unique. They are shared by virtually everyone, on both sides of the dam/no dam argument. There at the Madison River, the nation's premier dam-building agency, the Army Corps of Engineers, was in fact very active directly after the creation of the Madison Slide dam, but the Corps was trying to tear it down, not build it up. To dam proponents a man-made dam is good but one created by natural processes is bad. The fact that this is 180 degrees removed from my own opinion does not make it different. Preservationists and developers think they oppose each other, but their opposition is the stuff of mirrors. The view of the world that each reflects is fundamentally the same.

And fundamentally wrong.

Preservationists and developers both rely for the full acceptance of their beliefs on a failure to understand the fallacy of stasis. Things change. Delusion lies in trying to deny that change. And both sides are equally in denial.

Unbridled development requires nature to be in stasis. Nature to developers means raw materials. If there are going to be no limits on development, there can be no limits to nature. The supply of raw materials must be constant and unchanging; no matter how much we use or consume or modify, there must always be plenty left to develop later.

But preservation also requires nature to be in stasis. When we draw a line around a forest and "preserve" it, we are denying it the right to change into a grassland or a marsh as much as we are denying developers the right to change it into a housing development. If change continues, we have preserved nothing.

Neither of these positions is defensible.

Nature changes. The climax community of ecology is a convenient fiction which does not take into account the connections among ecosystems; there is always enough transfer along those connections to keep things stirred up. If a climax forest lasts "forever," how do you define *forever?* Forests evolve. Fires burn them; windstorms sweep them; avalanches knock them down. The long, slow heartbeat of climate modification moves them north and up, south and down, ever changing, never still. Glaciers shrink and advance; rivers change course. Not even the land is forever. At the time Christ walked the hills of Galilee, Lakes Superior, Michigan, and Huron were all one vast body of water in which, evidence suggests, whales swam. Natural processes ended that pretty scenario, not human activities. To think that similar natural changes will not occur simply because we have drawn lines on the earth is to delude ourselves drastically concerning our power over nature.

But that does not give carte blanche to the change-and-be-damned crowd. Changes affect one another, and if we do not take care about the changes we set in motion they are likely to twine around the chain of causation and kick us royally in the behind. The idea of a horseshoe nail that lost a kingdom is not as farfetched as some of us seem to think. It is safe to cut down all the trees on a watershed only if you don't need any water out of that watershed, and that presupposes another watershed over the next hill, and the next hill after that — always a next hill, always another source of water, world without end, amen, amen. Developers believe devoutly and unswervingly that the changes they bring about are insignificant in their effects because of the immense size and variety of the natural world. It's all right to use up the landscape for housing developments or clear-cuts or open-pit mines, they say; there is more where that came from. But it's not all right, and there isn't. A permanent supply of watersheds is no less a delusion than a permanent forest is. To accept change is to admit that we cannot cut all the timber we want to, and that we cannot develop all the suburbs we want to, as much as it is to accept the blunt, uncomfortable knowledge that the part of the forest we love the most may not be there tomorrow.

I noticed this morning that the apricot tree in the back yard is dying.

It has not been entirely unexpected. The apricot was old when we bought the place twenty-two years ago, and has barely borne fruit at all for the last decade. It is the only tree that remains from the days, long before our tenure here, when the hillside to the west was covered with a small orchard; its sole remaining companion from that orchard, twenty feet closer to the house, died six years ago and had to be cut down. Now this one is following. As May approaches in a wet year, none of its branches have leafed out. A few small shoots have appeared in the axils of the larger branches, next to the trunk, but even they do not look particularly healthy. We face the sad task of sawing down an old friend.

There are other changes in the yard. The black walnut sapling near the south fence — six feet high and whip-thin when we arrived — is now a healthy young tree, ten inches through and a good twenty-five feet tall. A peach and two new apricots have sprouted near the back alley, around the parking pad we leveled out for the cars some fifteen years ago; these have all now reached bearing age. Periwinkle and a butterfly bush have taken hold on the low bank above the flat lawn we created in a fit of landscaping passion that just happened to correspond to the summer we bought the croquet set. In the front of the lot the great California black oak, always a model of prime, vibrant health, has lately begun fighting a losing battle with mistletoe. A tree surgeon will be called in to make the final decision, but it looks as though the oak, like the apricot, will have to be cut down.

Life is that way. The essence of it is change. Living things are born; they mature, grow old, and die. They consume other living things, compete with them, crowd them, lose to them. The only way to force a living thing to stop changing is to kill it.

This knowledge needs to enlighten our attitudes toward human-caused change. It is qualitatively no different from natural change. Its scale and scope are often worrisome: but it is the scale and scope we need to be addressing in such cases, not the fact of change itself.

Southeast of my home about fifteen miles the Pacific Crest Trail meets Interstate 5 (the main north-south route for the

Pacific states) near the top of a 4,400-foot-high pass called Siskiyou Summit. The freeway is clearly far more massive and environmentally destructive than the trail is. Whole mountainsides have been moved to accommodate it. Its four lanes of white concrete, plus median and shoulders, cut a sterile swath hundreds of feet wide through the forest, creating a major barrier to wildlife migration. The chemical spoor of heavy vehicular traffic clings to the roadway and washes downhill with the rains; the exhalations of internal combustion beasts hang heavily over everything. If I-5 were suddenly to be abandoned, the scars on the land would remain for centuries, probably for millennia. There is every reason in the world to fight the imposition of more of these things on America's remaining wild areas.

Come with me, though, off the freeway for a moment. We turn off at the Mount Ashland exit, about half a mile below the summit of the pass, and find ourselves immediately on an older, parallel roadway, a two-lane, macadamized stretch of U.S. 99, known locally as "Old 99." Until the interstate was built, this was the main road through these mountains. Its construction, too, involved some serious earth moving — road cuts, fill, the laying of a precisely engineered roadbed — and its scale, like that of the freeway, is such that it would seriously have damaged any heretofore wild area it entered. The damage would have been only a third or so of that caused by the freeway, but it would have been enough that society might rightfully have questioned whether the road should be built.

A quarter mile or so up this stretch of Old 99, just beyond the first major road cut, a parking area opens on the right. We leave the car here and start walking west. We are on one of the last sections of the Pacific Crest National Scenic Trail to be constructed, a section whose completion was held up for years by negotiations with the private landowners over whose land it passes. The trail rises quickly through mixed conifers and hardwoods, passes around an open, meadowy corner marked by stone outcrops, and suddenly deposits us on another stretch of macadam. This, you might say, is the "third tier," the original paved road through these mountains. Narrower and curvier than Old 99, lying far more lightly on the land, it has been out of use since around 1940; a few isolated stretches, such as this one, are all that remain distinguishable. It is still clearly a road, still clearly a disturbance, but the differences between it and the trail have begun to blur — far enough that the trail designers could get away with using about three hundred yards of it as part of the trailbed. Should roads like this be kept out of our remaining wild areas? Probably; but the answer is far less certain than it was for Old 99 and the Interstate. Reasonable people could argue about it. From the freeway to Old 99 to this third tier — *old* Old 99 — we have passed through a difference in destructive impact of at least an order of magnitude. Can we justify treating them by the same rules? When we say we don't want any more roads, which type of roads do we don't want?

None of this should be taken to mean that we should open our parks and wilderness areas to unrestrained commercial development. It does mean that we should consider the possibility that some development may be compatible with the goals of these areas. If a proposed change is on such a scale that it cannot be accommodated by the natural systems it would disturb, then we need to question it seriously. If it is within the range of the system's adaptability, there are far fewer grounds for objection. If logging can be done in such a way as to be ecologically indistinguishable from the effects of fire, on what grounds do we allow the one and ban the other?

But the lesson is not over. On up the way a mile or so, just before a short side path that intersects the Mount Ashland Ski Road at a low place called Colestin Gap, the Pacific Crest Trail climbs a short way up a broad gully filled with green new growth, indistinguishable from other gullies and other green new growth on these hillsides. Near the top of the climb a small metal sign catches the eye. It identifies the gully as the route of the original stage road over Siskiyou Summit — the

Interstate 5 of its day, the main freight route up the Pacific tier of states. Here in this gully, where the coaches slowed to a near walk as the horses labored up the final incline, the famed highwayman Black Bart pulled off two major heists. That was only a little over a hundred years ago. Today, try as you may, you will be hard put to discover even a trace of a wheel's long-ago passage.

Notes

PROLOGUE: THE PEOPLE OF THE CLIFFS

1 My account of the Escalante expedition is based on that found in John Bartlett Brebner, *Explorers of North America, 1492–1806* (New York: Macmillan, 1933).

2 The information on Mesa Verde in these pages comes primarily from Dewitt Jones and Linda S. Cordell, *Anasazi World* (Portland, Oreg.: Graphic Arts Center Publishing Company, 1985).

5 The Adam Smith passage from *The Wealth of Nations* is quoted by Riddell, Shackelford, and Stamos in *Economics: A Tool for Understanding Society*, 3d ed. (Reading, Mass.: Addison-Wesley, 1987), p. 85.

6 Soma Golden's article in the *New York Times* for March 9, 1976, is reprinted in its entirety in Riddell, Shackelford, and Stamos, *Economics*, pp. 58–62.

9 Marsh on sight and seeing comes from Stewart L. Udall, *The Quiet Crisis* (New York: Avon, 1964), p. 83.

10 The quotes from Marsh and his reviewers cited on these pages are found in Udall, *The Quiet Crisis*, pp. 89 and 88.

11 The "ocean of organic being" quote is from George Perkins Marsh, *Man and Nature: The Earth as Modified by Human Action*, 2d ed. (New York: Scribner, Armstrong, 1874), p. 144. Marsh on "depravation, barbarism," and so forth, is quoted in Udall, *The Quiet Crisis*, p. 89.

18 "They seem not . . . above the green canyons." Jones and Cordell, *Anasazi World*, p. 34.
That the blame for the Southwest's air pollution lies with coal-fired power plants has been thoroughly documented. See, for

example, the editorial "The Pall over Grand Canyon," in the *Denver Post,* January 27, 1991.

ONLY ONE HOUSEHOLD

24 For further information on deepwell disposal, see my article on the subject in William Ashworth, *The Encyclopedia of Environmental Studies* (New York: Facts on File, 1991), pp. 96–97. The "serious and irreversible degradation" quote is from the Medford (Oregon) *Mail Tribune,* November 6, 1992 (hereafter cited simply as *Mail Tribune*); "scenic vistas . . . indistinct or invisible" comes from the *Mail Tribune* for January 14, 1993.

25 The Thoreau quote comes from the Norton critical edition of *Walden* (New York: Norton, 1966), p. 131.

26 Dan Quayle was quoted in *Wild Oregon* (Fall 1992), p. 16; the George Wuerthner quote is from *Wild Oregon* (Summer 1992), p. 12; Richard Darman's green vegetables are found in *Greenpeace* (September/October 1990), p. 2.

27 The figures on this page come primarily from the *Statistical Abstract of the United States* (U.S. Department of Commerce, Bureau of the Census, various dates).

OF LAWS AND REGULATIONS

31 The Florida developer's story comes from a Los Angeles Times News Service feature story printed in the *Mail Tribune* on December 27, 1992.

32 The Superfund material is taken from the General Accounting Office publication *Superfund: Problems with the Completeness and Consistency of Site Cleanup Plans.* Report to the Chairman, Subcommittee on Superfund, Ocean and Water Protection, Committee on Environment and Public Works, U.S. Senate, May 1992 (GAO/RCED-92-138).

33 "Dramatic new initiatives" and "precedent-setting" were the terms used in Great Lakes United, *Unfulfilled Promises: A Citizens' Review of the Great Lakes Water Quality Agreement* (Buffalo, N.Y.: February 1987), p. 1 and preface (unpaged). The actual phrasing was "The philosophy adopted for control

of inputs of persistent toxic substances shall be zero discharge." *Great Lakes Water Quality Agreement of 1978*, Annex 12, Paragraph (2)(a)(ii).
"We were shocked . . . contaminated fill into the Lakes." Great Lakes United, *Unfulfilled Promises*, preface (unpaged).

34 "We hereby formally request . . . intervention in this matter." *The Great Lakes United* 6:3 (Fall 1991), p. 1. The information in the rest of the paragraph is also from this source.

35 "Four years ago . . . single new guideline." Quoted in the *Mail Tribune*, December 31, 1991.

36 The Mellette County, South Dakota, story is from the Sioux Falls (South Dakota) *Argus Leader* for July 29, 1992; the Avtex Fibers case is reported in GAO, *Superfund: Problems with the Completeness and Consistency of Site Cleanup Plans*, p. 7.

37 Statistics on atmospheric loadings of lead are from the *1993 Information Please Environmental Almanac* (Boston: Houghton Mifflin, 1993), p. 89. I recounted the Cuyahoga story more thoroughly in William Ashworth, *The Late, Great Lakes: An Environmental History* (New York: Knopf, 1987), p. 143, and notes thereto.
The Smokies' smoke is analyzed in the *Smokies Guide* (Gatlinburg, Tenn.: National Park Service, Summer 1992), p. 6; Mount Washington's ozone levels were posted on an informational display in the Adirondack Club lodge at Pinkham Notch, New Hampshire, observed by the author on August 28, 1992.

38 The Los Angeles Plan was thoroughly analyzed in William Boly, "Smog City Wants to Make This Perfectly Clear," *Hippocrates* (April 1992), pp. 56ff; Supervisor Antonovich's quote is on p. 59. Italy's experience with banning private automobiles, and the quotes about it, are found in the *Mail Tribune*, January 12, 1993 (Los Angeles Times News Service).

39 The California gnatcatcher's problems were reported in the *Mail Tribune*, December 27, 1992 (Los Angeles Times News Service).

OF PARKS AND PRESERVES

42 The information on the history of the national parks movement comes primarily from Alfred Runte, *National Parks: The Amer-*

ican Experience, 2d ed., rev. (Lincoln: University of Nebraska Press, 1987), prologue and first two chapters.

44 Statistics on the extent of the national park system are from my own *Encyclopedia of Environmental Studies,* pp. 255–56; the quote from the Yellowstone Act is found in Runte, *National Parks,* p. 46.

The Adirondack Preserve chronology is thoroughly detailed in Norman J. Van Valkenburgh's prologue to Neal S. Burdick, ed., *A Century Wild: Essays Commemorating the Centennial of the Adirondack Forest Preserve* (Saranac Lake, N.Y.: Chauncy Press, 1985). Early redwoods preservation efforts are reported in Kramer Adams, *The Redwoods* (New York: Popular Library, n.d.), p. 112; the Olympic National Monument material comes from Ruby El Hult, *Untamed Olympics: The Story of a Peninsula* (Portland, Oreg.: Binfords & Mort, 1954), pp. 213–15.

46 My account of the intrusion into the South Warner Wilderness is based on the Forest Service's *South Warner Wilderness Area South Boundary Discrepancy Report* (Modoc National Forest, May 22, 1973); conversations with Betsy Ballard (Forest Service) and Luis Ireland (Sierra Club); and personal observation.

Information on the New River Preserve logging incident came to me from National Park Service sources via a printout of a piece of Park Service E-mail, "Ranger Activities Division Morning Report," dated February 8, 1993.

48 My copy of "1993 Goals & Objectives for the Southwest Region National Park Service" (National Park Service, Southwest Region, 1992) is courtesy of Scott Walker of Big Thicket National Preserve.

49 Information on the Devils Tower cottonwoods was obtained from the park ranger's fireside interpretive talk at Devils Tower National Monument on the evening of July 27, 1992.

The fate of the Fraser firs is reported in four articles: "Will Our Grandkids See a Fraser Fir Tree?"; "Pine Beetle Causing Orange Trees in Smokies"; "Air Pollution Is Damaging the Park"; and "International Biosphere Reserve," all in *Smokies Guide: The Official Newspaper of Great Smoky Mountains National Park* (Summer 1992).

50 For a more complete account, see the chapter entitled "Rain" in my book *The Late, Great Lakes,* with sources.

51 Sources for the Big Thicket story include Geyata Ajilvsgi, *Wild Flowers of the Big Thicket: East Texas, and Western Louisiana* (College Station: Texas A&M University Press, 1979); National Park Foundation, *The Complete Guide to America's National Parks, 1990–1991 Edition* (New York: Prentice Hall, 1990); and personal correspondence with Scott Walker dated December 23, 1992.

52 The Oregon Caves material is from "Islands of Hope," *Oregon Caves Underworld* (Oregon Caves National Monument visitors' newsletter) (Summer 1992), and from several conversations with John Miele, former supervisor, Oregon Caves National Monument. Material on the Herbert Hoover National Historic Park comes from park brochures and personal observation.

53 The date for the first development in the Everglades is found in Marjorie Stoneman Douglas, *The Everglades: River of Grass,* rev. ed. (Sarasota, Fla.: Pineapple Press, 1988), p. 284.
The East Everglades versus C-111 battle is recounted fully in Douglas, *The Everglades,* and in the *Visitors' Guide to South Florida's National Parks: Everglades, Biscayne, Big Cypress, Fort Jefferson* (Winter 1990–91), p. 1.

54 Statistics on Hurricane Andrew come from the *Mail Tribune,* September 6, 1992.
The information on exotic animals, including the quotes, comes from Dan Fesperman, "Call of the Wild Echoes in Florida after Hurricane," *Mail Tribune,* September 20, 1992 (Baltimore Sun News Service).

55 Exotic plant seeding by Hurricane Andrew was reported in Jon Nordheimer, "The Hurricane's Reshaping of the Landscape Isn't Over," *New York Times,* September 3, 1992; and in Carolee Boyles-Sprenkel, "Storm Warnings," *Nature Conservancy* (March/April 1993).
The Interior Department's internal audit was reported in the *Mail Tribune* for November 6, 1992; the National Academy of Sciences report showed up in the same paper on January 14, 1993.

PRIVATE RIGHTS, PUBLIC WRONGS

57 For an excellent textbook introduction to the ideas of Coase and his disciples, see Roger A. Arnold, *Economics* (St. Paul, Minn.: West Publishing, 1989), pp. 720–27 (and sidebars).

59 The "land ethic" is discussed by Aldo Leopold in *A Sand County Almanac* (New York: Sierra Club/Ballantine, 1971), pp. 237–64.

60 The story of Dorothy Irwin's Enchanted Forest (including the quotes) comes from the *San Francisco Chronicle,* September 28, 1992.

THE MIRROR FAILURE

62 The Mountain States Legal Foundation meeting was reported in the *Mail Tribune* on February 14, 1993 (AP); Congressman Smith's correspondence was printed in the same paper on February 28, 1993.

63 Pinchot's report of Senator Clark's speech can be found in *Breaking New Ground* (1947; reprint, Washington, D.C.: Island Press, 1987), p. 109.

64 The rise in forest products prices and Mr. Freeman's reaction to them were both reported in the *Mail Tribune* on February 14, 1993; the Congressional Research Service study was reported in the same paper on March 12, 1993.
The figures on economic growth are from the *Mail Tribune* for March 16, 1993.

65 The rate of increase in joblessness can be found in the *Mail Tribune* for March 4, 1993; the reactions to it by Bill Clinton and Dave Meikle come from a copyrighted story by Sharon Cohen of the Associated Press printed in the same paper on March 14, 1993.
The page in question was in the business section of the *Mail Tribune* for March 16, 1993.
The best textbook account of the Phillips curve story that I know of is that in Arnold, *Economics,* pp. 322–31.

THE DEER IN THE MALL

68 The Hidden Valley bollard was reported in the *Mail Tribune* on February 2, 1993; the deer in the Mountain View Mall showed up in the same newspaper ten days earlier, on January 23.

69 The information for this paragraph on oil spills came from three separate articles in the *Mail Tribune,* dated January 10, 1993 (Washington Post News Service); January 12, 1993 (AP); and January 22, 1993 (AP).

The trials of modern mushroom hunters were reported in the *Mail Tribune* on May 11, 1993.

70 Judge Hogan's ruling and the reactions to it were reported in the *Mail Tribune* on December 29, 1992.

OF MYTHS AND PARADIGMS

73 The history of *paradigm* is more completely told in the *Oxford English Dictionary,* 2d ed., vol. 11 (Oxford: Clarendon Press, 1989), p. 183.

74 The remarks by Frederick Jackson Turner come from his paper "The Significance of the Frontier in American History," reprinted in Daniel J. Boorstin, ed., *An American Primer* (Chicago: University of Chicago Press, 1968), pp. 545ff.

76 For a succinct account of the enclosure movement, see the article on "enclosure" in the 1992 edition of the *Academic American Encyclopedia* (New York: Grolier, 1992) (my copy is on CD/ROM and is thus unpaged).

The "wilde beastes and wilde men" are found in William Bradford, *History of Plimoth Plantation,* ed. William T. Davis (New York: Barnes & Noble, 1959), p. 96.

79 Homestead National Monument's history was learned from National Park Service interpretive exhibits at Homestead National Monument, observed by the author on July 31, 1992.

82 The quote on Cumberland Gap, and the history of the Gap's role in the Civil War, come from National Park Service interpretive materials at Cumberland Gap National Recreation Area observed by the author on August 5, 1992.

SPACESHIP GAIA

83 The earliest reference by Fuller to "Spaceship Earth" that I
have been able to find is in *Prospect for Humanity* (1964), as
quoted in *Bartlett's Familiar Quotations,* 16th ed. (Boston:
Little, Brown, 1992), p. 691.
The "Earth is a beautifully designed spaceship . . ." quote is
from R. Buckminster Fuller, "Technology and the Human Environment," in Robert Disch, ed., *The Ecological Conscience:
Values for Survival* (Englewood Cliffs, N.J.: Prentice-Hall, 1970),
p. 174.

84 Charles Elton's crowbar image was used in Elton, *Voles, Mice
and Lemmings: Problems in Population Dynamics* (Oxford:
Clarendon Press, 1942), p. 105.

85 This account of the Gaia hypothesis was recast from the article
I wrote on the subject in Ashworth, *The Encyclopedia of Environmental Studies,* pp. 158–59.

THINKING LIKE A FOREST

89 DuWayne Gebken used the "sideways" analogy in a conversation with the author in his office at the Wisconsin Department
of Natural Resources in Madison on July 7, 1983.

90 My immediate source for this well-known Muir quotation
was David Brower, ed., *Gentle Wilderness: The Sierra Nevada*
(New York: Sierra Club/Ballantine Books, 1968), p. 146; "Everything is connected . . ." is from Barry Commoner, *The Closing
Circle: Nature, Man & Technology* (New York: Knopf, 1971),
p. 33; the John Osborne quote is from *Luther* (New York:
New American Library, 1963), p. 73.

92 The Jane Elder quote is from a conversation with her on July
7, 1983, in the Midwest Office of the Sierra Club in Madison,
Wisconsin.
Aldo Leopold's attempt at an "extension of the social conscience" is found in *Sand County Almanac,* p. 246.

93 The Aldo Leopold quotes are from *Sand County Almanac,*
pp. 201–2.

SCARCITY

97 This account of the Chernobyl disaster is adapted from my article in Ashworth, *The Encyclopedia of Environmental Studies,* p. 65; the information on the restarting of the reactors is from the *Mail Tribune* for December 14, 1992.

VALUE

102 Adam Smith on the diamonds-and-water paradox is quoted in Riddell, Shackelford, and Stamos, *Economics,* p. 69.
"One of the few places in North America . . ." Since I wrote these words, the discoverers of a major diamond deposit in northern Canada have gone public.

MARGINS AND OPPORTUNITIES

106 The professor with the chocolate bars was Dr. Richard Stuart at Whitman College (Walla Walla, Washington) when I was a student there in the early 1960s.

MARKET ECOLOGY

115 The Andrew Bard Schmookler quote is from *Fool's Gold* (San Francisco: HarperSanFrancisco, 1993), pp. 176–77.
Daniel D. Chiras's *Lessons from Nature* was published by Island Press (Washington, D.C.) in 1992.
My source for the Thomas Carlyle story was Arnold, *Economics,* pp. 49–50.

119 For Gifford Pinchot's views on monopolies, read Pinchot, *Breaking New Ground,* pp. 332–33, 506–8.

LIMITS

124 Donella H. Meadows, Dennis L. Meadows, Jorgen Randers, and William W. Behrens III, *The Limits to Growth* (New York: Potomac Associates, New American Library, 1972).

128 Accounts of the Kaibab deer explosion are widespread in ecological literature. This one is retold from my earlier report in
Ashworth, *The Carson Factor* (New York: Hawthorn Books,
1979), pp. 141–43; that account, in turn, was based primarily
on Lorus J. Milne and Margery Milne, *The Balance of Nature*
(New York: Knopf, 1960), pp. 78–82.

133 The cottonwood experiments of Boise Cascade and Potlatch
were reported in the *Mail Tribune* on March 30, 1993.

134 Louisiana Pacific's deal for Venezuelan timber was recounted
in the same paper on April 3, 1993.

THE WHOLE IS NOT THE TOTAL

138 Buckminster Fuller on synergy is quoted from Fuller, "Technology," p. 175.

139 See Arnold, *Economics*, p. 16. The fallacy of composition is
also the principal topic of economist Thomas C. Schelling's
provocative and highly recommendable little volume *Micromotives and Macrobehavior* (New York: Norton, 1978).

143 Information on Storm King was gathered from numerous sources,
including (but not limited to) Gene Marine, *America the Raped*
(New York: Avon, 1969), pp. 88–101; New York–New Jersey
Trail Conference, *New York Walk Book* (Garden City, N.Y.:
Doubleday, 1971), pp. 95–97; my article on Storm King in
Ashworth, *Encyclopedia of Environmental Studies*, pp. 371–
72; and personal observation at the mountain.

THY NEIGHBOR'S SACRIFICE

146 An excellent textbook treatment of the ideas discussed in this
chapter can be found in Douglas F. Greer, *Business, Government, and Society* (New York: Macmillan, 1983), pp. 31–33.
The interested reader should also see Schelling, *Micromotives
and Macrobehavior*, pp. 110–33.

OTHER PEOPLE'S GARBAGE

153 The General Accounting Office's look at the EPA was published as *Environmental Enforcement: Penalties May Not Re-*

cover *Economic Benefits Gained by Violators,* U.S. General Accounting Office Report to Congressional Requesters, June 1991 (GAO/RCED-91–166); the financial-gain data appears on p. 5, the information about the content of the reporting forms on pp. 9–10.

154 The "laugh test" is described in GAO, *Environmental Enforcement,* p. 12.

NOT IN MY BACK YARD

155 Mayor Welch's comment on garbage is quoted in Eugene A. Glysson, James R. Packard, and Cyril H. Barnes, *The Problem of Solid-Waste Disposal* (Ann Arbor: University of Michigan College of Engineering, 1972), p. iii.

159 For information on the Detroit trash incinerator, see, for example, the *Detroit MetroTimes,* June 8–14, 1988, pp. 6, 14, and 16.

THE PRISONERS' DILEMMA

161 An excellent description of the math behind the prisoner's dilemma (including versions involving more than two players) may be found in Schelling, *Micromotives and Macrobehavior,* chap. 7 ("Hockey Helmets, Daylight Saving, and Other Binary Choices").

WHAT DOES IT COST TO RUN A COUNTRY?

168 The Jackson County/Orange County comparisons come from an article by Paul MacComber in the *Mail Tribune,* December 12, 1992.

169 "For every dollar . . . open farmland." *Density-Related Public Costs* (Washington, D.C.: American Farmland Trust, 1986), p. 41.

GROWING PAINS

174 David Brower's "sermon" is quoted from John McPhee, *Encounters with the Archdruid* (New York: Farrar, Straus and

Giroux, 1971); the cancer comparison appears on p. 83, the compression of Earth's history into a single year on p. 80.

175 Chiras, *Lessons from Nature,* p. 70.

George Bush's comments on growth appeared in the *Mail Tribune* on October 29, 1992.

176 "Any human activity . . . could flourish." Meadows, Meadows, Randers, and Behrens, *The Limits to Growth,* p. 180.

177 "Growth is a means . . . where it may and where it should." Donella H. Meadows, "A Company Decides Not to Grow," *Los Angeles Times,* December 27, 1992.

FLOWS AND FUNDS

181 Steve Reynolds made his remark in an interview with the *National Geographic*'s Thomas Y. Canby, who put it in the magazine (Thomas Y. Canby, "Water — Our Most Precious Resource," *National Geographic* [August 1980]; quoted in William Ashworth, *Nor Any Drop to Drink* [New York: Summit Books, 1982], p. 113).

NATIONAL WEALTH AND THE WEALTH OF NATIONS

192 This account of Simon Kuznets and the GNP has been assembled from several sources, notably the article on Kuznets in *Funk & Wagnalls New Encyclopedia,* vol. 14 (New York: Funk & Wagnalls, 1975), p. 470; Chiras, *Lessons from Nature,* pp. 55–56; and Arnold, *Economics,* pp. 320–31.

197 The MEW is fully explained in Arnold, *Economics,* p. 118.

198 A good account of the Human Development Index appears in Lester Brown, Christopher Flavin, and Sandra Postel, *Saving the Planet* (New York: Norton, 1991), pp. 125–26; my source for both the PQLI and the ASEDI was Paul Ekins, Mayer Hillman, and Robert Hutchison, *The Gaia Atlas of Green Economics* (New York: Doubleday Anchor, 1992), p. 62.

The ISEW is covered thoroughly by Ekins, Hillman, and Hutchison, *The Gaia Atlas,* and Brown, Flavin, and Postel, *Saving the Planet.*

199 "Even a burglar couldn't have said it better." Mark Twain, "Glances at History," in *Letters from the Earth: New Uncen-*

sored Writings of Mark Twain, ed. Bernard DeVoto (New York: Crest Books, Fawcett World Library, 1963).

201 Buckminster Fuller's definition of wealth comes from Fuller, "Technology," p. 177.

GETTING OUR MONEY'S WORTH

206 For an interesting contrast in views on the topic of global warming, see Cheryl Simon Silver, "Greenhouse Warming," in the *1993 Information Please Environmental Almanac,* and Wilfred Beckerman, "Global Warming: A Skeptical Economic Assessment," in Dieter Helm, ed., *Economic Policy Towards the Environment* (Oxford, U.K.: Blackwell Publishers, 1991).

208 The Department of Interior lawsuit against the state of Florida is detailed in "Water Quality Issue May Be Headed for Resolution," *Visitors' Guide to South Florida National Parks* (Winter 1990–91), p. 6.

For information on the Michigan Environmental Response Act, see, for example, Dawson Bell, "State Identifies 257 More Sites of Toxic Waste Underground Tank Leaks," *Detroit Free Press,* August 10, 1989.

The Montrose Chemical suit settlement was reported in the *Mail Tribune* on November 6, 1992 (Los Angeles Times News Service).

209 Information on the ALCOA sites came from James Ransome, "ALCOA Guilty of Environmental Crimes," *The Great Lakes United* (Fall 1991), p. 5.

The Astoria plywood mill story was reported in the *Mail Tribune* on January 17, 1993.

213 The immorality of clear-cuts is examined in Colin Fletcher, *The Secret Worlds of Colin Fletcher* (New York: Vintage Books, 1989), p. 236; for the source of the "land ethic" quote, see the notes to the chapter "Private Rights, Public Wrongs."

213 Zane Smith made his comments to me beside Azalea Lake in what is now the Red Buttes Wilderness on July 4, 1978.

214 The information on Rancho Seco comes primarily from the *1991 Sacramento Municipal Utility District Annual Report;* the quote about the Scattergood Award is on p. 2.

215 Ed Smeloff made his comment about the "albatross" during a

panel discussion at the Labor-Environmental Solidarity Network Conference in Portland, Oregon, on March 21, 1992.

217 "A piece at a time." 1991 *Sacramento Municipal Utility District Annual Report,* p. 4.

My conversation with the information booth attendant at SMUD took place on June 2, 1992.

FALSIFYING THE MARKET

219 For admiring articles on feebates, see, among other sources, Amory and Hunter Lovins, "The Energy Saboteurs Are in the White House," *Los Angeles Times,* January 21, 1991; and William H. Miller, "Energy: The Solutions Are Obvious," *Industry Week,* January 6, 1992.

PAY AS YOU GO

229 A succinct account of the history of U.S. government revenue raising can be found in the *Information Please Almanac,* 1990 ed. (Boston: Houghton Mifflin, 1990), p. 77.

231 For another view of user fees for recreation, see Paul Rauber, "What Price a Walk in the Woods?" *Sierra* (May/June 1993), pp. 46–49.

Although many states run park permit systems, the best model for a national nature-access permit system is probably the Texas Conservation Passport, the annual parks permit issued by the state of Texas. See any of numerous brochures on the subject available from the Texas Parks and Wildlife Department.

233 The quotes from Representative Bob Smith on this page come from a letter the congressman sent to his constituents on April 7, 1993.

235 Side payments, and Ronald Coase's analysis of them, are thoroughly analyzed in Dieter Helm and David Pierce, "Economic Policy Towards the Environment: An Overview"; and in Karl-Göran Mäler, "International Environmental Problems," both in Helm, *Economic Policy Towards the Environment.*

THE PUBLIC LANDS

239 A succinct account of this period in American history is provided in Ray Allen Billington, *The Westward Movement in
the United States* (Princeton, N.J.: D. Van Nostrand, 1959),
pp. 29–30.
241 The case for privatization as an environmental protection tool
is cogently but ultimately unpersuasively argued in Walter E.
Block, ed., *Economics and the Environment: A Reconciliation*
(Vancouver, B.C.: The Fraser Institute, 1990).
244 "Drive through Incline Village . . ." or try driving around Lake
Arrowhead, in the San Bernardino Mountains above Los Angeles. The only public access to this fairly large lake is a concrete walkway behind a strip mall, one end anchored by a tiny
park, the other by a boat ramp behind the local McDonald's.
The rest of the shore is covered by houses, which also completely fill the mountain basin the lake sits in.
246 Larry James showed me around the proposed Issaquah development on June 18, 1992; the quotes attributed to him come
from that tour.
247 For a complete, highly cogent explanation of the marketization
alternative, see Randal O'Toole, *Reforming the Forest Service*
(Washington, D.C.: Island Press, 1988).

HOW MUCH IS A RIVER WORTH?

254 The Leontief analysis example is retold from Wassily Leontief,
"Environmental Repercussions and the Economic Structure:
An Input-Output Approach," *Review of Economics and
Statistics* (August 1970); reprinted in Robert Dorfman and
Nancy S. Dorfman, eds., *Economics of the Environment: Se-
lected Readings* (New York: Norton, 1972), pp. 403–22.
257 "Air, water and land . . . environmental impact of its prod-
ucts and services." Frank P. Popoff and David T. Buzzelli, "Full-
Cost Accounting," *Chemical and Engineering News,* January
11, 1993, p. 8.

259 The Vermont potty problem was reported in the Burlington *Free Press* on August 26, 1992. Vermont is hardly alone; perhaps this is the time to spring on an unsuspecting public the song I wrote on U.S. 287 in east Texas, somewhere between Beaumont and Palestine.

The Texas Potty Song
In the Great State of Texas the thing that perplexes
Is where you can find a commode;
By the Mexican border they think that you oughter
Just hold it until you explode.
In the wide open spaces, just looking for places
To pee can take most of your time;
You could go in the gutter, but that would be utter-
Ly gauche, and besides, it's a crime.

When your bladder capacity says that you hasta pee,
Texas is no place to travel.
You can drive till you burst or (whichever comes first)
Till your kidneys begin to unravel.
There's mechanical steers and they drink lots of beers
In the bars, so they say, hereabouts;
When a cowboy's been boozin', just what is he usin'
That I don't know nothin' about?

260 Buckminster Fuller on "affording" things comes from Fuller, "Technology," p. 177.
263 For Gifford Pinchot's views on monopolies, read Pinchot, *Breaking New Ground*, pp. 332–33, 506–8; the figures on pollution from starting and stopping an internal combustion engine, versus merely idling it, come from an article in the *Mail Tribune* for July 2, 1992, which cited as its source "an EPA study."

My source for the developers' rules of thumb is Joel Garreau, *Edge City* (New York: Doubleday, 1991), pp. 463–71.
264 The potential Walden Pond development is discussed in Garreau, *Edge City*, pp. 94–97.
266 The full citation for Alexander's book is Christopher Alexan-

der, Sara Ishikawa, and Murray Silverstein, with Max Jacobson, Ingrid Fiksdahl-King, and Shlomo Angel, *A Pattern Language: Towns, Buildings, Construction* (New York: Oxford University Press, 1977).

ECONOMIC JUSTICE, ENVIRONMENTAL JUSTICE

271 The figures on U.S. consumption compared with that of the rest of the world are all calculations from data recorded in the *Statistical Abstract of the United States* and the *Information Please Almanac,* 1990 ed.

273 William Stanley Jevons on marginal returns is quoted in Arnold, *Economics,* p. 443.

274 For the record, I should probably state here that my wife and I did indeed raise three daughters — all, for a space of several years, simultaneously in their teens — in a house with just one bathroom. It is not always comfortable, but it can be done.

276 The garbage recycling effort in Victoria, British Columbia, was reported in Tom McFeely, "Disposing of British Columbia's Waste Worries," *British Columbia Report,* June 8, 1992, p. 7.

277 The Farmington, Minnesota, material (including the quote from Bob Williamson) comes from the Minneapolis *Star-Tribune* for February 14, 1991.

IS THIS JOB NECESSARY?

280 David Chism's statement was made during a panel discussion at the Labor-Environmental Solidarity Network Conference, in Portland, Oregon, on March 21, 1992.

Tony Mazzochi's remarks came a few minutes earlier, during his keynote address to the conference. The extended quote on the "Superfund for workers" is taken from Mazzochi's foreword to Lucinda Wykle, Ward Morehouse, and David Dembo, *Worker Empowerment in a Changing Economy: Jobs, Military Production and the Environment* (New York: Apex Press, 1991), p. ix.

284 My conversation with Ed Kupillas took place outside the South Medford High School auditorium in Medford, Oregon, on May 2, 1989.

286 Tony Mazzochi's remarks on defense conversion were made during a panel discussion at the Labor-Environmental Solidarity Network Conference, in Portland, Oregon, on March 21, 1992.
The quotation from Dr. Cook is taken from an article in the
Ashland (Oregon) *Daily Tidings* for July 14, 1989.

ACCESS TO NATURE

290 A succinct account of Carhart's role in the protection of Trapper Lake can be found in John C. Hendee, George H. Stankey,
and Robert C. Lucas, *Wilderness Management* (Washington,
D.C.: USDA–Forest Service Miscellaneous Publication No. 1365,
October 1978), pp. 34–35.

291 "To run a line . . . uses the term." From Arthur H. Carhart,
*Planning for America's Wildlands: A Handbook for Land-use
Planners, Managers and Executives, Committee and Commission Members, Conservation Leaders, and All Who Face Problems of Wildland Management* (Harrisburg, Pa.: The Telegraph
Press, 1961), p. 21. The quote a few lines later about "constant change" is found on p. 41 of the same source.
"May I interpolate this thought . . . one-use land management." Carhart, *America's Wildlands,* p. 59.

BROWSE LINES

299 See Joel Garreau, *Edge City.*

302 "No one stopped to consider . . ." Well, almost no one. For a
cogent analysis of what was wrong with South Florida's building codes, see Sharon Cohen and Fred Bayles, "Development
Couldn't Cope with Storm's Power," *Mail Tribune,* September
6, 1992, p. 4A (AP).
"As much as a thousand miles away . . ." Los Angeles gets
part of its water supply from the Colorado River, putting it in
direct conflict with Denver for water rights. See my analysis in
William Ashworth, *Nor Any Drop to Drink* (New York: Summit Books, 1982), pp. 84–98.

306 George Tinker's thoughts on indigenous peoples are spelled out
in an interview, "With Drum and Cup," published in *Sojourners* (January 1991), pp. 15–18; in George Tinker, "For All

My Relations," *Sojourners* (January 1991), pp. 19–21; and in George Tinker, "The Full Circle of Liberation," *Sojourners* (October 1992), pp. 12–17.

THE WORLD IS NOT A WAX MUSEUM

308 Buckminster Fuller on nature's experiments was quoted in the Minneapolis *Tribune,* April 30, 1978.
309 My account of the history of the Madison Slide is taken primarily from interpretive materials at the site as they existed in the summer of 1991, plus my own memories of the event.
310 For a concise geological history of the Great Lakes region, see the second chapter of my book *The Late, Great Lakes.*

Bibliography

I have organized the materials in this bibliography into two groups. Group I may be thought of as the "seminal" group: it contains those works I found particularly stimulating, thought-provoking and/or original, and which I leaned upon heavily while developing my own ideas. In geological terms, these are the parent materials out of which the soil of the present work evolved. Group II contains other works I found useful during the writing process, either for corroborating evidence or as jousting partners against which to sharpen my swordsmanship. If we stick with the geological metaphor, these are erratics — interesting, valuable even, but essentially foreign to the local environment, even though they may have contributed important elements to it. I should probably add that the line between the groups is by no means hard and fast, and it was sometimes difficult to decide in which group a particular work belonged. Al Gore's *Earth in the Balance* and Jack Brill and Alan Reder's *Investing from the Heart* are especially strong examples of these borderline items; I have placed Gore's book in Group I and Brill and Reder's in Group II, but each of them might just as easily go in the other category.

GROUP I

Alperovitz, Gar, and Jeff Faux. *Rebuilding America: A Blueprint for the New Economy.* New York: Pantheon Books, 1984.

Billington, Ray Allen. *The Westward Movement in the United States.* Princeton, N.J.: D. Van Nostrand, 1959.

Cairncross, Frances. *Costing the Earth: The Challenge to Governments, the Opportunities for Business.* Boston: Harvard Business School Press, 1993.

Carhart, Arthur H. *Planning for America's Wildlands: A Handbook for Land-use Planners, Managers and Executives, Committee and Commission Members, Conservation Leaders, and All Who Face Problems of Wildland Management.* Harrisburg, Pa.: The Telegraph Press, 1961.

Fuller, Buckminster. "Technology and the Human Environment." In *The Ecological Conscience: Values for Survival,* edited by Robert Disch. Englewood Cliffs, N.J.: Prentice-Hall, 1970.

Garreau, Joel. *Edge City.* New York: Doubleday, 1991.

Gore, Al. *Earth in the Balance: Ecology and the Human Spirit.* Boston: Houghton Mifflin, 1992.

Johnson, Warren. *Muddling Toward Frugality.* San Francisco: Sierra Club Books, 1978.

Leopold, Aldo. *A Sand County Almanac.* New York: Sierra Club/ Ballantine Books, 1971.

Marsh, George Perkins. *Man and Nature: The Earth as Modified by Human Action.* 2d ed. New York: Scribner, Armstrong, 1874.

Meadows, Donella H., Dennis L. Meadows, Jorgen Randers, and William W. Behrens III. *The Limits to Growth.* New York: Potomac Associates, New American Library, 1972.

Pinchot, Gifford. *Breaking New Ground.* Conservation Classics ed. 1947. Reprint, Washington, D.C.: Island Press, 1987.

Schelling, Thomas C. *Micromotives and Macrobehavior.* New York: Norton, 1978.

Schumacher, E. F. *Small Is Beautiful.* New York: Harper & Row, 1973.

Smith, Adam. *An Inquiry into the Nature and Causes of the Wealth of Nations.* New York: Modern Library, 1937.

Turner, Frederick. *Beyond Geography: The Western Spirit Against the Wilderness.* New Brunswick, N.J.: Rutgers University Press, 1983.

Warsh, David. *The Idea of Economic Complexity.* New York: Viking, 1984.

GROUP II

Adams, Kramer. *The Redwoods.* New York: Popular Library, n.d.

Ajilvsgi, Geyata. *Wild Flowers of the Big Thicket: East Texas, and Western Louisiana.* College Station: Texas A&M University Press, 1979.

Arnold, Roger A. *Economics*. St. Paul, Minn.: West Publishing, 1989.

Ashworth, William. *The Late, Great Lakes: An Environmental History*. New York: Knopf, 1987.

Block, Walter E., ed. *Economics and the Environment: A Reconciliation*. Vancouver, B.C.: The Fraser Institute, 1990.

Brebner, John Bartlett. *Explorers of North America, 1492–1806*. New York: Macmillan, 1933.

Brill, Jack A., and Alan Reder. *Investing from the Heart: A Guide to Socially Responsible Investments and Money Management*. New York: Crown, 1992.

Brown, Lester R., Christopher Flavin, and Sandra Postel. *Saving the Planet: How to Shape an Environmentally Sustainable Global Economy*. New York: Norton, 1991.

Brown, Lester R., et al. *State of the World 1992: A Worldwatch Institute Report on Progress Toward a Sustainable Society*. New York: Norton, 1992.

Burdick, Neal S., ed. *A Century Wild: Essays Commemorating the Centennial of the Adirondack Forest Preserve*. Saranac Lake, N.Y.: Chauncy Press, 1985.

Chiras, Daniel D. *Lessons from Nature: Learning to Live Sustainably on the Earth*. Washington, D.C.: Island Press, 1992.

Commission on the Adirondacks in the Twenty-First Century. *Adirondack Park in the Twenty First Century*. Albany: State of New York, 1990.

Commoner, Barry. *The Closing Circle: Nature, Man & Technology*. New York: Knopf, 1971.

Density-Related Public Costs. Washington, D.C.: American Farmland Trust, 1986.

Dorfman, Robert, and Nancy Dorfman, eds. *Economics of the Environment: Selected Readings*. New York: Norton, 1972.

Douglas, Marjory Stoneman. *The Everglades: River of Grass*. Rev. ed. Sarasota, Fla.: Pineapple Press, 1988.

Ehrenfeld, David. *Beginning Again: People and Nature in the New Millennium*. New York: Oxford University Press, 1993.

Ekins, Paul, Mayer Hillman, and Robert Hutchison. *The Gaia Atlas of Green Economics*. New York: Doubleday Anchor, 1992.

Environmental Enforcement: Penalties May Not Recover Economic Benefits Gained by Violators. Washington, D.C.: General Accounting Office, Report to Congressional Requesters, June 1991 (GAO/RCED-91-166).

Foster, Charles H. W. *The Cape Cod National Seashore: A Landmark Alliance.* Hanover, N.H.: University Press of New England, 1985.

Glysson, Eugene A., James R. Packard, and Cyril H. Barnes. *The Problem of Solid-Waste Disposal.* Ann Arbor: University of Michigan College of Engineering, 1972.

Greer, Douglas F. *Business, Government, and Society.* New York: Macmillan, 1983.

Helm, Dieter, ed. *Economic Policy Towards the Environment.* Oxford, U.K.: Blackwell, 1991.

Hult, Ruby El. *Untamed Olympics: The Story of a Peninsula.* Portland, Oreg.: Binfords & Mort, 1954.

Jones, Dewitt, and Linda S. Cordell. *Anasazi World.* Portland, Oreg.: Graphic Arts Center Publishing Company, 1985.

Lambert, Darwin. *Great Basin Drama: The Story of a National Park.* Niwot, Colo.: Roberts Rinehart Publishers/Great Basin Natural History Association, 1991.

Leatherman, Stephen P. *Barrier Island Handbook.* College Park: University of Maryland Laboratory for Coastal Research, 1988.

Makower, Joel. *The E Factor: The Bottom-Line Approach to Environmentally Responsible Business.* New York: Times Books, 1993.

Marine, Gene. *America the Raped: The Engineering Mentality and the Devastation of a Continent.* New York: Avon, 1969.

McPhee, John. *Encounters with the Archdruid: Narratives about a Conservationist and Three of His Natural Enemies.* New York: Farrar, Straus and Giroux, 1971.

Naisbitt, John, and Patricia Aburdene. *Megatrends 2000: Ten New Directions for the 1990's.* New York: Morrow, 1990.

National Geographic's Guide to the National Parks of the United States. Washington, D.C.: National Geographic Society, 1989.

1993 Goals & Objectives for the Southwest Region National Park Service. Santa Fe, N.M.: National Park Service, Southwest Region, 1992.

Petulla, Joseph M. *American Environmental History: The Exploitation and Conservation of Natural Resources.* San Francisco: Boyd & Fraser, 1977.

Riddell, Tom, Jean Shackelford, and Steve Stamos. *Economics: A Tool for Understanding Society.* 3d ed. Reading, Mass.: Addison-Wesley, 1987.

Runte, Alfred. *National Parks: The American Experience.* 2d ed., rev. Lincoln: University of Nebraska Press, 1987.

Schmookler, Andrew Bard. *Fool's Gold: The Fate of Values in a World of Goods.* San Francisco: HarperSanFrancisco, 1993.

Seneca, Joseph J., and Michael K. Taussig. *Environmental Economics.* Englewood Cliffs, N.J.: Prentice-Hall, 1974.

Thoreau, Henry David. *Walden and Civil Disobedience.* New York: Norton, 1966.

Toffler, Alvin. *Future Shock.* New York: Random House, 1970.

Udall, Stewart L. *The Quiet Crisis.* New York: Avon, 1964.

Unfulfilled Promises: A Citizens' Review of the Great Lakes Water Quality Agreement. Buffalo, N.Y.: Great Lakes United, February 1987.

U.S. Senate Committee on Environment and Public Works, Subcommittee on Superfund, Ocean and Water Protection, Report to the Chairman. *Superfund: Problems with the Completeness and Consistency of Site Cleanup Plans.* May 1992 (GAO/RCED-92-138).

Wijkman, Anders, and Lloyd Timberlake. *Natural Disasters: Acts of God or Acts of Man?* Philadelphia: New Society, 1988.

World Resources Institute. *The 1993 Information Please Environmental Almanac.* Boston: Houghton Mifflin, 1993.

Wykle, Lucinda, Ward Morehouse, and David Dembo. *Worker Empowerment in a Changing Economy: Jobs, Military Production and the Environment.* New York: Apex Press, 1991.